A Journey through Peapack and Gladstone

Jacqueline Tutton

December 1993

A Journey through Peapack and Gladstone

JACQUELINE TUTTON

Friends of the Peapack-Gladstone Library
1993

The Friends of the Peapack-Gladstone Library wish to thank HarperCollins Publishers, Inc. for their permission to reprint "The Fox of Peapack" from *The Fox of Peapack and Other Poems* by E. B. White. Copyright 1932 by E. B. White.

❧ *Dedication* ❧

The Friends of the Peapack-Gladstone Library dedicate this book to the memory of Marge Smith, long-time member of the Peapack-Gladstone Woman's Club, which founded the library and funded it for many years. Marge was a dedicated library patron and volunteer, and an avid gardener. Her daughter-in-law, Helen Smith, recalls teasing Marge that she spent two-thirds of her time in her garden and the remaining one-third in the library. On her death in 1979, the Friends of the Peapack-Gladstone Library sought a means to create a suitable memorial for Marge. Peter Smith, Gladstone artist and grandson of Marge, graciously donated his prints of local historic scenes to be reproduced on note cards and sold by the Friends of the Library. As Marge had an abiding interest in local and Smith-family history, it was decided that profits from the note cards were to be used to fund the publication of a history of Peapack-Gladstone in her memory.

The Friends would also like to acknowledge the most generous financial donation given by the late Victor Huyler to help defray the cost of publishing this book. Victor was a third-generation native of Peapack-Gladstone and served the community in many capacities. He had a great love for this area and the people living here and was very enthusiastic about this project. Shortly before his death he read a rough draft of the manuscript and was reported to chuckle at times and say, "I remember that!" It is because of Victor's generosity that the Friends are able to make this publication more accessible to all those who may wish to purchase it. ·

The Friends of the Peapack-Gladstone Library

❧ *v*

❧ *Contents* ❧

❧ *Preface* ❧

Surely our local history is a treasure for sire to bequeath to son, not in tradition but in truthful print. . . . Every year old men die and old documents perish, and with them pass away forever interesting data. For the small part this Magazine has taken in collecting these materials of history, we hardly believe the next generation will regret.

—*Our Home: A Monthly Magazine of Original Articles*

Edited by A. V. D. Honeyman, later editor of the *Somerset Gazette*, *Our Home* was devoted to local and general literature and contained forty-eight pages of original articles, stories, and poetry; a year's subscription cost two dollars. Published in Somerville during 1873 by Cornell & Honeyman and printed in Newark at the offices of the *Daily Advertiser*, *Our Home* ceased publication after one year because of financial problems. This quotation appeared on page 565 of the final issue (December 1873).

To live in Peapack-Gladstone is a privilege, one that I appreciate all the more fully for having delved into its past during the research and writing of this book. History is the examination of change, for if everything remained the same, there would be no need to research the past. Progress is inevitable, and desirable, but we must be careful to respect and retain what is historically valuable. Historic treasures that surround us in Peapack-Gladstone include significant architectural structures, cultural traditions, scenic vistas, and a pristine environment. I hope the reader is convinced that our heritage is well worth conserving.

Jacqueline Tutton
Peapack, New Jersey
January 1993

NOTE TO READERS: Full publishing information for items mentioned in the footnotes can be found in the bibliography.

❧ *Acknowledgments* ❧

I wish to acknowledge the following institutions, which made their resources available to me: The New Jersey Historical Society, Newark; the Special Collections Section of Rutgers University Library, New Brunswick; the New Jersey Section, Somerset County Library, Somerville; the Bernardsville Public Library; the Clarence Dillon Library, Bedminster; the Morristown Public Library; and the Peapack-Gladstone Public Library.

I am specifically indebted to the following individuals: George N. Smith, former Peapack resident and retired principal of Morris Knolls High School, for reading the original manuscript and giving me many useful comments and suggestions; Florence Vander Beek, president of the Friends of the Peapack-Gladstone Library, for her patience, tact, and confidence in this project; Marion Kennedy, dedicated volunteer archivist of the Spinning Collection of the Bernardsville Public Library, who cheerfully researched many questions for me; Barbara Westergaard, editor, for her skillful work, attention to detail, and patience—her fine hand is responsible for bringing order and logic to my original manuscript; Judith Martin Waterman, book designer, for her creativity, organizational skills, and enthusiasm.

Finally, I would like to express my gratitude to the following individuals who so graciously helped me with this history by giving me interviews, information, and suggestions, and trusting me with their precious photographs and artifacts: Professor George F. Adams, John Amerman, Irene Aspell, Marcus Canfield (deceased), Alex Cassells, Harold Chesson, Daisy Cooper, George DeSesso, Edith Gambrill (deceased), Marge Gould, Mayor Mary Hamilton, Homer Hill, T. Leonard Hill, John Ike, Terry and Steve Kostew, Canon John Morrow, Katie Ryan, Helen Smith, John C. Smith, Peter Smith, Percy Terry, Mary Tiger, Ruth Thomson, Diana Villa (deceased), the Reverend Paul Walther, Ethel and Thomas Ward, Norman Welsh, and Ann Winston. I apologize if I have failed to mention here any of the many who have helped with this project.

A Journey through Peapack and Gladstone

The Property
of
W. A. Von Dern Esqr
1858

❦ *Prologue*

Life within a vital community includes occasions for celebration. Such celebrations, whether they are small at-home gatherings or much grander occasions, are historically revealing, for they are times when we pause to mark an event as noteworthy. Let us begin our journey through Peapack-Gladstone's past by looking at a few such occasions celebrated within our community.

❦ *General Knox Commemorates the French Alliance*

What was perhaps one of the grandest events on record happens to have been one of the earlier ones. On February 18, 1779, General Henry Knox commemorated the first anniversary of the French alliance with the revolutionary forces with a gala held at his headquarters in Pluckemin.

Sketch of the William Van Doren Mill and Home. The William Van Doren gristmill and home, a primitive sketch copied from a photograph, artist unknown, dated 1858. Note the pennant flying from a tree at the house, which carries the words "James Buchanan for President 1859," the stone arch bridge and stone blacksmith shop, and the out-of-scale proportions. Sketch courtesy of the Reverend Paul Walther Collection.

The following account of the celebration was published at the time:

The anniversary of our alliance with France was celebrated on the 18th ultimo, at Pluckemin, at a very elegant entertainment and display of fireworks, given by General Knox, and the officers of the corps of artillery. It was postponed to this late day on account of his Excellency General Washington's absence from camp. General Washington, the principal officers of the army, Mrs. Washington, Mrs. Greene, Mrs. Knox, and the ladies and gentlemen, for a large circuit around the camp, were of the company. Besides these, there was a vast concourse of spectators from every part of the Jerseys.

The barracks of the artillery are at a small distance from Pluckemin, on a piece of rising ground, which shows them to great advantage. The entertainment and ball were held at the academy of the Park. About four o'clock in the afternoon, the celebration of the ALLIANCE *was announced by the discharge of thirteen cannon, when the company assembled in the academy to a very elegant dinner. The room was spacious, and the tables very prettily disposed, both as to prospect and convenience. The festivity was universal, and the toasts descriptive of the happy event, which had given certainty to our liberties, empire, and independence. In the evening was exhibited a very fine set of fireworks, conducted by Col. Stevens, arranged on the point of a temple, one hundred feet in length, and proportionally high. The temple show[s]* THIRTEEN *arches, each displaying an illuminated painting. The centre arch was ornamented with a pediment, larger than any of the other[s]; and the whole edifice supported by a colonnade of the Corinthian order.*

The illuminated paintings were disposed in the following order:

The 1st arch, on the right, represented the commencement of hostilities at Lexington, with this inscription:—"The scene opened."

2nd, British clemency. Represented in the burning of Charlestown, Falmouth, Norfolk, and Kingston.

3rd, The separation of America from Britain. A magnificent arch broken in the centre, with this motto: "By your tyranny to the people of America you have separated the wide arch of an extended empire."

4th, Britain represented as a decaying empire, by a barren country, broken arches, fallen spires, ships deserting its shores, birds of prey hovering over its moldering cities, and a gloomy setting sun. Motto: "The Babylonian spires are sunk, Achaia, Rome, and Egypt mouldered down; Time shakes the stable tyranny of thrones, And tottering empires crush by their own weight."

5th, America represented as a rising empire. Prospect of a fertile country, harbors and rivers covered with ships, new canals opening, cities arising amidst woods, splendid sun emerging from a bright horizon. Motto: "New worlds are still emerging from the deep, The old descending in their turns to rise."

6th, A grand illuminated representation of LOUIS *the sixteenth. The encourager of letters, the supporter of the rights of humanity, the ally and friend of the American people.*

7th, The centre arch. The Father in Congress. Motto: "Nil desperandum reipublicae."

8th, The American Philosopher and Ambassador extracting lightning from the Clouds.

9th, The battle near Saratoga, 7th Oct., 1777.

10th, The Convention of Saratoga.

11th, A representation of the sea-fight, off Ushant, between Count D'Orvilliers and Admiral Keppie.

12th, Warren, Montgomery, Mercer, Wooster, Nash, and a crowd of heroes who have fallen in the American contest, in Elysium, receiving the thanks and praises of Brutus, Cato, and those spirits who in all ages have gloriously struggled against tyrants and tyranny. Motto: "Those who shed their blood in such a cause shall live and reign forever."

13th, Represented peace, with all her train of blessings. Her right hand displaying an olive branch; at her feet lay the honors of harvest; the background was filled with flourishing cities; ports crowded with ships, and other emblems of an extensive empire and unrestrained commerce.

When the fireworks were finished, the company returned to the academy, and concluded the celebration by a very splendid ball.

The whole was conducted in a style and manner that reflects great honor on the taste of the managers.

The news announced to congress from the Spanish branch of the house of Bourbon, arriving at the moment of celebration, nothing could have so opportunely increased the good-humor of the company, or added to those animated expressions of pleasure which arose on the occasion.[1]

❧ *Peapack-Gladstone Celebrates Washington Bicentennial*

On June 16, 1932, the *Peapack-Gladstone Exponent* recorded the borough's celebration of the Washington Bicentennial:

The borough of Peapack and Gladstone had a real celebration of the Washington Bicentennial celebration on Saturday. Not only was there a massive parade, but an attractive one. It was truly a patriotic celebration.

Pelham St. George Bissell, Justice of the Court of New York, Lt. Col. in the U.S. Infantry Reserve and District Commander of the American Legion of New York, delivered a stirring address.

Mayor Reginald B. Rives accepted the flag for the borough from Somerset Hills Post 216, American Legion, which was raised in attractive ceremonies in the Borough Park, close to the memorial tablet bearing the names of those serving in the World War.

Preceding the ceremonies in the park, a street parade was held. The parade was a massive one and started at the entrance to the Blair estate and passed north to Smith's store, then west to Van Derbeek's corner, then south to the Borough Park. The reviewing stand was upon the public school grounds, opposite the Borough Park. The marshals in the parade were Roger D. Mellick, Charles Scribner and Kenneth B. Schley, of Far Hills, and Clarence V. S. Mitchell and Frank E. Johnston, of Peapack. The judges were Mrs. Robert D. Mellick, Mrs. Reginald B. Rives and Mrs. Charles Scribner. Mayor Reginald B. Rives was the general chairman and Frank Fenner the chairman and deserve much credit for their untiring effort in making the event such a success.

Martin B. Huyler, the only surviving Civil War veteran in the borough, and a member of the G.A.R. Post in Morristown, occupied a place of honor in the parade. About 200 school children sang and took part in the ceremonies. Among the many floats in the parade was a tallyho entered by Richard V. [M.] Gambrill. There were also [entries] by the churches, the Essex Fox Hounds Hunt Club, Woman's Auxiliary of the Legion Post, the Somerset County Past Councillors Association, Jr. O.U.A.M., many business men, etc.

The unveiling of a water fountain donated by the W.C.T.U., was also attractive. Fire companies from several community towns were in the parade as well as a few bands. Before and after the parade J. O. Perry of Stroudsburg, Pa., formerly of Gladstone, and a World War veteran, gave an exhibition of stunt flying with two aeroplanes and there [were] also two parachute jumps.

Luncheon was served the visiting fire companies and bands at the firehouse. A block dance was held in the evening on Willow Avenue, near the Jr. O.U.A.M. building.

The first prize for having the largest percentage of members in line was given to the Mendham Fire Company. The first prize for float was awarded to the Italian organizations of the borough for their float picturing Washington Crossing the Delaware. The second prize for float was awarded to Daniel H. Van Doren picturing Washington at the Forge. The car prize was awarded to the Alabama Blackberries Club, it being an Austin car trimmed as the Washington Monument.

A special donation was awarded the borough school for their part in the program. This will be used for a picnic.

A very pretty float representing the sixth grade of the public school caught fire and burned just before it entered the parade.

Many expressed themselves as it being the finest celebration yet among the many that have taken place. It is estimated that there were about 800 in the line of march.

Mrs. Elizabeth Sherrer, who is about eighty-two years old, was attractively attired as the mother of Washington, and was on the Methodist Church float depicting Washington kneeling before his mother and receiving her blessing.

❧ *A Moroccan Fantasy*

The purchase of the Kate Macy Ladd estate in 1983 by King Hassan II of Morocco inspired the Somerset Friends of Channel Thirteen (Public Broadcasting System) to sponsor a Moroccan Fantasy as a gala benefit on June 25, 1983. Six months in the making, the gala, hosted by the Carmen Paternitis on their Far Hills estate, was chaired by Mrs. John W. Pyne, assisted by Mrs. Francis E. Johnson, chairperson of the organization, and fellow committee persons and neighbors Malcolm S. Forbes, Mrs. Jane Englehard, Mrs. Millicent H. Fenwick, and Miss Doris Duke.

The magic began the moment fantasy-clad guests stepped over the threshold of the gracious Carmen Paterniti Far Hills estate. . . . The

The stone house at the entry to Natirar is said to have been the stopping place for the stagecoach. From the Borough Archives.

sense of excitement mounted as they were drawn by the throbbing beat of Moroccan music into a richly brocaded maroon and gold draped souk or Middle Eastern bazaar. Ladies in caftans and harem pants, magnificently jeweled, gentlemen in jebullahs and Arabian style head dresses and fezes gravitated to a small wooden platform on which Krisha, a native belly dancer was undulating to the sensuous rhythms of Casbah flutes and drums. . . . Delighted party goers admired and purchased gold-embossed Moroccan leather picture frames, pillows and hassocks, stunning brass trays, vases and urns, and silver dressing table trays fitted with exotic silver perfume shakers. A library table was piled with a collection of rare books on traditional Islamic craft and Moroccan architecture. . . . Fantasy drew more celebs than any one party in the history of the Hills, including His Excellency Ali Benjelloun, Ambassador of Morocco and Mrs. Benjelloun, who drove up from Washington for the affair; His Excellency Abdellatif Filali, former Moroccan ambassador to the United Nations and presently special advisor representing King Hassan II; Governor and Mrs. Thomas H. Kean; Mr. and Mrs. Nicholas Brady; Mr. and Mrs. Douglas Dillon; Miss Doris Duke; Mrs. Millicent Fenwick; and Mr. and Mrs. Cyrus R. Vance.[2]

The article goes on to describe the Moroccan dinner for 450 guests, set in a dining tent draped with clouds of white chiffon, tables covered with silver and gold sari cloths from Morocco. Following the meal, H.O.H. Frelinghuysen conducted a lively auction of gifts donated by King Hassan II, including a seven-day excursion to Casablanca and Marrakesh, a dinner for two at the American embassy, and a first-class Moroccan trip for two.

The evening was further described by an article in the *New York Times*:

> *"Never has Peapack had a party such as this," said Mrs. Pyne, the chairman of the benefit committee. "Peapack will never be the same." . . . Fresh figs, stuffed grape leaves, stuffed dates and rumaki (chicken livers wrapped in bacon) were passed among the guests. A band sent from Morocco at the King's request played Moroccan music. . . . The highlight of the evening was Mr. Forbes's balloon team. Shortly before the guests arrived, a jeep, a Mercedes bus, and a pickup truck pulled into Mr. Paterniti's paddock. A team of 25 men and women wearing yellow trousers and red shirts embroidered with the words "Forbes Magazine Balloon Ascension Division" filed onto the grass and began inflating two enormous balloons.*
>
> *One, the Chateau de Balleroy, is a likeness of Mr. Forbes's chateau in France. . . . For $20 and $10 guests could take a ride, and the balloons were filled until nightfall. They did not go far, however, because the balloons were tethered. Mr. Forbes was at the controls.*[3]

❧ Seventy-fifth Anniversary of Incorporation

On June 6, 1987, Peapack and Gladstone marked the seventy-fifth anniversary of its incorporation as a borough with a day-long celebration. The festivities began with a parade which included numerous bands, floats, a company of marching mummers (elegantly feathered and spangled), antique automobiles, Scouts, the First Aid Squad and Fire Company, and visiting fire companies.

James Barrett, borough councilman, was the master of ceremonies who introduced honored guests and speakers, including Borough Mayor Mary Hamilton, State Senator John H. Ewing, Somerset County Freeholder Director Christine Todd Whitman, and Bedminster Mayor Robert Lloyd.

Music enlivened the festivities. Country Krunch, a country-folk foursome played during the afternoon while the crowd enjoyed hot dogs and sodas. In the evening, after a chicken barbecue, a concert was presented by the Lakeland Winds Community Band.

The afternoon program included the Gladpack Equine Event featuring a coach and four, a dressage free-style demonstration, a vaulting demonstration, and a driving surrey class. Inside the municipal complex a variety of displays was organized by the Cultural Heritage Committee, the Environmental Commission, the Friends of the Library, the Woman's Club, the Happy Rockers (a senior citizens group), the Matheny School, and the police department.

A parchment scroll of the Act of Incorporation was given to all attending as a memento of the day. The calligraphy was done by Nora Schulte of Gladstone.

❧ *Malcolm Forbes's Scottish Spectacular*

On May 28, 1987, Malcolm S. Forbes hosted more than one thousand guests at his estate, Timberfield, to mark the seventieth anniversary of *Forbes* magazine, founded in 1917 by his father, Scottish immigrant B. C. Forbes.

The details of the evening were described by Sandy Stewart in the *Bernardsville News*. The spectacular event was staged in a Scottish castle setting simulated by huge tents and theater sets. Forbes, dressed in a kilt of the family's blue and green tartan, stood for more than three hours in the receiving line, along with his hostess for the evening, actress Elizabeth Taylor. Guests arriving by helicopter or chauffeured limousine approached the gala by a long canopied walkway that was lined with photographers and reporters, all jockeying for the chance to catch one of the many celebrities in attendance. The thirty guests who were flown in by helicopter to alight on an illuminated landing pad were shuttled to the walkway via a chauffeured golf cart.

Celebrities and dignitaries in attendance included White House Chief of Staff Howard Baker, Dr. Henry Kissinger, CIA Director William Webster, Governor Thomas Kean, United States Senator Bill Bradley, CBS Chairman William Paley, newspaper tycoon Rupert Murdoch, soprano Beverly Sills, and real estate magnate Donald Trump, as well as many others from the fields of film, music, and fashion.

> *As twilight slipped into darkness, the woods surrounding the cocktail tent came alive with the haunting sounds of bagpipes. Marching two-by-two, the brigade of kilt-clad pipers filed through (artificial) fog past a replica of a Scottish cathedral ruins.*
>
> *The pipers and drummers lined up in formation in front of the cocktail tent and played a moving rendition of "Amazing Grace," one of Forbes' favorite songs.*
>
> *Then, calling the guests to dinner, the bagpipe band marched toward the main tent, which covered an area roughly the size of a football field. "Couldn't they have just used a dinner bell," asked one guest, holding his hands over his ears to block out the din.*
>
> *In keeping with the Brigadoon theme, the dinner tent sported a large mural of a castle facade against one wall and smaller castle turrets disguising the entrances to the food preparation tents. The "moat" leading into the tent was crossed by means of [a] drawbridge guarded by knights in suits of armor.*
>
> *The guests, carefully assigned to places at 103 round tables, dined on cold pheasant, baked Scottish salmon, potatoes and baby vegetables. For dessert, each table received a cake with the cover of the first issue of "Forbes," created in icing. . . .*
>
> *The grand finale of the evening was a 20-minute fireworks and laser light show, choreographed to music by the Grucci family. Staid* CEO's *in penguin suits grinned like little kids as the bangs and booms echoed across the hills and flashes lit the skies.*[4]

In that same issue of the *Bernardsville News*, contributing writer Allen Crossett of Gladstone, wrote:

> *While the elite supped on cold pheasant and sipped chilled imported wines within the huge tents on the Forbes' estate, an odd distillation of tweeds and denims gathered along the public roads which border the property.*
>
> *No fancy invitations were needed for this affair. Guests arrived not by helicopter or stretch limo but on foot or in aging Fords and Chevys.*
>
> *Most were there to watch the fireworks and laser light show and while the area could easily have been cleared by the abundant security personnel, there was an implicit understanding: no loud noise, no distractions, no trouble or confrontation, enjoy the show but keep your distance. Fair enough.*
>
> *Many of us found comfortable seating on the bank of the road opposite that part of the open field where the helicopters had been arranged in rows. We saw them first in the darkness, strange fish-like shapes silhouetted by the floodlights which washed over the schools of waiting limousines.*
>
> *As we continued down an adjoining road, we were able to see the band pavilion and we could hear the music drifting across the field.*
>
> *Several of us seized the moment to create a lasting memory. We danced to the music of Lester Lanin at the 70th anniversary gala for Forbes magazine and who really would need to know years from now that we were shuffling our two-step in the middle of a dirt road. . . .*
>
> *And then, almost unexpectedly, we heard a dull booming sound from the distant field and the sky exploded. We could hear faint strains of*

Wagner's "Ride of the Walkures," and with the helicopters before us and the fireworks above us, we were reminded of the striking imagery in the film Apocalypse Now. . . .

As we walked back to our car, we became part of a festive recessional, a line which included what seemed to be an endless stream of Lincolns and Cadillacs, Mercedes and Rolls.

We may have missed the pheasant and the chilled imported wine but we will tell our grandchildren that at this party of the century, we were among the appreciative guests.[5]

❧ Notes

1. John W. Barber and Henry Howe, *Historical Collections of the State of New Jersey*, pp. 441–442.
2. Karla Wiley, *Bernardsville News-Observer Tribune*, June 30, 1983.
3. *New York Times*, June 27, 1983.
4 Sandy Stewart, *Bernardsville News*, June 4, 1987.
5. Allen Crossett, *Bernardsville News*, June 4, 1987.

Postcard of the old stone arch bridge over Peapack Brook on Jackson Avenue, date unknown. The bridge was damaged in a flood and later replaced. From the Harold Chesson collection.

Setting the Scene

A Note on Geology

Peapack-Gladstone, situated as it is in a fertile river valley surrounded by blue hills, is noted for the beauty of its landscape. Millenniums of geological activity have formed the terrain that gives the Somerset Hills their particular look. Traversed by a seismic fault line, the area encompasses deposits of volcanic rock, iron ore, and an economically significant amount of limestone.

George F. Adams, a retired professor of geology from the City University of New York, and a specialist in investigating geological phenomena that are in danger of being obliterated by development, kindly provided the author with a historical description of the geological phenomena of our area.[1]

Peapack-Gladstone exhibits a complex of highlands and lowlands which form part of a fault ramp. Within this fault ramp, individual ridges and valleys have been etched out along rock belts of different ages, types, and resistance to erosion. For example, Peapack Brook follows a limestone belt skirting the edge of the older, more complex granitic and other resistant rocks of the Highlands. We say the stream is adjusted to the limestone structures.

The North Branch of the Raritan is an interesting exception. It cuts across the Highlands infrastructure but follows the general southerly slope of the fault ramp. Such rivers generally start on gently sloping sedimentary rock, long since removed. The leading candidate here is the Brunswick formation now underlying most of the Raritan lowland to the south and east. The North Branch, where it cuts a deep but wide valley through the Highlands is called a superimposed stream. The rocks cut by this river are more than six hundred million years old, but the river itself is somewhat less than two hundred million years old.

In contrast to the North Branch, Peapack Brook has cut into two limestone formations running parallel with the brook. The limestone is some four hundred million years old and has been affected by compressional faults, perhaps three hundred million years ago. The limestone may present a hazard to buildings because of the possible collapse of cavern roofs or the settling of glacial debris in sink holes. Caves briefly opened to the public in 1902 presented sufficient hazard to be quickly closed.

As the Peapack and the North Branch unite, they flow through the shales and sandstones of the Brunswick formation. At the stream junction the red shales dip gently southward away from the Highlands, which here slope abruptly and probably disappear into the sands and shales. Farther west, these beds steepen to thirty to fifty degrees southwest, as they once rose northward to the steeper ramp slopes and then leveled off in Mendham at Mt. Paul.

A volcanic pipe related to the basaltic lava flows of the Watchung Mountains makes up a single lozenge-shaped hill northeast of the North Branch-Peapack confluence. This pipe is on the property of the King of Morocco and so is difficult to access. Such pipes are rare along the Ramapo Border fault system. The pipe, of a dark granular pepper-and-salt appearance, stands at a junction of the three main rock types in Peapack: the granites, limestones, and sandstones described above. At one time it may have fed a volcano now removed by erosion.

Professor Adams notes that there is no indication of any recent activity along the seismic faults here and no greater chance of an earthquake here than in other regions where there are no obvious seismic faults.

According to Dr. Robert Sheridan, professor of geophysics at Rutgers University in New Brunswick, the Ramapo fault begins in New York State and is approximately fifty-five miles long and twenty thousand feet deep, having been formed two hundred million years ago after the North American continent separated from the continent of Africa. Running parallel to Route 202, it crosses through Bernardsville and Peapack-Gladstone, and from there stretches toward Somerville.[2]

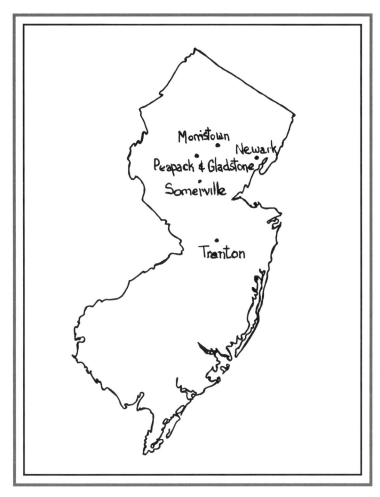

❧ *The Lenni-Lenape*

The Indians who inhabited this valley when the first white settlers arrived were known as the Lenni-Lenape. Classified as Algonquin, they were part of the Iroquois nation. Now known as the Delaware, the Lenni-Lenape referred to themselves as "The Original People" and to the land they occupied between the Hudson and Delaware rivers as "Scheyichbi." They were peaceful and nature loving, simple in their ways, but by no means were they "savages." "They had a definite form of government, a system of villages, a genuine religion, a devoted family relationship, a moral code, and a rudimentary educational system in which boys and girls learned what they needed to know to cope with their particular environments."[3]

These Indians relied on raising maize and on hunting and

What is now the Borough of Peapack-Gladstone was originally part of a large tract of land purchased from the Dutch in 1701. The tract, known as the Peapack Patent (see "The Peapack Patent" in "Early History" below), extended north of the Lesser and Larger Crossroads, across the Township of Bedminster, into the Townships of Bedminster and Bernards, and below Pluckemin. Peapack became a part of Bedminster Township when it incorporated in 1749 and remained so until 1912, when Peapack and Gladstone chose to secede from the township and incorporate as a twin borough. The borough (as shown on the map of New Jersey) is situated close to the northern boundary of Somerset County on County Route 512 near U.S. highways 202 and 206.

fishing for their livelihood. They created tools and weapons of flint and quartz, and fashioned canoes by burning out the centers of great trees, and many Indian arrowheads and other relics have been uncovered in the Somerset Hills.

According to Lenni-Lenape legend, they were descendants of a people who had migrated from the northwest to the east until they came to the ocean and the sunrise. The Iroquois Indians to the north were warlike. They kept the Lenni-Lenape from their territory and

> called them "The Old Women," looking upon them as weak and foolish and not worth attacking. The kindest interpretation of that nickname was that the Lenni-Lenape loved peace and served as intermediaries in the councils of war or after the intermittent trailside tomahawking by other tribes. Undoubtedly the Lenni-Lenape lived in peace, and in their relationship with the first settlers, this proved most helpful for the colonists rather than the Indians.[4]

At first they received the white settlers with friendly curiosity and gifts. However, the relationship was doomed, as were these peaceful Indians. The hostilities between the colonists and the Indians escalated during the Dutch rule in New Amsterdam, with many skirmishes and casualties on both sides. After wresting the territory from the Dutch in 1664, the English handled matters differently, using the English methods of titles and deeds in transfers of territories. The historian John Cunningham points out that although no violence was involved in these transactions, they were not altogether fair. Some of the Indians, who did not understand written documents, may have had no idea that they were signing away all rights to their lands for a few knives and commodities. Rather, they may have been under the impression that they were ceding the use of the land in return for hunting and fishing rights.

The eventual decline of the Lenni-Lenape in New Jersey is a sad story of disease, as smallpox decimated the tribe. Alcoholism and, consequently, indolence and poverty further contributed to diminishing numbers. It is estimated that there were two thousand Indians living in New Jersey in the early seventeenth century when the Dutch arrived and that less than a fourth of that number remained at the beginning of the next century. Between 1755 and 1757, the French and Indian War brought another period of violence. Peace was reached in 1758 when the New Jersey Assembly established the first Indian reservation in America at Edge Pillock (now Indian Mills). In exchange the Indians ceded all rights to New Jersey except for hunting and fishing rights. By 1802, the reservation having been a failure, the remaining two hundred Lenni-Lenapes left New Jersey to join some of their fellow tribesmen who had migrated to New York. The invitation extended to them by the Mohicans was welcome: "Pack up your mats," they said, "and come and eat out of our dish which is large enough for all, and our necks are stretched in looking toward the fireside of our grandfather till they are as long as cranes."[5] The New Jersey Indians were invited to spread their mats before "our fireplace, where you will eat with your grandchildren out of one dish and use one spoon."[6] They sold all remaining rights to the three-thousand-acre reservation to settle their debts. The Original People no longer inhabited the Scheyichbi as a tribe.

A few of the Lenni-Lenape did remain behind in the Somerset Hills. The Roxiticus were a subtribe of the Lenni-Lenape. According to local lore, an Indian chief named Paul A. Roxiticus is buried overlooking what was his village just north of Peapack. Chief Paul brought the first hemlock tree here from New Brunswick; legend has it that he carried it himself the entire distance and planted it. Wishing to gaze upon his beloved village of Peapack in perpetuity, Chief Paul requested that he be buried beneath the hemlock tree. The site was for many years the property of Colonel and Mrs. John Winston; they named it Mt. Paul Farm. Chief Paul's tree propagated, and now the site is adorned by a ring of hemlock trees. The Winstons gave 184 acres of Mt. Paul Farm to the Morris County park system; that acreage included Chief Paul's grave.

❧ *The Origin of the Name Peapack*

Peapack! The name either intrigues or amuses people who hear it for the first time, and they invariably remark upon it.

The borough's name may be one of the only original native Indian names in Somerset County to have continued as a town name in something near its original spelling.

No one explanation of the meaning of the word Peapack has been accepted as authoritative. It is known that the "Peapack Path" was the name of a native Indian thoroughfare that ran from east to west through northern New Jersey, crossing the Lamington River at its falls; it was frequently mentioned as a boundary in early land grants. In her history of Peapack Rachel Potter included the following:

> *The late Mr. A. D. Mallick, Jr. considered it dated on written records from 1711, when in the return of the survey made by order of Colonel Lewis Morris for an English Company, known as the west Jersey Land Society (survey covering nearly 92,000 acres), the description referred to the "Peapack Path" as crossing "the north branch of the Raritan River." A village named "Pepock" is mentioned in the deed recording the sale by the Lenni Lenape Indians of a large tract of land to new settlers. In 1715 John Reading, surveyor, spelled the name "Pepack" in his journal.[7]*

The word Peapack has several possible derivations. "Pe" is the Lenni-Lenape word for water. "Pepock" or "Papeck" means pond. The name may have signified where the "pepacktunk" or "water root" began. According to Rachel Potter, John Burrows referred to "Peapackton" as an Indian name meaning the "marriage of the waters."[8] The fact that the Raritan River and the Peapack Brook form the boundaries of the borough and meet at its east end gives credence to this definition. "Pee," "pea," "bi," or "bee" are Lenape words for water; "packy" or "pachy" signified location in their language.

An Indian trail from the Raritan to the Musconetcong extended further to the Minisink country, and there was evidently a small Indian village along that trail that occupied the site of what is now known as Peapack. Perhaps the village was a place where water was located, where travelers on the trail could stop to rest and drink.

Donald Becker, a former principal of the Peapack-Gladstone School, lists the following sources for origins of the name:

> A. *The Brinton-Anthony Dictionary defines a term,* PEPACHGANK, *as "calamus root or sweet flag." Related to the designation,* PEPACHGANK, *is the word* PAPEEK, *defined in Zeisberger's* Dictionary *as "pond."*
>
> B. *The* Origin of New Jersey Place Names *lists the source as* PE, *"water,"* PACK, *"roots."*
>
> C. *Footprints of the Red Men, by Mr. Edward Ruttenber, contains the following entry:* "PENPACK *(Somerset County, New Jersey) apparently corrupt Dutch from* PAANPACHT, *'low, soft land or leased land' (Peenpack, Paan, Paen, Pien, Penn)."*
>
> D. *An unclassified newspaper reference to Peapack suggested the translation of the Indian word to mean "marriage of waters."*
>
> E. *The reader is referred to an interesting speculation in similarity*

of sound. Note citation "B," PAPACHK, *under the entry* PAPAKATING, *above.*

Variations: Pachpeck (1901), Pepack, Pepock, Peepock, Popock, Pechpek, Peapock.[9]

A *New York Times* article of May 28, 1898, describing the Smith family picnic (see "Pleasant Valley or O-Wan-A Massie" in "Early History" below), declared: "Peapack is the Indian name for Smith."

❧ *Notes*

1. Dr. Adams, who received his doctorate from Columbia University, retired from CUNY in 1978 and moved to Bridgewater; he wrote the Environmental Impact Statement for Bridgewater. Dr. Adams is particularly interested in the Second Watchung Mountain area and the Moggy Hollow Valley, site of the Leonard Buck Gardens.
2. *Bernardsville News*, October 26, 1989.
3. John T. Cunningham, *New Jersey: America's Main Road*, p. 17.
4. Ibid., p. 18.
5. Ludwig Schumacher, *The Somerset Hills*, p. 25.
6. Cunningham, *New Jersey*, p. 23.
7. Rachel Potter, "Historical Facts and Places of Interest in Peapack-Gladstone."
8. Ibid.
9. Donald William Becker, *Indian Place Names in New Jersey*, pp. 58–59.

Early History

Prerevolutionary Bedminster Township

Knowing something of the complicated history of prerevolutionary New Jersey, particularly the conflicts engendered over issues of land ownership, helps us understand more clearly how the village of Peapack-Gladstone evolved as a community and the ways in which it has altered over time. In 1664, the English monarch, Charles II, granted his thirty-year-old brother James, the duke of York and heir apparent, the largest territory ever bestowed by an English sovereign. According to the charter, James was sole proprietor not only of the present state of New York, but of all the region between the Connecticut and Delaware rivers.

Also included were the present state of Maine east of the Kennebec, Long Island, Martha's Vineyard, and Nantucket.

The duke appointed Richard Nicolls deputy governor, armed him with four frigates, and directed him to set forth to secure the new properties. On August 18, 1664, Peter Stuyvesant surrendered the territory to Nicholls without a shot having been fired. As a result, New Amsterdam was renamed New York; Fort Orange renamed Albany; and Fort Casimir on the Delaware renamed Newcastle; the entire province was renamed New York.[1]

According to his charter, the duke was sole proprietor of this vast grant, to do with as he wished, without consideration of the inhabitants therein. One of his first arbitrary acts was to present to two of his friends, Sir George Carteret and Lord John Berkeley, who were proprietors in the Carolina colony, all the land between the Delaware and Hudson rivers. The grant was an award in recognition of their loyalty to the crown during the English civil war. The territory was called Nova Caesarea, or New Jersey, in honor of Carteret's defense of his native Isle of Jersey against Cromwell's forces. The inhabitants of the grant were a small population of English and Dutch settlers. York, however, had blundered by not telling Colonel Nicolls of his grant of New Jersey to Carteret and Berkeley. Three months before the duke's grant, when Nicolls forced the surrender of the Dutch, he had begun appropriating land across the Hudson and selling land grants,

promising self-government to the buyers. Subsequently, Carteret and Berkeley also effected sales and property transfers. This confused series of events gave rise to one of the most vexing problems of the Colonial era. Disputes arose over the issue of quitrents, which were levies the two proprietors claimed the right to collect under the duke of York's grant; grantees under Nicholls felt they were exempt from such royalist fees, as did those who traced their titles to purchases from the native Indians. The difficulties resulting from the conflict continued well into the eighteenth century.

Somerset County was one of the trouble spots in this conflict; here land claims and counterclaims overlapped one another. As in other colonies, rioting broke out among land-grant purchasers. Local jails were broken into and emptied of prisoners who had refused to pay quitrents. Andrew Johnston addresses some of the issues from a proprietor's point of view in his journal, portions of which are excerpted in the appendix.

The deeds of release granted to Berkeley and Carteret gave them territorial rights, but no political control. In 1665, seeking to exercise governmental authority, the proprietors issued the "Concessions and Agreements of the Proprietors of New Jersey," which, according to *The Oxford History of the American People*, was "the most liberal grant of political privileges made by an English colonial proprietor to the people."[2] Freedom of conscience was guaranteed, generous land grants were promised, and a representative assembly was formed, which first met, at Elizabethtown, now Elizabeth, in 1668. However, disputes among the proprietors arose, and in 1676, a partition of the territory was agreed to, Carteret taking for himself East Jersey, Berkeley taking West Jersey. East Jersey was managed by a board of twenty-four proprietors. Carteret died in 1680, and his will specified that his proprietary title be sold to retire his debts. The trustees of the will conveyed the property, for thirty-four hundred pounds, to a group of Quakers, who, in turn, sold shares in East Jersey to men in Scotland. East Jersey subsequently had an assembly at Elizabethtown, and was in the possession of twenty-four proprietors; West New Jersey, with its assembly at Burlington or Salem, belonged to three or four other men. In 1702, because of the confusion and disputes over land titles, the proprietors agreed to surrender their governmental powers to the crown. Thus the two New Jerseys were united as the Royal Province of New Jersey. The two groups of proprietors retained their property rights. Even though the crown was the governing body, it held no rights or title to the land itself.[3] This semblance of royal government continued until the summer of 1776. In those months the Provincial Congresses met at Burlington and adopted a state constitution; became the "Convention of the State of New Jersey," a free and independent Commonwealth; and deposed the royal governor, William Franklin, the illegitimate son of Benjamin Franklin.

Somerset County

Somerset County dates from May 14, 1688, when it was separated from its neighboring county of Middlesex by act of the Provincial Assembly, in Amboy. The preamble of the act sets forth the reason for separation:

> *The Upper part of the Raritan River is settled by persons, whom, in their husbandry and manuring their lands are forced upon quite different ways and methods from other farmers and inhabitants of Middlesex County. Because of frequent floods that carry away their fences on the meadows, the only arable land they have and by consequences of their interests, are divided from the other inhabitants of said County.*[4]

Six-Mile Run, Hillsborough, and Somerville were successively the county seats.

The Peapack Patent

In 1701 a grant known as the "Peapack Patent" transferred lands from the twenty-four proprietors of East Jersey to George Willocks and John Johnstone.[5] The two, as joint tenants, received a parcel of land that evidently embraced within its boundaries the entire township of Bedminster, extended below Pluckemin, and went from the North Branch of the Raritan River to the east, to the Lamington River to the west.

> *Beginning at the upper corner of George Willocks' thousand acres and*

ascending and including the Lamington River to its falls between two steep hills near the Morris County line; thence continuing Easterly to the head waters of the North Branch of the Raritan; thence Southerly following that stream to a point where it veers Westerly below the mouth of Mine Brook; thence to the top of the first mountain South of Pluckemin; thence following the crest of that mountain Southeasterly to the Northeast corner of Ann West's thousand acres; thence Westerly along the North line of this land to the East line of George Willocks' thousand acres, which lay at the conflux of the North Branch of the Raritan and Lamington Rivers; thence along his East and North line to the upper corner, which is the place of beginning.[6]

When it was bought, the Peapack Patent was thought to encompass about three thousand acres. When it was actually surveyed, however, the total area was found to exceed ten thousand acres.

Andrew Mellick, Jr., in *The Story of an Old Farm*, published in 1889, tells us that in New Jersey, according to early laws, settlers were made to settle the claims of the native Indians before acquiring legal title to lands. According to Mellick, Willocks, who was from Kinny in Scotland, had acquired large tracts of land from the proprietors in Middlesex, Monmouth, Hunterdon, Bergen, and Somerset. He actually acquired the property in 1698, but title to the land was formalized three years later, in 1701, when he and Johnstone purchased the tract from the Indians Tallquapie, Nicolas, and Elalie.

From the *Somerset County Historical Quarterly* we learn that title to property in East Jersey was first conveyed from David Barclay, of Urie, Scotland, to James Johnstone of Spotswood, Scotland. The deed, dated April 20, 1684, was evidently drawn in Scotland, but is now recorded in the Office of the Secretary of State in Trenton. The transfer of " $\frac{1}{10}$ of $\frac{1}{48}$ part of East Jersey" was witnessed by John Johnstone, P. Falconer, and John Swinton. James Johnstone sailed from Scotland in July of 1684 and arrived in East Jersey after an eighteen-week voyage. From East Jersey he wrote letters to his brother, Dr. John Johnstone, "Drugest in Edinburgh," describing his pleasant new life. James was appointed to serve as one of the commissioners to confirm the Acts of Assembly. He died June 22, 1690. His brother John sailed from Scotland to East Jersey the following year on the vessel *Henry and Francis*. It was he, with George Willocks (one of the founders, in 1698, of St. Peter's in Perth Amboy, the first Church of England parish in East Jersey), who purchased what is called the Peapack Patent, which, after the Twenty-Four Proprietors Rights, is the basis for many land titles in Bedminster (including Peapack) and Bernards Township.[7]

Here is the text of the Peapack Patent, as transcribed by Potter:

The Proprietors of the Province of East Jersey to all to whom these Presents shall come, Greetings:

Whereas the said Proprietors of the said Province for divers[e] good causes and considerations them thereunto moving, did grant and allow to John Johnstone of the County of Monmouth, Esq. fifty acres of land for importing himself into said Province, and 25 acres for each servant and other person by him imported, etc., and whereas the said John Johnstone and George Willocks of said County of Monmouth, merchant, purchased of David Lyell of New York, Goldsmith, 1,000 acres of land within said province; and whereas the said George Willocks holdeth 1,200 acres in right of Sir Thomas Lane, Knight, one of the alderman of London, and the rest of the West New Jersey Society or Company as Proprietors of said East New Jersey.

Now know ye the said Proprietors of East New Jersey have Aliened, bargained, sold, released and confirmed, and by these present doth alien, grant, bargain, sell, release and confirm unto the said Johnstone and George Willocks in severalty, their respective heirs and assigns forever; All that tract of land situate, lying and being in the County of Somerset and Middlesex in said providence; together with all and all manner of rivers, rivulets, ponds, pools, pits, waters, waterfalls, trees, woods, underwoods, mines, minerals, quaries, huntings, hawkings, fowlings, fishings, royalties, wafes and franchises and whatsoever unto the said tract of land belonging or appertaining and the reversion of the same, etc. etc.

George Willocks and their respective heirs and assign forever, yielding and paying for the said 1,200 acres of the said John Johnstone to the said Prop[r]ietors yearly the sums of twelve pence sterling on every five and twentieth day of March forever hereafter, if lawfully demanded, and for the remainder of the said tracts the proportion of the chief or quit rent issuing out of the Province to the King.

In witness whereof the said Proprietors have caused these presents to be signed by the Governor of said Province and the major part of his Council for the time being, and the common seal of said Province to be thereunto affixed, the 7th day of June in the 13th year of the reign of William the Third over England, Scotland, France and Ireland, King, etc., 1701.

(signed by) And. Hamilton, Benj. Griffith, Samuel Leonard, Sam'l Dunnes, Sam'l Hale, John Bishop.

Potter added that "Andrew Hamilton was the Acting-Governor of New Jersey and brother-in-law of John Johnstone, and the other five signers were members of his Council."[8]

Andrew Johnston, one of the sons of Dr. John Johnstone, was subsequently president of the Proprietors Association from 1748 until his death in 1762. He left a journal of his survey of the land involved in the Peapack Patent. It is of interest because it mentions the names of many of the original grant holders, and it touches on the ever-present issue of proprietary rights. Johnston was naturally an advocate of the claims of the original proprietors, none of whom ever acknowledged the validity of claims arising from Colonel Nicolls's grants. James Parker, a printer with royalist sympathies, purchased extensive property within the Peapack Patent from the executors and heirs of John Johnstone.

The following information regarding the "Indian Towne of Peapack" was also cited by Potter:

Reference is frequently made of Peapack in Bedminster Township, as one of the oldest towns in Somerset County. . . . The late Mr. A. D. Mallick, Jr. considered it dated on a written record from 1711, when in the return of the survey made by order of Colonel Lewis Morris for an English Company, known as the West Jersey Land Society (survey covering nearly 92,000 acres), the description referred to the "Peapack Path" as c[ro]ssing "the north branch of the Raritan River."

There was published however in the New Jersey Law Journal *of 1893 the copy of an Indian deed from eleven Indians owning a tract they called "Mockreta Cohunge," to Peter Fancomie, Nathaniel Bonnel of Elizabethtown and three others, for a section of land in which "another Indian Towne called Peapack" formed the southwest corner, and this deed was dated Aug. 13, 1708. In consideration was kettles, axes, hoes, powder, knives, rum, etc. On Nov. 4th of the same year Peter Sommans, an East Jersey Proprietor, gave a patent to nearly the same persons, including Nicholas Bonnell of 30,000 acres, extending from near present Morristown, Southerly through part of Somerset Co., and in the one of the course mentioned as an "Indian Town called Pepock," and states that Bonnell had paid a consideration to the native Indians to the value of $200.*

Evidently the two deeds relate to the same land, and they are undoubtedly the earliest co[n]veyance of the northern portion of our County.

In 1715 John Reading, surveyor, spelled the name "Pepack" in his "Journal." [9]

❧ The Revolutionary War

No historic marker stands within our community commemorating a significant skirmish or "Battle of Peapack" during the Revolutionary War. Yet, the inhabitants of the old village were keenly involved in the momentous events that led to the insurrection and eventual war.

In *The Story of an Old Farm* Andrew Mellick paints a compelling picture of the citizens of Bedminster Township and their experiences during the time of the Revolutionary War. Set forth here is a summary of the events that most directly affected local history as condensed from Mellick's account and other sources.

Fueled by the excesses of the royalist government, anti-British sentiment escalated steadily within the colonies. By the 1770s, when it became clear that war was inevitable, the patriots in local communities had taken it upon themselves to marshal arms and defenses in preparation for the impending conflict.

In 1774 a general Committee of Correspondence was appointed by the Provincial Assembly in New Jersey. The body was composed of nine members whose purpose was to persuade prominent citizens of the need of united resistance against the British and to keep people well informed on matters of mutual interest. Hendrick Fisher was chosen to represent Somerset County in this body.[10]

A series of meetings was held in the New Jersey provinces in June and July to organize defenses for war. By this time sentiment for resistance had escalated, although pockets of loyalist sentiment remained in various parts of the state.

After April 1775, when news of the Battle of Lexington reached New Jersey, a general Committee of Correspondence convened. The chairman was directed by the committee to call a provincial congress at Trenton. The Provincial Congress ordered New Jersey to prepare for war, passed the first militia bill, and imposed a war tax of ten thousand pounds, nine hundred pounds to be Somerset's levy.

The first militia bill initiated obligatory one-year service for all men between the ages of sixteen and fifty. Monthly wages were five dollars, and each man was required to supply his own firearms and ammunition. The clothing issued to privates in the Jersey line "was to each man one felt hat, one pair of yarn stockings, and one pair of shoes."[11] Men were enrolled in local militia companies formed by regional Committees of Safety. These companies were often incorporated into regiments throughout the state.

The second New Jersey enlistment provided that "in addition to their monthly pay, the privates and noncommissioned officers received one hundred acres of land and an annual kit of clothing comprising two linsey hunting shirts, one pair of overalls, a waistcoat of wool or leather, one pair of breeches, a hat or leathern cap, two shirts, and two pairs of hose and shoes."[12]

During this time the minutemen of New Jersey were raised under direction to go anywhere needed on a moment's notice. They were given the option of joining the Continental Army, which, according to Mellick, most of them did, and they were soon phased out of New Jersey's forces.

A local Committee of Observation and Inspection was formed in Bedminster to gather arms and ammunition. Stephen Hunt, whom we meet in a later chapter as the architect of "Hunt's Folly," is mentioned by Mellick as the man chosen by the Bedminster Committee of Observation and Inspection to go to New York to buy arms.

This committee scoured the countryside and farms for arms of any kind. The Provincial Congress had directed such committees to "collect all the leaden weights from windows and clocks; all leaden weights of shops, stores, mills, of one pound weight and upwards; also all the lead in and about houses and other places."[13] Mellick further relates that "Bedminster was soon denuded of what had suddenly grown to be considered a precious metal, many of the families even cheerfully sacrificing their pewter dishes and platters, which were much valued by Colonial housewives."[14]

So the sons and fathers of Peapack and neighboring Bedminster Township, most of whom had heretofore known only the pastoral life of the family farm, armed themselves and prepared to fight.

General Washington's headquarters in Morristown and

General Knox's encampment at Pluckemin were subsequently the focus of important revolutionary activities. During these tumultuous times the people of Bedminster Township were witness to the momentous events of the war that unfolded, day by day, within their own community. According to Mellick's narrative, from the time of the fall of Fort Lee on November 19, 1776, until the end of the war,

> the soil of New Jersey was the board upon which many of the most desperate Revolutionary games were played, and her territory was much of the time the fighting ground or plunder of the enemy. It is claimed that her losses in proportion to wealth and population were greater than that of any other state save South Carolina. With the exception of the winter of Valley Forge and the Virginia campaign against Cornwallis in 1781, the Continental troops were constantly in or on the confines of the state. In addition, her militia was constantly called upon by the Commander in Chief for special services or to swell the number of the American Army.[15]

With the fall of Fort Lee, and the subsequent retreat of the Continental Army through Somerset to Trenton and across the Delaware, New Jersey became a British-occupied territory. Although the British forces were billeted far to the south of Bedminster Township at New Brunswick, the area was nevertheless the target of raids by British soldiers who roamed the countryside in search of spoils, and many times kidnapped and murdered people they suspected of being supporters of the patriot cause. The British, in turn, were continually harassed by the revolutionaries.

In one incident a squadron of British cavalry executed a particularly vicious raid in Pluckemin, robbing and insulting the villagers, and vandalizing property. They broke down the door of the Lutheran Church and destroyed pews and the pulpit. Mellick tells us that they were in search of Captain Isaac Van Arsdale, who managed to escape into the woods and later help the local population harass the British.

The last months of 1776 were dark days in New Jersey. General Lee had yet to bring his troops to meet with General Washington's army, which languished in its Pennsylvania encampment. The occupying British forces continued to maraud the countryside, plundering and murdering, abusing and insulting women. Some of the militia were so demoralized that they became insubordinate and returned to their farms, abandoning the revolutionary cause altogether.

When General Lee's troops finally made their way to New Jersey, the exciting news must have been carried from farm to farm, from miller to blacksmith.

> At the close of this twelfth day of December, 1776, when Lee's army crossed the North Branch of the Raritan and entered Bedminster, his battalions with clank of arm and swing of saber pressed on along the Lamington highway until the head of the column had passed a considerable distance beyond the crossing of the Peapack road; the troops then deployed to the right and encamped, the greater part of them occupying the lands of Peter Melick. When the moon climbed the heavens that night it illumined with its mellow gleam a strange spectacle for this quiet Bedminster country. The roads and fields were

encumbered with cannon and baggage-wagons, and stamping horses were tethered to trees and fences. Campfires gleamed on the hillsides, around which were stretched tired, bronze-faced men with ragged blankets for a covering and with knapsacks and bundles for pillows. Sorry-looking soldiers they were, with their antiquated cross-belts and cartouch boxes. A strange spectacle indeed, upon which the moon looked down, with naught to break the stillness of the sleeping camp save now or then the whinneying of a picketed horse or the occasional challenge of a pacing sentry.[16]

Mellick tells the sad story of the capture and eventual disgrace of General Lee at Basking Ridge, where he had stopped the night instead of continuing on to Bedminster with General Sullivan and the army.

It is probable that General Sullivan, who was second in command, quartered that night at Aaron M[a]lick's house, as it was among the most substantial of the neighborhood. At least family traditions aver that the house was full of officers, who arrived mounted. It is pleasant to learn something of the personality of the leaders of the Revolution who campaigned in this Bedminster country. Sullivan at this time was thirty-seven years old; possessed a well-proportioned and commanding figure, animated by the ruddy hue of health. His voice was deep and melodious, and in his military career he used it to great advantage, for it was always quick to respond alike to stern and gentle emotions. In the morning an officer came in great haste to the Old Stone House and announced the capture of the commanding general.[17]

Washington recrossed the Delaware to Trenton on December 25, 1776, and proceeded to march toward Trenton. On January 3, he surprised and defeated the British forces, encamped for the night near Princeton, who were on their way to join forces with Cornwallis at New Brunswick. Washington's army, together with General Mercer's forces, routed the enemy troops and caused them to retreat in a battle reputed to have lasted only thirty minutes. General Mercer was mortally wounded in the skirmish. It was Washington's desire to march to New Brunswick and attack Cornwallis, but as his army was exhausted and its resources depleted, he chose instead to regroup. He camped that night at Millstone and on the afternoon of January 4, deployed his forces to Pluckemin.

The encampment at Pluckemin was visited often by the people of the area, whether to gain news of events and loved ones, or to attend some of the military parades and celebrations. Mellick describes the excitement engendered by the presence of the Commanding General Washington:

Sunday the fifth of January was a great day for Pluckemin. The news of Washington being in Bedminster had rapidly spread, and, while it was yet early, on the roads and lanes leading to the village numerous parties of country people could be seen, all hurrying to visit the soldiers and learn for themselves the latest news of the campaign. Throughout the entire day the place was astir with an animated multitude, and excitements of all kinds ruled the hour. Squads of infantry and artillery men were everywhere. Farmers' wagons laden with provisions came rolling in from the neighborhood of Peapack, Lamington, and the valley.

Stern, brown-visaged officers in heavy boots and tarnished uniforms were mounting here, dismounting there, and clattering through the streets in every direction. Foraging parties were being dispatched; couriers and express messengers rode off in hot haste; horses neighed, men shouted, and on all sides were handshakings and congratulation. The martial instinct of the people seemed alert; eyes sparkled and all hearts beat quickly. Every little while brought new arrivals of country people, and the details of the famous victory must be gone over again and again. Although the war was yet young, the soldiers had plenty to tell of marches and countermarches, of camp life and bivouacs, of attacks, routs, wounds, and hardships. And then the newcomers were carried off to the Lutheran Church, which was surrounded by a cordon of sentinels. And through its doors and windows, what a brave show!—two-hundred and thirty British soldiers; broad-shouldered, big-boned Scotchmen, stalwart grenadiers, and dragoons brilliant with color-caged lions, who looked with gloomy stares upon the inquisitive and rejoicing Americans, whom the experiences of the past few days had taught them to better appreciate as soldiers and freemen.[18]

And further:

In after years Aaron often told of the aspect Pluckemin presented on those memorable days. He especially delighted in reminiscences of the generals whose names grew greater as the war progressed—of Greene, tall and vigorous, with the air of one born to command; of Sullivan, alert and soldierly; of Knox, whose broad, full face beamed with satisfaction; but above all, of the conspicuous figure of Washington, who seemed a king among men as he moved amid the throng, with high-born eye, lofty but courteous port, and a calm, strong face reflecting a mind full of the tranquillity of conscious power.[19]

❧ *Early Development*

The first settlers in the area were farmers who bought large tracts of land from the Indians and from George Willocks's and John Johnstone's property, "the Peapack Patent." Most of the Indians left the area for good between 1750 and 1775.

Peapack's early development is archetypal of the prerevolutionary rural community. Farmers require certain services and products, and thus the commercial enterprises established in those early years were primarily farm-related: blacksmiths' shops, gristmills and sawmills, tanneries, a wheelwright's shop, distilleries, limestone kilns, and general stores.

Early eighteenth-century farming methods were primitive and arduous. Before the revolutionary war, farm implements were made of wood. Seed was sown by hand, sickles and scythes were used for harvesting. In 1776 the first wrought-iron plowshare was introduced to the area. Natural meadows provided fodder for animals until clover seed was introduced to Somerset County in 1800. In *The Story of an Old Farm*, Mellick carefully describes the details of life on the earliest Bedminster farms.

Rachel Potter was born in Chester Township April 19, 1888 (d. April 8, 1967). She lived in Peapack with her aunt

VANARSDALE COTTAGE
PEAPACK, N.J.

A postcard featuring "The Van Arsdale Cottage" circa 1910, still standing at 176 Main Street. This is now the Bailey Funeral Home. From the Reverend Paul Walther collection.

and uncle, Mr. and Mrs. George Van Arsdale, in the house they built at 176 Main Street, now the Bailey Funeral Home. She wrote an undated and undocumented history of the village which is on file at the Peapack-Gladstone Library. Her main sources seem to have been *The Story of an Old Farm*, Snell's *History of Hunterdon and Somerset Counties*, and stories told by long-time residents. In her history she lists the names of those who owned land in Peapack before 1763: Robert Allen, 112 acres; Robert Allen, Jr., 212 acres; John Allen, 50 acres; Jas Doren [*sic*], 200 acres; Robert Allen, 107 acres; William Logan, 50 acres; Stephen Hunt, 76 acres. She also names Alexander Kirkpatrick as a surveyor and merchant in residence here before 1800.

The general-store ledger of John Bryon, 1793–1798, includes the following names: Allen (Robert, James, Samuel), David Amerman, Walton Craig, Hugh Gaston, Henry Riker, Peter Sutphen, William Smith, Todd (Capt. William and Samuel), Jacob Tiger, Van Doren (Gilbert, Jacob, William, Aaron),[20] John Wortman, and Samuel Wills, Esq.[21]

It is important to note that the New Jersey Proprietors leased many of their properties, and in many cases eventually sold some acreages to their tenants. So although a family name may occur in the records as early inhabitants, there are not always records of deeds on file to support the claim of early land ownership.

A map of Peapack in the 1808 *Atlas of Somerset County, New Jersey* shows the Mellick house to the south of Peapack (The Old Farm); the D. Jeroleman property, which consisted of a house, three tanning vats, and grist- and sawmills; an Indian trading post; and the Van Doren properties, consisting of two houses, the mill, and the millpond.

Three separate areas developed quite early within the boundaries of today's Peapack-Gladstone: Lower Peapack, Upper Peapack, and Pleasant Valley. Basically self-sustaining, each area eventually was served by a general store, mills, and other agricultural services.

Lower Peapack

JOHANNES LOWRANCE'S MILL. ❧ There are records of several early mills in Peapack; one of the earliest documented ones was the Lowrance Mill and homestead.[22] This property is located at 109 North Main Street and is currently the residence of Peter Hogeboom. It was restored by Mr. and Mrs. Sydney F. Austin, who lived there from 1942 until 1959.

Johannes and Anna Margaretta Lowrance immigrated to New York from the Palatinate area of Europe, where France, Switzerland, and Germany meet. They brought four daughters; and a son, Alexander, was born in 1708 on the ship *Medford* during their crossing. Two more sons were born in America. Johannes in 1721 signed a lease giving him the use of land in Peapack owned by the proprietor Andrew Johnston

OLD MILL HOUSE 1670

PETER T. SMITH

Old Lawrence Mill House still standing at 109 Main Street in Peapack, built before 1720. Drawing courtesy of Peter Smith.

(see above). He agreed to plant orchards and build fences, but to sow no winter grain. There is no documentation as to when he actually settled here. There was probably a bargain struck between Johannes and Johnston that changed the terms of their agreement from leasing to ownership, but no documentation of such a pact was found by the author of this history.

> *April 24th, 1744 Went to look for Lawrances division line and found [illegible] markt trees, and one small hickory with 3 notches and 2 blases on the N. and S. sides and 3 notches and one blase on the East side, 77 [illegible] the North side. We run from s'd tree N. 20 deg. E. 59 ch; thence N. 46 deg., E. [illegible]ch; thence N. 71 deg e. 6 ch to the white oak markt for the corner of lot No. 6 on Axtells line near Richard Comptons.*[23]

Johannes Lowrance died in 1745, and in his will, which was registered in Trenton, he disposed of his land and improvements as if they were owned. The property was left to his son Daniel. However, the will does include the phrase "and the Proprietors Dew not disturb," perhaps meaning that their agreement may have been an informal one. A deed dated November 11, 1763, from James Parker, Lord Stirling, and others to Daniel Lowrance, conveyed a tract of 231 acres on Lowrance's Brook in Bedminster called Lot #8 of the Peapack Patent; it is dated after Andrew Johnston's death.[24]

The house may have been built as early as 1670, an undocumented conclusion drawn when old coins were found during restoration. A sketch of the house appears on page 37 of *The Old House Picture Book* by Marion Nicholl Rawson, and the subtitle lists it as a "Peapack farmhouse, before 1720." Johannes Lowrance, occupation miller, is the first recorded occupant of the house, which faces south and stands between Main Street and Lowrance's Brook (later known as Peapack Brook).

The house was built on three levels, in three stages, the oldest part being that on the west side on the lowest level. The interior of the house is noteworthy in that it has four large fireplaces on the first floor which contains large rooms. The room currently used as a dining room is on the second level, and was apparently the main room of the original structure, referred to in Johannes Lowrance's will as "the east fire room." The fireplace in that room contains an old crane and what remains of an oven. The later sections are those on a third level, including a main hall and stairway. The remains of an old lime kiln stand behind the house on the west side of Peapack Brook.[25]

Hugh Gaston, Jr., was a later owner of the Lowrance mill. Nicholas Jeroleman purchased the mill and property in 1808. The small Jeroleman family cemetery can be seen at the corner of Highland Avenue on the east side of Main Street. The Lowrence house property was owned and last operated as a mill in the early 1900s by the H. (Hamp) Miller family.

A raceway to operate the mill wheels was created by

diverting part of Peapack Brook into a narrow trough, which started at a point near what is now Liberty Park Pond. This headrace (water flowing toward the mill) ran along Main Street to the mill wheel and then into a "tailrace" from which the water flowed back into the brook. When stores were built along Main Street, boardwalks were placed over the millrace at the entrance to each building.

Stories of misadventures involving the millrace include one news item from 1908: "Theo Potter badly pounded, kicked and threw his brother-in-law, David Philhower, Jr., into the mill race on Tuesday evening of last week, leaving him partly unconscious. . . . The work is said to be an old grudge."[26]

When a disastrous fire struck the commercial buildings on Main Street in 1909, water from the millrace was used to fight the flames.

> *It is recalled by several towns-people present at the time how two of our firemen, Mr. Daniel M. Todd and Mr. Tay Handville, were handling a hose line on the roof on one of the buildings. They signaled for more water. As the pressure was increased at the pumper, the hose began to snake to the point that they lost their footing and their hold on the hose line and a short time later were fished from the mill race, none the worse, fortunately, for their experience.*[27]

The mills, with their huge rotating wheels and heavy grindstones, were also hazardous and were occasionally the cause of accidents.

> *Miss Verna Miller met with an accident at the mill on Saturday which fortunately did not prove serious. The wind blew her skirt against the projection from a revolving grindstone which quickly wound the skirt around the shaffing wrapping her tightly and drawing her body to the stone. Irving Trimmer heard her screams and rushed to her assistance. Realizing her position he quickly held her arms and face from the revolving stone and threw his weight upon the belt, breaking the belt at the lacing and freeing the child. She escaped with a few severe bruises.*[28]

In 1919 the Liberty Park Association purchased the mill property, including the mill, millpond, millrace, tailrace, all water rights and lands, and the house (which was at the time the property of H. N. Miller). Liberty Park Pond was created by building a dam on the brook (see "Community Services" below), and that was the end of the millrace in Peapack. What remains of the tailrace can be seen running between numbers 89 and 95 Main Street. When road work was done on Main Street in the 1960s, part of the old millrace was uncovered in front of what is now the Copper Kettle.

ALLEN'S MILL AND HUNT'S FOLLY. ❧ Andrew Johnston gave Abraham Drake permission to build a mill at the fork of the North Branch of the Raritan River and the Lowrance Brook. Reference to Drakes Mill is made by Andrew Johnston in his journal entry for April 20, 1743. The mill was sold to William Allen in 1750.[29] Allen died in 1761, leaving the mill to his sons, Robert and Joseph.[30]

An old bridge that once crossed
Peapack Brook behind the H.N.
Miller feed mill. From the
Norman Welsh collection.

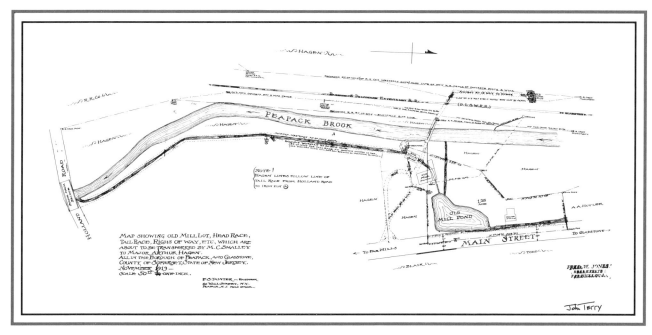

November 1919 survey map showing old mill lot, headrace, tailrace, and right-of-way, which were to be transferred by M. C. Smalley to Major Arthur Hagen. From the Harold Chesson collection.

May 5th—Got to my plantation. My expenses this journey 9/4. or nine shillings and four pence. Agreed with Wm. Allen for a small lot of the lands bought of Mrs. Leslie above Molicks land on Lawrence brook, it being a ruffy stoney lot; agreed to take 35/-pr. acre, payable 1st May next, and entered into articles with him.[31]

Before 1763 Robert Allen purchased 112 acres on the east side of Peapack Brook and by 1787 owned 212 acres.[32]

Mellick speaks of the mill:

The number of vats [tanning] below the dam was increased to eighteen and the water power much improved. This latter was done in connection with the joint owners of the water rights on the opposite side of Peapack Brook, who utilized their portion in grinding grist and sawing lumber. The exact date of establishing a flouring mill at this point has not been ascertained, but it is well known to have been the first mill in the township.[33]

It became clear to Allen that the flow of the brook was inadequate to turn the three mill wheels of the operation. In 1765 Allen enlisted the service of an engineer, Stephen Hunt, later a colonel in the Revolutionary Army, to solve the water problem. Hunt proceeded to build a dam on the North Branch to divert some of the river water. He selected a site where the two bodies of water ran most closely parallel, at a distance of about three hundred feet. At this point they were separated by a narrow ridge, then called the "hogback." There he built a dam, creating a reservoir. A one-hundred-foot tunnel through the ridge was dug, which, according to

Mellick, "created an aqueduct six feet high and three feet broad; it being on an incline, a considerable quantity of additional water was led through it, into the smaller stream, thus greatly augmenting the powers of the latter stream in serving the mills near its mouth."[34]

Digging of the tunnel was undertaken simultaneously from either side of the hill. However, the workers miscalculated, and the tunnels failed to meet in the middle as planned, so it was necessary to incorporate a double curve into the project. The project was an engineering success, but a financial failure for Allen. He was forced to sell the mills to Stephen Hunt on December 25, 1766. From that time forward the project was referred to as "Hunt's Folly."

In 1792 Hunt sold the property to Nicholas Arrowsmith, who came to the area after the revolutionary war and in 1787 owned seventy-six acres. Arrowsmith married Ellen Sutphen. His granddaughter Louise married Cornelius W. Schomp, and they settled on the homestead. Schomp was a member of the state legislature in 1855 1856; his son, Cornelius W., was elected to the state legislature in November 1880.[35]

Upper Peapack

THE VAN DOREN FAMILY. & The Van Doren family, early settlers in Peapack, were responsible for many improvements and civic contributions to the community. Jacob Van Doren emigrated from Holland to Long Island with his parents about 1660. He later moved to Monmouth County, New Jersey, where he married and sired ten children. His son Jacob Van Doren, Jr., born January 21, 1703, married Maria Schenck; they also had ten children. After her death he married Rachel Longstreet.

John Van Doren, son of Jacob and brother of Aaron Sr., married Agnita Schenck in 1756 and around 1760 purchased a large tract of land on the west side of Peapack Brook from Dr. John Johnstone. He moved to Peapack in 1766. Later, he sold the land to his brother Aaron and moved to Chester.

Jacob's son Aaron was born September 14, 1744, and died July 14, 1830. He sired twelve children by Geshea Schenck. A land deed of 1766 conveyed 175 acres in Peapack to him from his brother John. A land deed of December 23, 1769, conveyed 178 acres to him from his brother John.[36]

Aaron Van Doren, Sr., built a flour mill and millhouse in 1808. The mill and pond and two houses are indicated on the 1808 *Atlas of Somerset County* map. The 1850 *Atlas* map shows an added Van Doren house, built by William Aaron Van Doren, as well as a distillery. The mill and pond were located on the site of the field that stands across from the Methodist Church, and the millhouse is still standing on Church Street, directly opposite the front door of the church. In the early

Map of Peapack, 1850, in the *Atlas of Somerset County*. From the Harold Chesson collection.

The home built by William Van Doren, circa 1814. Located at the southwest corner of Main Street and Jackson Avenue. Around 1900 it was owned by William Vander Beek who operated a general store and coal business there; it was rented from him in 1908 by Oscar Smith, who ran a grocery and meat market on the premises. From the Reverend Paul Walther collection.

1800s Aaron Sr. built what was called "the mansion house," on the property now known as "Trestle Brook," on Old Chester Road, now owned by Harold Chesson. The house was sold to Jacob Dellicker in 1840 and to Peter Apgar in 1857. The Fred Condits owned the improved property before they sold it to Harold Chesson.

Aaron Jr. was born in Peapack on June 8, 1787, married Elizabeth Finley, and had four children, John (b. 1812), Eleanor (b. 1814), Elizabeth (b. 1818), and Mary (b. 1822). Aaron Jr. was deeded property by his father on August 28, 1813, and he built a house on that land. The house on Old Chester Road was owned in 1990 by Rev. Paul J. Walther, minister of the Peapack Reformed Church. No documentation has been found regarding the exact date that Aaron Jr. built the house, but historical research by Reverend Walther suggests that the house was a "two-build," the first and smaller section having been built circa 1808 by Aaron Jr. when his father's mill was opened (Aaron Jr. was a miller there), and the second and larger section built as his family expanded. Aaron Jr. moved away in 1844, and the house was sold. It was renovated by Whitfield and Ella Benjamin in the 1940s after World War II.

Aaron Sr.'s eighth child, William Aaron Van Doren, was born in Peapack July 26, 1781 (d. July 14, 1871). He married Elsie Sutton and they had ten children. William inherited a part of his father's property and purchased additional land.

He built a house in 1814, which is located on the corner of Main Street and Old Chester Road, and is now owned by Mr. and Mrs. William Timmons.

Lewis Van Doren, ninth child of William, born March 24, 1824 (d. August 20, 1902), married Henrietta Vroom Kline; he was also a miller and farmer. He lived in the house for a time, possibly after William's death. The house burned in the 1880s and was renovated in the Victorian style. In 1908 the property was owned by William Vander Beek, who had a coal business. Later it was rented by Oscar Smith for his grocery and meat business.

William Aaron Van Doren was a remarkable man:

> He was one of the most enterprising and highly esteemed citizens of Somerset County. . . . William A. at the age of nineteen left home to see the world and seek his fortune. He went to Pittsburgh, and thence in a "flat-boat" down the Ohio and Mississippi Rivers to Natchez where he began to raise cotton. He cultivated the growing crop much in the same manner that he did corn, and was quite successful, thus doing three-quarters of a century ago what planters are just now learning to do in some parts of the South. At the end of two years, not liking a state of society where difficulties were settled by a resort to the knife or pistol, he returned home.
>
> Peapack was then a little hamlet, with its post-office at New Brunswick, and subsequently at Somerville, until by his influence an office was opened there. With the proceeds of his cotton he began business in a store, and extended it until he had also a large farm, mill,

lime-kiln, and other branches of business. He took more pleasure in helping his family and friends and the neighborhood than in accumulating property. He became identified with all the improvements of the place. By purchasing various strips of land he straightened the roads, had bridges built, and set an example to others in draining and clearing the land. He introduced the first threshing machine in that vicinity, and other implements now so common, though there were many evil predictions concerning them.

In public life he was well known, his integrity securing for him continuously some office of trust or honor. Such was the confidence in which he was held that, though always an ardent politician, he was continued through all the changes of party for thirty-five years in the office of justice of the peace and judge of the Common Pleas, and, as an indication of the soundness of his judgment, though an immense amount of business came before him, his decisions were never set aside nor an appeal taken but in three instances.

He was a man of great firmness and dignity of character; his habits were temperate, and all his appetites and impulses under remarkable control. His vigor of body and mind was retained to an advanced age, so that he was able to prosecute improvements at a stage of life when men generally think such work out of the question. When nearly eighty years of age he enlarged his water-power and rebuilt his mill, superintending the getting out of the timber and going upon the roof of the mill to see that the work was well done. He lived to see a dozen years after the work was completed, almost reaching the rare age of ninety years.

His life was rigidly moral and upright, and he had been brought up in the strictest manner. Although not connected with any church as a member, he was an earnest supporter of religion, and at one time raised the subscription money for building a Reformed church in the place; but, owing to some opposition of their pastor at Bedminster, it was not until afterwards that the building which now stands was erected.[37]

Records of deeds of Van Doren family properties in the Hall of Records of Somerset County, Somerville, appear in the following:

B 629; A. Mellick to Van Doren; 10/20/1801
E 370; John Smiley to Aaron Van Doren; 12/20/1808
E 437; John Van Doren to Aaron Van Doren; 5/9/1809
F 735; G. Parker to Aaron Van Doren; 6/22/1812
F 830; Nicholas Jeroleman to Aaron Van Doren Jr.; 6/17/ 1812
I 138; William A. Van Doren to Aaron Van Doren; 11/11/1815
K 15; Aaron Van Doren Sr., to Aaron Van Doren Jr.; 1/13/1821
E 8 148; Lewis Van Doren to William Vander Beek; 5/17/1896
E 2 521; Lewis Van Doren to William Vander Beek; 7/28/1896

Pleasant Valley or O-Wan-A-Massie

The beautiful pastoral area east of Peapack-Gladstone, known as Pleasant Valley, is historically significant as the original site of the Smith family homestead and the later Smith family picnic reunions. Pleasant Valley actually straddles Peapack, Mendham Township, and Bernardsville.

Anne O'Brien, the noted Bedminster historian, who died

SMITH PICNIC BRIDGE 1918

PETER T. SMITH

Smith Family Picnic Bridge over the Raritan River on Willow Avenue, 1918. Drawing courtesy of Peter Smith.

in 1987, compiled an extensive folk history of Pleasant Valley based on the recollections of long-time residents of the area, land surveys, maps, Smith family genealogy and family records, and historical texts. The history, compiled by her between 1982 and 1984, was printed in 1985 and distributed to residents of the area. That history was made available to this author through the courtesy of the John Dayton Smith family. A portion of the following material is a condensation of Mrs. O'Brien's history and is included as a tribute to her dedication as a historian of Bedminster Township.

The rich bottom glade from Union Schoolhouse to Smith Picnic Bridge is Pleasant Valley. The cleaving hills of the Ramapo Fault embrace the vale and the riverhead of the Raritan. Iron was mined from the western ridge, and sandstone quarried in the eastern rise. Crops and dairy cattle, sheep and pigs, horses and pheasants have flourished in the valley.

There once were Indians. Owanamassie is said to be the name of their chief or, alternatively, the Indian word for Pleasant Valley. In spring when the Smith Picnic grounds are plowed a wide black ring is visible in the soil. A great campfire burned here when the Indians came up river. Spearheads and arrowheads have been found by the stream.

The red man relinquished his claim to the valley in 1701. The land east of the river was acquired by John Harrison, an agent of the Lords Proprietors of East New Jersey. Title to the west of the Raritan was conveyed to the Proprietors by three Indian chiefs, N[a]cholas (Nicholas), Elalie, and Tallaquapie, in an instrument known as the Peapack

Patent. A more engaging story is that the seller was Pequod; that Peapack is a corruption of Pequod; and that Pequod or Peapack is the Indian name for Smith.

Zachariah Smith was an early settler in Pleasant Valley. He was the youngest son of Johannes Heinrich Schmidt (1718–1791) who came from Holland as a servant indentured to a farmer in Staunton. Johannes changed his name to John Henry Smith, married the farmer's daughter, Christiana Hassel, and begat 17 children. The children were, in order: Christopher, Magdalena, Martin, John, Elizabeth, Charity, Mary Ann, Peter, Andrew, Catherine, Rebecca, Jacob, Sarah, Christiana, Joseph, Isaac, and Zachariah. All married, settled in central and northern New Jersey and New York State, and had between 3 and 14 children each.

Zachariah Smith (1780–1848) came to Pleasant Valley as a young man about 1800. He bought 227 acres of land in 1801 and built a double log house, a sawmill, and a brush block factory. The mill dam is gone, but part of the millrace and sawmill remain. Traces of the log house could be seen in 1881, and a flagpole marked the site at that time.

Zachariah married Mary "Polly" Smith (1779–1858), no relation, and sired 13 children. They were, in order: Christiana, Jane, John Z., Jacob Z., Peter Z., Elizabeth, William Z., Zachariah, Mary, Gertrude, Abraham, Margaret, and Celinda.

The shingle-over-clapboard house at Smith Picnic Bridge was built by Peter Zachariah Smith (1808–1893), a son of Zachariah. Peter Z. was a miller, a drover, and captain of a militia regiment of 80 men in Bedminster Township from 1837 to 1870. He drove cattle and sheep in from western New York State, and operated his father's sawmill and brush block factory. Both were still in use in 1881. In the 19th Century the area was known as "The Branch," after the River. Peter Z. Smith initiated the Smith Family Picnics and Charles VanArsdale Smith (b. 1875) later continued the tradition.[38]

❧ *The Smith Family and Friends Re-Union Established 1876*
The Smith Family of New Jersey in acknowledgment of their ancestral devotion, feeling grateful for the prosperity attending their general welfare, and prompted by the social and religious influences to which their fathers so strictly adhered, do hereby re-unite and form an Association for the purpose of encouraging those social qualities which should accompany every Christian body; thus, in memory of their ancestors, the descendants of John Smith and Christiana Hassel, his wife, down to the seventh generation, have organized and established the Smith Family and Friends' Re-Union.

Signed by Peter Z. Smith, Abraham Smith, Z. Z. Smith, John D. Smith, James Smith, W. A. Smith[39]

The famous Smith family picnics were initiated by Peter Z. Smith in 1876 on the site of the original log house. According to the Smith Family and Friends' Re-Union records, twenty-five hundred descendants of John Henry and Christiana Smith attended, some arriving in the 483 carriages counted. The picnics became an annual event with ever-growing attendance, and press coverage was extensive. In 1890 the *New York Times* extolled Peapack and the picnic:

Peapack! The spot is neither a city, a town, nor a village. It is only a spot consisting of two houses, a blacksmith shop, a creek, a horse-clipping machine, and a church. It is connected with the outside world merely by a narrow road running along the side of Mine Mountain, much like a hoop around a keg. Peapack is the Indian name for Smith [only according to this reporter].

The children of the Peapack Smiths have been especially blessed. From scores they grew into hundreds, and from hundreds into thousands. Until today they are marching onto the 3,000 mark with the lustre of seven generations enfolding them as they shout hosannas to the Lord at the annual Peapack Picnic. These Smiths are all members of the church and staunch Democrats. They stuff themselves with the delicacies of the Peapack kitchens, chicken patties, all sorts of cold meats, homemade pickles, 17 kinds of cakes, pure clear spring water, lemonade, pink and white. Every female of the Peapack Smiths is a born housewife and an accomplished cook.

The Smith girls have taken much to the Garrabrants and Coles. The picnic register has almost as many of those names as it has Smiths. But all are Peapack Smiths. In this century the picnic was moved west of the river to the site since known as the Smith Picnic Grounds. As many as 5,000 people would attend, as automobiles replace carriages as the means of transportation.[40]

The last picnic on the grounds of the old homestead took place in 1901.

Peapack New Jersey, August 28—The Peapack Smiths held their twenty-sixth annual reunion here today at the old Smith homestead,

The first Smith family reunion picnic, 1876. From the Helen Smith collection.

The Smith family
reunion picnic, circa
1930. From the
Helen Smith
collection.

near the headwaters of the Raritan River just east of the village where
stood the old log cabin of Zachariah Smith over one-hundred years ago.

The property, it is said, is to be sold, it being the last tract of land
in the vicinity not bought by the Ravine Association Syndicate. It was
expected the transfer would occur during the year, but as the property
is still in the hands of the Smith family, they decided to continue the
celebration on the old spot at least once more. The Valley, however, is
building up and the surrounding hills are dotted with magnificent
residences of wealthy New York people, so that it is safe to say there will
not be many more reunions at the old homestead.[41]

The Smith family purchased property on Branch Road in the early 1920s, and the picnics were reinstated. The sixtieth annual Smith family picnic was held in 1934 and was attended by more than a thousand family members and friends with Governor Hoffman as the principal speaker. The picnic grove was decorated by a huge painting of John Smith and his wife, Christiana Hassel, and trees were hung with family photographs. The picnics were discontinued after 1935 during the Depression years.

After a lapse of fifty years, the picnic was revived by John Dayton and Helen Smith on Saturday, September 14, 1985. A banner reading "In Memory of Our Ancestors" that was hung at the first reunion in 1876 had been preserved and was displayed in the meadow. About 120 Smith family descendants, ranging in age from seven weeks to eighty-seven years, attended the affair.

THE HOMESTEAD CHANGES HANDS. ❧ The Peter Z. Smith homestead and farm were purchased by George B. Post around 1860, before Post went to fight in the Civil War. Post was a prominent architect who designed the New York Stock Exchange and a number of other important buildings. Post never lived in the valley. He owned another farm on Mine Mountain, and in 1907 built "Claremont," a mansion still retained by his family.

The Smiths continued to live in the homestead and farm the land. Peter
Z.'s son, John Dayton Smith (1845–1919), and grandsons, Oscar
Smith and C. V. (Charles Van Arsdale) Smith were born there. The
boys went to school at Union Schoolhouse (in use 1851–1928).

Peter Z. Smith died in 1893 at age 84. His brother, Abraham,
became the patriarch of the Smith family, and represented Peter Z.'s
heirs in the sale of the farms to the Ravine Association.

Abraham Smith, born in 1830 at Mendham, became an apprentice in the carriage-making trade at Lesser Crossroads. He moved to Plainfield in 1851 and returned to Peapack in 1859. He was next a journeyman with David Apgar and later started his own wagon and carriage-building business. In 1865 he started an undertaking business.

The heirs of Peter Z. Smith were his widow, Jane, his sons and their
wives, Isaiah and Elizabeth, Oscar and Henrietta, and John Dayton
and Denia, and his daughter, Anna F. Wilson.

C. V. Smith became a commission merchant in New York and
brought the first Puerto Rican pineapples to the city. He lived in

Plainfield, but he had a special feeling for the valley. In 1919 he purchased Owanamassie and three acres from the Cole family—the Smith family daughters married Coles and Garrabrants and returned to Pleasant Valley to live. In 1922 he bought the 86-acre Pleasant Valley Farm from Fred McMurtry for $9,000. He had repurchased lands owned by the Smiths more than a century before.[42]

PLEASANT VALLEY FARM.   ❧   Pleasant Valley Farm and the other structures on Branch Road have been home to the Smith family since they purchased the properties in the early 1920s. The farmhouse is thought by the John Dayton Smith family to have been built circa 1670, builder unknown. It is a handsome example of early domestic architecture with beamed ceilings and masonry work. According to Smith family history, the foundation for the house was dug about three hundred years ago and used for a few years as the family's residence until further construction occurred. That early basement, which runs beneath the entire first floor, was used by the family as a summer kitchen years ago. On the porch at Pleasant Valley Farm is the gravestone of John Henry Smith, dated 1791. He is interred in an old Smith family burial ground near his bandbox house on Springtown Road in Staunton.

In a letter on file with the Hunterdon County Historical Society, New Jersey historian Hiram Deats wrote about Johannes Smith:

"They lived about two miles from me. I found his gravestone in the attic of a house once occupied by Willard Smith. I turned it over to the officers of the Smith Family Association. I wanted it placed in the Newell Cemetery, as more of his descendants are interred there."

In 1922 the family living in the house requested that it be removed from the attic of the house. It is thought that Oscar Smith (1886–1966) was the Smith Association representative who removed the tombstone at the request of Hiram Deats.[43]

O-Wan-A-Massie, as we know, is probably the Indian name for Pleasant Valley, and that name has been given to the stuccoed-brick bank house on Branch Road that overlooks the pond and open meadow south of the Smith-family farmhouse. Owned by landscape architect John Smith, it is thought to be an early eighteenth-century house and, according to the Smiths, has been in the family since 1718. The original house consisted of one room on the main floor with a fireplace and two bedrooms on the second floor, reached by a narrow stairway. The dining room, formerly a woodshed, was joined to the main body of the house when a second living room and kitchen were added about 1920.

Just across Branch Road from "O-Wan-A-Massie" is "The Mill House," built circa 1925, when the Smiths purchased the property. The house occupies the site of an old sawmill on the Raritan River. The pond was built about 1945 to power a waterwheel that for many years generated electricity for the other two Smith houses. The upper level of the structure, once a playhouse, has been converted to a private residence, another side having been added in 1971.

There are a number of mid-to-late nineteenth-century houses in Pleasant Valley that are believed to have been built by Smith family descendants. The names Cole and Garrabrant appear on 1850 and 1873 maps, and it is known that these families and the Smiths intermarried. The small settlement of Pleasant Valley had an early general store at what was later know as Blazure's Corner.

Teviotdale, a wood frame and fieldstone New Jersey farmhouse, was built circa 1840, probably by some member of the Smith family. The 1850 map indicates that is was the property of A. Cole. It was purchased by Palmer Campbell in the 1920s and sold soon after to William J. Hutchinson, who owned and farmed the entire Pleasant Valley, east of the river, in the 1920s. It was purchased by the architect William Turnbull in 1939; he made alterations and additions. The farm was named Teviotdale after the river Teviot, ancestral home of a branch of the Turnbull family.

One of the oldest houses in Pleasant Valley, probably prerevolutionary, is just to the north of Teviotdale. It is a perfect example of a New Jersey farmhouse, wood frame, with slate roof, hand-hewn beams, plaster on wood lath, and handwrought nails.

The Murray McDonnell house is an early nineteenth-century New Jersey farmhouse with alterations and additions, which was probably built by a member of the Smith family. The 1855 and 1873 maps indicate its owner was A. S. Garrabrant. The property changed hands over time, most recently in 1952 when the house and fifty acres were purchased from Mr. and Mrs. Malcolm McKay by Mr. and Mrs. T. Murray McDonnell. The barn and part of the land were sold to Mrs. Elizabeth Chace Burden (a sister of Mrs. James C. Brady) in 1950. She converted the barn to a house, and sold it Mrs. Jacqueline Kennedy Onassis about 1970.

The Arthur Turnbull house, located at the west end of Campbell Road, near its junction with Lake Road and Willow Avenue, was built in 1912 and 1913 for Mr. and Mrs. Arthur Turnbull, Sr., on land that once belonged to Mrs. Turnbull's father, George B. Post. The site is contiguous to the hundred acres that George B. Post bought from the Smith family when he went to fight in the Civil War. The architect was William Sloane Post, son of George B. Post, and a member of his father's New York architectural firm, George B. Post and Sons.[44]

❧ *The Mellick Family*

Andrew D. Mellick, Jr., published *The Story of an Old Farm* in 1889.[45] In this history he traces the lives of his ancestors who lived in Bedminster Township before him. Many local people are familiar with the book, and with the old stone house that still sits on Old Dutch Road today. Mellick was not only a historian, but a marvelous raconteur. The history is a colorful account of events as they unfolded in Bedminster Township and Somerset County during the Colonial period, the revolutionary war, and the early years of Independence.

Mellick had been a vital and active person early in his life, having been a real estate investor and businessman. An accident forced him into a sedentary life, but fortunately for us, Mellick spent the years after his impairment researching and writing his invaluable book. He combed official records and had access to family papers, letters, and legal documents. In addition to the written data, he had as a living source his grandfather Daniel, the grandson of Johannes Mellick, who was the first family member to settle in America.

The historical material that pertains to Peapack-Gladstone from the Colonial period through the mid-nineteenth century is sketchy and rather general. In this history of Peapack-Gladstone the author has taken the liberty of excerpting portions from Mellick's book that relate most directly to our borough because of the fascinating historical tapestry so skillfully woven by him. His book is certainly required reading for a complete local history education.

A Brief Sketch of the Mellick Family

Johannes Mellick emigrated to this country, with his wife and four children, from Bendorff, Germany, about 1735. They settled at first near what is now Readington, New Jersey. On November 1, 1751, Johannes purchased a 367-acre tract of land from George Leslie. The tract had been part of the Peapack Patent, purchased from the Indians and the New Jersey Proprietors by Dr. John Johnstone and George Willocks.

Mellick's purchase was described by Snell: "This tract extended east to Peapack or Lawrence Brook and the North Branch; south to the north line of the Major Daniel Axtell tract, the present east and west road being then of the line, having been laid out in 1745; north to the north line of the Indian tract."[46]

Mellick's book describes in detail the rigors and rewards of life on a family farm. The Mellicks built a log house at first, opposite the site where the stone house was later constructed. They proceeded to carve out of the tract a farm and tannery. Johannes died in 1763, and his eldest son, Aaron, assumed responsibility for running the family farm. Under his administration the tanneries were expanded, and a drying and currying shed adjoined the area.

Aaron Mellick died in 1809, and much of his personal property was sold at public auction, although the farm and house remained the property of the Mellick family. A copy of "The Estate of Aaron Mellick Record Book 1809–1818" is on file in the Manuscript Collection of the New Jersey Historical Society, and from it we can learn much about the life of Somerset County farmers in the late eighteenth century.

Among the household items listed for sale in the estate book were:

> one eight-day clock
> one feather bed
> one table and two stands
> one looking glass
> two spreads and one quilt
> one cupboard
> one old poplar desk and book case
> six silver teaspoons
> six delph [sic] plates
> one grindstone
> two old knives
> one old tub

The estate book also listed farm animals and implements that were to be sold, and, what may surprise many readers, the book includes a list of slaves to be sold at that public sale. Slaves were in fact a part of many of the Somerset County farmers' property. Census figures list the slave population in New Jersey before the Revolution as between 300,000 and 400,000. In 1725 Somerset County had a total population of 4,500, of whom 732 were slaves. Although the American Congress had prohibited the slave trade in 1776, the 1800 Census of Somerset County included 1,863 slaves out of a population of 12,813, so it is obvious that the practice prevailed in the North as well as the South. Slave ships called at Perth Amboy, and it was there that slaves were auctioned. Between 1804 and 1820 a series of laws intended to lead gradually toward abolition was enacted in New Jersey. These laws provided that every child born of a slave mother in the state of New Jersey after July 4, 1804, should be nominally free, but should remain the servant of the owner of the mother until age twenty-five for males, twenty-one for females. By 1830 full slaves in Somerset County numbered only 78.

Andrew Mellick, in *The Story of an Old Farm*, avers that Aaron Mellick had no slaves until he was quite an old man, in deference to his wife's wishes, she being a Quaker. However, finding himself short-handed at the tannery in 1786, he agreed to buy "Old Yombo" from his brother-in-law Jacob Kline. Later other slaves were purchased for the farm, who, according to Andrew Mellick, were generally well treated and happy. When Aaron died in 1809, the fate of each of the slaves was not to be known until his will was read. This led to a period of uncertainty for the people involved, as described by a poignant note (probably written by the administrator of the estate) penned in ink in the margin of the estate book (punctuation and spelling are as they appear when legible):

> *The question with the negro children and the white ones of their age was not who shall buy the old bay horse or the old Brindle cow but who will buy Dian, who'll buy Sam or who ll buy Ben. Where will they*

go. Will we never see them more and how will they get on with their new master. All these things came up for consideration and between talk and tears the time wore heavily on to the day of sale. But thanks to good masters, to a good name, to honesty, the clouds lifted to show a silver lining. Uncle Dick Aunt Nance and Ann were Bid off to Daniel Melick for [illegible] Dollars. Dian to Jonathon Dayton Esq. of the City of Elizabeth to be miss Daytons servant until 25 years old. She is [illegible] now and has the promise of coming to see the old folks Christmas each year. Sam to Revd John McDowell for 225.00 until he is 28 year old Dick to William R. Smiley for 225.00 until he is 28 year old.[47]

On another page the notes explore the ages of the slaves when they were acquired by Mellick:

Dick was older than Nance by perhaps ten years and Nance was supposed at the time of the sale to be about 51 or 2 year old—while Dick was considered sixty five at the time of Dicks purchase from Capt. Jms Taylor he was about 49 years old The purchase was, Dick, Nance his wife 37 Diana called Deon 6 years old, Sam 3 years old and Dick 10 mos old.

It would appear that yombo had been bought some time before Dick & family in about 1786 or 7 he had a wife at Elizabethtown. I think that he became the property of Jacob Kline and was sold to Aaron Melick by him. He was a good tanner and leather finisher, worked in the Currying Shop and went bare headed (chewed tobacco) had rings [barely legible] in his ears and was a shiny black and said that he was a son of a negro King in [illegible].[48]

The slaves who were sold are listed as follows in the estate book:

One old negro named Yombo, a slave	*$ 25*
One [illegible] Dick, a slave	*$ 40*
One old negro wench, Nance, a slave	*$ 40*
One old negro wench name Dianah born 9th August 1791 and appraised for her time till she is 25 yrs of age	*$ 90*
One negro boy named Sam, born September 1794 and appraised (for his time) till he is 28 years of age	*$160*
One negro boy named Dick born in December and appraised (for his time) till he is 28 years of age	*$160*
One negro boy named, Joe, born 4th March 1800 and appraised (for his time) till he is 28 years of age	*$120*
One negro girl named Ann born 4th March 1806 and appraised (for her time) till she is 21 years of age.[49]	*$ 35*

Mellick explains in his book that Aaron provided for the indenturement of the young slaves so as not to thrust "pauperism" on them by freeing them, which would have caused an "incubus" for the estate, "as they would have to be supported."[50]

Other Early Families

The Tiger Family

Forebears of the Tiger family emigrated from Holland to the United States after 1773. Tigers are known to have served in the War of 1812 and the Civil War. Those who enlisted in the Civil War First Battalion of the Second Regiment of the Somerset Brigade include Corp. Jacob Tiger, Jr., Corp. Peter Tiger, and Capt. John Tiger (buried in Union Cemetery).

Jacob John Tiger (son of Capt. John Tiger) was a farmer in Chester Township and Mendham. He owned property covering several hundred acres in Bedminster Township in the Ski Hill area. He bought the Peapack farm in 1862 from the estate of George Luce, who died the same year. The property included 113 acres and was purchased for $16,500. Administrators of Luce's estate were Ed Schomp and William Hillard. Included with the land were the stone barns (built in 1829); the smaller stone building behind them, which was a wagon house; and the large sheep barns (now "The Stable"). The property extended from the brook below to the top of what is now the Tiger Hill development. A spring house that fed a reservoir was at the top of Tiger Hill. Below the stone barns a meadow extended to the brook, and in it stood an old stone shelter for livestock. That parcel is now Main Street and the Gladstone train station. The reservoir was behind the barns, and the Tigers gave the railroad access for its coal-burning engines.

Jacob John Tiger, whose wife was named Sophia, began to build the new house located at 248 Main Street in 1868, but did not live to see its completion. In his will of February 24, 1868, he bequeathed land for the Reformed Church cemetery. His will stated that if at any time the church failed to keep the property clear of "ground thistle and other foul weeds," the property was to revert to the heirs to his estate.

The house he built has remained in the family. It is now occupied by Marcus A. Canfield, whose wife was Edith Tiger (deceased). They had two children, Ellis Canfield (deceased) and Barbara Neil.

Jacob Tiger's son, Ellis Tiger, married Arabella Opdyke. They raised four children: William, Vernon, Anna (Smith), and Edith (Canfield). Ellis founded Ellis Tiger & Co., a lumberyard and general merchandise store located along the railroad tracks, in 1893. He was a cofounder and first president of the Peapack-Gladstone Bank. The next business started by Ellis was a hardware store in what is now Conover Corners Building on the northwest corner of Mendham Road and Main Street.

Ellis Tiger left the land that is Tiger Hill to his four children. Vernon and William took over the businesses. Vernon ran the hardware store and owned the stable. His children were Doris (Studer) and Bernice (Epler).

THE STONE BARN 1829

PETER T. SMITH

Tiger family farm stone barns, Main Street,
Gladstone, 1829.
Drawing courtesy of Peter Smith.

ELLIS TIGER HARDWARE STORE   1905   PETER T. SMITH

The Ellis Tiger Hardware Store, built in 1905.
Drawing courtesy of Peter Smith.

Eldridge M. Ward and employees of his plumbing, heating, and sheet metal business in Peapack-Gladstone, circa 1918. Mr. Ward is at left with son Tom and daughter Blanche. Note Red Cross poster in the show window. The Ellis Tiger Hardware Store on the right is now Conover's Corner. Tiger's Garage, now Gladstone House, was built a few years later on the vacant lot behind the men. From the Thomas Ward collection.

"A visit to the Tiger's store is an experience in itself. Name it, he has it! He may take time to find it, but while he is hunting you can look around. Be sure to look up! It is unbelievable to see how high the shelves are and the number of things hanging from the ceiling."[51]

William built the Tiger Building (now Gladstone House) in 1923 as an automobile dealership. He was the first Ford dealer in New Jersey (see "Crossroads and Automobiles" in "From Rural Village to Incorporated Borough" below). He had two children, William Ellis and Frances T. Lynch.

The other Tiger family descendants include Anna (Mrs. Oscar Smith), whose children are Gladys Roper and Edith Loring.

The Hill Family

Theodore Sutphen Hill, who had been a farmer in Mendham for many years, settled in Peapack-Gladstone and purchased an old hotel from Oscar Vliet, which he converted into a two-family house. In 1850 this structure had served as a tavern, with W. A. Mellick its proprietor. The building still stands at 291 Main Street and is owned by T. Leonard Hill.

Garner Ferris Hill, better known as G. F., bought property in Gladstone in 1900 with his father, Theodore Sutphen Hill. G. F. decided to pursue a different career from his father and daily took the Delaware and Lackawanna train from Gladstone to Newark, where he attended business school. In his first business venture he purchased a team of horses and contracted to dig foundations for some of the large estates being constructed in the area. He then added a livery service to his enterprises, which operated out of a barn that stood on the site of the Scout Cabin (see the appendix). That barn stands now on Lackawanna Avenue across from Dominick's Pizza. The livery service employed fourteen or fifteen horses constantly, pulling carriages and wagons that transported people and supplies. Garner bought a hearse from the undertaker, Mr. Forsythe, whose business was located on the corner of Mendham Road and Dewey Avenue (now owned by the Tiger family), and two jet black horses were used to pull the hearse. On one occasion Garner drove the local basketball team to the Morristown YMCA in a horse-drawn sleigh to participate in a game. The horses were also used to pull the fire company hose carts before fire trucks were used. He next expanded his business to include a feed mill, adjacent to the railroad, convenient for unloading carloads of feed. The mill stood until 1979 when it was destroyed by a fire, believed to have been arson.

Garner's business ventures expanded further in 1921, when a new bank was organized locally. He put up a building on the corner of Main Street and Lackawanna Avenue to house both the bank and a hardware store. A Chevrolet agency followed in 1923, which was later run by his son, T. Leonard Hill, who went on to run all parts of the business, including a lumber-and-coal yard which was located across Peapack Brook behind the railroad tracks, and an International Harvester agency which is now the Beval Saddlery.

Garner F. Hill feed mill, circa 1910. From the T. Leonard Hill collection.

The Garner Hill
Livery Service, 1907.
From the
T. Leonard Hill
collection.

First taxi, circa
1910, operated by
Garner Hill Livery
Service. From the
T. Leonard Hill
collection.

Garner F. Hill feed mill. Built in 1904,
destroyed by fire in 1979.
Drawing courtesy of Peter Smith.

The Ludlow Family

Charles Ludlow (1800–1866) lived in Peapack on his family homestead located near what is now the foot of Ravine Lake.[52] He raised four sons, Josiah (1839–1913), Charles Jr. (1847–1916), James Irving (1852–1940), all of Peapack, and Henry, who moved to Far Hills. The family epitomizes the entrepreneurial spirit that arose here in the mid-1800s.

Josiah and James Irving created an internationally known hub factory—Ludlow Brothers, Manufacturers of White Oak, Elm and Warner Hubs—at the homestead. The hubs were crafted by hand of white oak and elm, and the area was dubbed "Hub Hollow." When C. Ledyard Blair and other developers decided to create Ravine Lake by damming the Raritan River, in 1895, they began acquiring the farms located along the river at approximately eighty dollars per acre.[53] Hub Hollow was one of those properties, and its sale prompted the Ludlows' move to Peapack. They built a new factory on the site now occupied by Komline-Sanderson Corporation. Later the factory was sold to a Frenchman who manufactured printed candy wrappers, and subsequently it was sold to Cleaveland Laboratories, Inc., which manufactured plastic-coated cloth. It burned to the ground in July 1945.

Ludlow business letterhead. From the Kostew family collection.

The Ludlow Brothers Hub Factory, circa 1913. From the Harold Chesson collection.

Peapack
N.J.

F.P.C.
123

The Ludlow family home built by James Irving Ludlow and his son William, circa 1900, still standing on the northeast corner of Main Street and Highland Avenue. From the Reverend Paul Walther collection.

The remains of the Ludlow meat-market barns at 68 Main Street, built by Charles Ludlow circa 1870. The building was razed in 1990. Photograph by Jan Gordon, October 1990.

James Irving was also a prosperous coal merchant, who together with his son William Irving (1878–1957) built the imposing Victorian house on the northeast corner of Main Street and Highland Avenue. Their coal yard stood behind what is now the Komline-Sanderson factory.

Charles Jr. started a butcher shop and meat market which was continued by his son Walter (1874–1936). They delivered meat to customers in a horse-drawn wooden wagon, from a barn they erected on Main Street which housed their horses and meat-processing operation; during the Civil War it was used to board horses. The butcher shop occupied the stucco building at 68 Main Street. In 1990 the barn was razed, and today only the stone foundation remains of what was a landmark of the early rural development of Lower Peapack. The foundation is located between 66 and 70 Main Street.

Henry Ludlow moved to Far Hills where he started the lumberyard. Several of the Victorian houses on Holland Avenue were built by the Ludlows.

When Josiah Ludlow died in 1913, the local paper ran the following obituary:

> *Josiah Ludlow, an aged and very highly respected citizen of this place, passed to the life beyond on Saturday morning, at about 3:30, from a complication of diseases. Deceased was seventy-four years of age and was a life-long resident of this vicinity. He was greatly loved and respected by all who knew him; being possessed with the kindest spirit and having so many of the finer qualities which so few possess, he was one of those men of whom it could be said "To know him was to love him." This vicinity has lost one of its best citizens in his death.*
>
> *Deceased was born and grew to manhood in a house which formerly stood where the cottage now stands at the foot of Ravine Lake. Before a railroad extended to this vicinity he drove a stage from Liberty Corner to Bound Brook, carrying the mail and passengers. He also worked at the wheelwright business until 1868 when he started the hub business, being one of the pioneers in that business and remaining in that business until about two years ago, when his failing health compelled him to retire. He started the business with a turning lathe which was run by a horse and saw the business develop until the present large factory was occupied. He moved into the village about twenty-two years ago and took much interest in improvements and the growth of the village, and assisted the church and all things that were good.*
>
> *Deceased is survived by a widow and three children—F. H. Ludlow, Miss Cora Ludlow and Miss Edith Ludlow, all of this place. Also the following brothers—Henry Ludlow, of Far Hills, and Charles Ludlow and James Ludlow, of this place.*
>
> *Funeral services were held at the Reformed Church on Tuesday afternoon, Rev. T. M. Simanton officiating. Interment was made in the Reformed Churchyard by Funeral Director W. A. Smith.*[54]

The Craig Family

The Craig family was an important part of the early rural development of Peapack. Moses Craig, second son of Moses Watson Craig and his wife, Hannah Allen Craig, was born near Peapack in 1796 and died in 1874. His house, still standing at 158 Main Street, is said to have been the first town meeting hall, and later, in 1850, a retail store. Craig built the large gray house next to it in the 1800s. He was one of the founders and builders of the First Christian Church in 1838.

> *January 11, 1838 a meeting was held at the home of Moses Craig, in Peapack and the following trustees were elected: Abraham Wortman, Philip Lawrance, Stephen Rush, David Apgar, Moses Craig, John Jeroleman and Hugh Runyan, Jr. These persons certified that they had taken upon themselves the name of "Free Christian Society." A stone church was erected on the west side of Main Street and services were conducted by the Rev. Moses Cummings and Austin Craig and others for a year or two, then discontinued. The building was afterwards used for services by the Baptists for a time, and these also were discontinued.*[55]

In 1868 the building was sold to Peter Z. Smith, who converted it to a store with living quarters in the rear, where he lived until 1874. Moses' son Austin Craig, D.D. (1824–1881) married Adelaide Churchill. He became a teacher and college chaplain and later was president of Antioch College and pastor of the Christian Church at Yellow Springs, Ohio. His son Moses (1863–1913) is buried in Union Cemetery in Gladstone. Emeline Craig (1828–1891) was born in Peapack and married Edward Perry, M.D. (1820–1892). Dr. Perry was the local physician, and he and his wife lived in the house on Main Street between the lime kilns and Blair Drive.

The Philhower Family

John Philhower (1798–1876) was a farmer in Upper Peapack who married Barbara Apgar (1802–1890). They had seven children. John acquired land from Nicholas Arrowsmith in 1828.[56] He donated the land on which the Methodist Church was built, and later twelve acres for Union Cemetery. His son Elias (1832–1913) followed his father as a Gladstone farmer with major landholdings that comprised most of what is now Gladstone. Elias's sister Sophia (1822–1887) married Jacob John Tiger (1817–1868), and his sister Rachel (1825–1920) married William T. Mellick (1821–1898). His children were Mrs. Rachel Rodenbaugh of Peapack ("The Rachel" steam locomotive of the Rockaway Valley Railroad was named for her by her husband, a train engineer; see "The Rock-a-Bye Baby," in "From Rural Village to Incorporated Borough" below); Mrs. Johnathan Thorp, Dover, Delaware; Mrs. E. H. Dekyne, Plainfield; and Mrs. Amos Blain, Peapack. George R. Mosle purchased the land on which he built his estate from the Philhower family.

On February 12, 1909, the following appeared in the *Weekly Exponent*:

> *We publish below a few items taken from an old account book of John Philhower, who owned the farm in town purchased by G. R. Mosle. The accounts are mainly those of about 1850. Although they are not*

as valuable as many published of a much later date, they give an idea of prices of articles and labor about fifty or sixty years ago. This farm then extended over about all the land now occupied by the pretty, thriving little town of Gladstone, which was then represented by three or four buildings. A few of the accounts are as follows:

April 7, 1849	*2 bushels of oats*	*.60*
April 14, 1849	*4 bushels of oats*	*1.20*
Aug. 29, 1849	*1 bushel of rye*	*.79*
July 10, 1851	*1 load of hay*	*4.00*
Aug. 4, 1851	*2 pounds butter*	*.32*

The accounts show that a farm laborer received from $96 to $100 a year.[57]

The Huyler Family

Martin Huyler, the last living Civil War veteran in Peapack and the first marshall in Peapack-Gladstone, farmed on the John Tiger farm on Peapack Road. He and his wife, Aletta, lived in a house just south of the present site of St. Brigid Catholic Church; the house was later moved to Far Hills. The Huylers had two sons, Fred and Charles.

Fred, a member of the first Council of Peapack-Gladstone, was a local contractor and builder in business with Mr. Flomerfelt in the early 1900s. One of the buildings he built was the Van Arsdale home, now the Bailey Funeral Home, at 176 Main Street in Peapack. He married Margaret Van

Horn, and they had two sons, Fred Dumont Huyler and Victor Martin Huyler. Fred was singled out by James Cox Brady to manage Hamilton farm, built in 1911. He held the post for fifty years, helping Brady in a wide range of activities (see "Hamilton Farm" in "The Grand Estates and the Resultant Changes" below).

Victor Martin Huyler was born in 1898 and lived in Peapack-Gladstone. He was employed by the Peapack-Gladstone Bank. A long-time Board of Education representative, he was treasurer and Consistory member of the Peapack Reformed Church. He was extremely interested in the local history of the borough. He died in 1990, having expressed to the Friends of the Library his wish that funds from his estate be used to help defray the costs of publishing this history.

❧ Notes

1. Samuel Eliot Morison, *The Oxford History of the American People*, p. 77.
2. Ibid.
3. Andrew D. Mellick, Jr., *The Story of an Old Farm: or Life in New Jersey in the Eighteenth Century.*
4. *Somerset County Historical Quarterly*, vol. 3, 1914.
5. The family name of John Johnstone and his descendants was spelled both Johnstone and Johnston in early documents. It is not until the eighteenth century, with Andrew Johnston, that the final "e" was officially dropped.
6. According to Frederick Walter, "the earliest recorded transaction in

Bedminster Township was the purchase in 1690 by Margaret Winder of a thousand acres lying on both side of the North Branch. She was the daughter of Governor Rudyard and after her husband, Samuel Winder, died, she married George Willocks." In *The Township of Bedminster: Published for the New Jersey Tercentenary (1664–1964)*, p. 13.

7. *Somerset County Historical Quarterly*, vol. 3, 1919.
8. Rachel Potter, "Historical Facts and Places of Interest in Peapack-Gladstone." The text of the Peapack Patent can also be found in Ludwig Schumacher, *The Somerset Hills*, p. 121.
9. Potter, "Historical Facts."
10. Schumacher, *The Somerset Hills*.
11. *Lesser Crossroads*, edited by Hubert G. Schmidt, p. 186.
12. Ibid., p. 187.
13. Ibid., p. 156.
14. Ibid.
15. Ibid.
16. Ibid., p. 188.
17. Ibid., p. 189.
18. Ibid., p. 210.
19. Ibid., p. 211.
20. Members of the Van Doren family also used the spelling Van Dorn.
21. The ledger is in the manuscript file of the New Jersey Historical Society.
22. Lowrance was the spelling used by Johannes; his descendants called themselves Lowrence.
23. Andrew Johnston's journal, 1743–1754, reprinted in *Somerset County Historical Quarterly*, vol. 1 (1912).
24. John Lawrence Ely, "Supplement to *The Old Farm* by Andrew D. Mellick, Jr.: Regarding the Ancestors of Alice Louise Lawrence Ely & Interesting to Her Descendants."
25. Hogeboom Collection.
26. *Weekly Exponent*, December 4, 1908.
27. *Peapack and Gladstone Fire Department: 1905–1955*, Fiftieth anniversary celebration souvenir booklet, 1955.
28. *Weekly Exponent*, July 23, 1908.
29. Mellick credits Allen with having established the mill.
30. "Supplement to *The Old Farm*."
31. Andrew Johnston's Journal of 1755.
32. James P. Snell, *History of Hunterdon and Somerset Counties, New Jersey*, p. 708.
33. Mellick, *Story of an Old Farm*, p. 267. Note the disparity here between the Lowrance Mill dates and Mellick's account.
34. Ibid., p. 268.
35. Ibid., p. 708.
36. Peter Ellis Van Doren, *Combined Recorded History of the People of Peapack-Gladstone Born before 1900 with Children*.
37. Snell, *History of Hunterdon and Somerset Counties*, p. 733.
38. Condensed from Anne O'Brien, "Pleasant Valley."
39. William Francis Smith and Beverly B. Smith, *John Smith 1718–1791: Descendants*, p. 361.
40. As quoted in the *Bernardsville News*, July 25, 1985.
41. *New York Times*, August 29, 1901.
42. O'Brien, "Pleasant Valley."
43. Smith and Smith, *John Smith*, pp. 306–307.
44. The house descriptions are condensed from O'Brien, "Pleasant Valley."
45. Mellick, *Story of an Old Farm*. Hubert G. Schmidt prepared an edited reprint that appeared under the title *Lesser Crossroads* in 1948, and an abridged version that was printed in 1961.
46. Snell, *History of Hunterdon and Somerset Counties*, pp. 704–705.
47. The Estate of Aaron Mellick Record Book, 1809–1818.
48. Ibid.
49. Ibid.
50. Mellick, *Story of an Old Farm*, p. 610.

51. J. H. Van Horn, *Historic Somerset*, p. 173.

52. All of the Ludlow family dates are taken from Van Doren, *Combined Recorded History of the People of Peapack-Gladstone*.

53. Allison Wright Post, *Recollections of Bernardsville*, p. 15.

54. *Weekly Exponent*, August 29, 1913.

55. From Rachel Potter's "Historical Facts and Places of Interest in Peapack-Gladstone."

56. The Philhower family dates are from Van Doren, *Combined Recorded History of the People of Peapack-Gladstone*.

57. As quoted in the *Bernardsville News*, January 9, 1975.

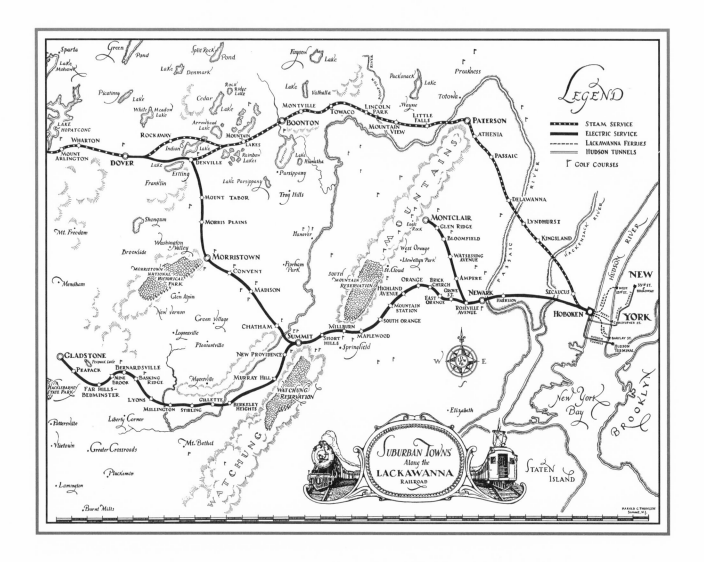

LEGEND

- **□□□□** STEAM SERVICE
- **━━━** ELECTRIC SERVICE
- **- - -** LACKAWANNA FERRIES
- HUDSON TUNNELS
- ⌐ GOLF COURSES

Suburban Towns Along the **LACKAWANNA** *Railroad*

HAROLD C. THOMSON
Summit, N.J.

From Rural Village to Incorporated Borough

The Turn of the Century Transformation: The Iron Horse

The Delaware and Lackawanna

The transformation of Peapack-Gladstone from an isolated rural village to the suburban community it is today was generated by the extension here of the Delaware and Lackawanna Railroad in 1890. Before that time, travel had been limited to horse and carriage on poorly maintained, unpaved roads. Journeys were tedious, uncomfortable, and

A map of the Erie Lackawanna Railroad route as printed on a restaurant placemat. From the Homer Hill collection.

time consuming. But within a few years of the extension, a once-limited horizon opened outward to vistas beyond rural Peapack; inversely, a once-remote pastoral village became accessible, and, because of its beauty, attracted the world beyond its immediate boundaries.

The resounding whistle of locomotives, the rumbling of train wheels, and the screeching of brakes have long been a part of the daily scene in Peapack-Gladstone. Each morning and evening passengers board the trains that carry them to and from their places of employment. Many of them travel to Hoboken and transfer to the tubes and on to New York City. Students climb aboard for the trip to and from area high schools, such journeys having been made by borough adolescents since 1912.

The modern electric train system that Peapack-Gladstone commuters use today evolved from a rivalry between early New Jersey railroads. The challenge was to build a line from the tidewater areas that would extend west across the state to cross the Delaware and reach the coal fields of Pennsylvania.

The Jersey Central Railroad had reached the Delaware River at Phillipsburg in 1852 under the leadership of its president, John Taylor Johnston. Two other magnates with interests in the Pennsylvania coal fields were equally eager to connect with the coast for shipping: John I. Blair, who had helped found the Delaware Lackawanna & Western Railroad, which connected the Lackawanna coal fields with the Delaware; and Asa Packer, who helped charter what was to become the Lehigh Valley Railroad from Mauch Chunk, Pennsylvania, to Easton in 1846. Packer later built a two-level bridge across the Delaware River and connected his railroad with the Jersey Central Railroad in Phillipsburg. He began buying up interests in railroads, including the Passaic Valley & Peapack, which was renamed the New Jersey West Line in 1870. Packer's Lehigh Valley Railroad reached Perth Amboy in 1875. Before he died in 1879, Packer founded Lehigh University.

Two railroads had bypassed the Somerset Hills area: the Morris and Essex to the north could offer service between Morristown and New York as early as January 1838; and the Jersey Central to the south from Elizabethtown to Plainfield by 1839. It was not until March 1865 that the Passaic Valley & Peapack Railroad was incorporated to construct a railway from Essex County to Peapack. In 1870 construction was begun on a line from Summit to Bernardsville; it was completed in 1872. At this point the line began to encounter financial difficulties, eventually going bankrupt, before being sold to the Delaware Lackawanna & Western. Later it was reorganized as a new corporation, the Passaic and Delaware Railroad, and leased to the Delaware Lackawanna & Western. The terminus of this line was now to be Gladstone.

The railroad's extension to Far Hills and subsequently to Gladstone was accomplished through the influence of Grant

B. Schley, the founder and great benefactor of Far Hills. He developed an abiding interest in the Somerset Hills while visiting Seney's Bernardsville mountain resort; subsequently he built his estate in Far Hills.

Construction on the new line was begun in April 1890 in Bernardsville, and by October of the same year the "Millionaire's Express" was making eight runs daily between Gladstone and Hoboken. Accommodations for passengers on this line included a dining car and a club car with special attendants. There were but seventy-six members of the club car, and there was always a long waiting list to buy individual subscriptions. Prospective subscribers were asked to submit two letters of recommendation. The club car, it was rumored, was reserved for those subscribers who paid one thousand dollars per year for the privilege of riding in it. The club car was rather spartan, considering the cost. The passengers sat in wicker armchairs placed on each side of the car under the windows. The cars did feature a special porter, mahogany paneling with small teak inlays, and air-conditioning. Contrary to what one may think, no alcoholic beverages were served. Each morning, after the commuters were seated and immersed in the *New York Times* or *Wall Street Journal*, the porter would come through the car offering ice water. On the way home soup, tea, soft drinks, and, perhaps, cookies were offered. The porter was reimbursed for his expenditures by the passengers at the end of each month. The air-condition-ing system was quite primitive. Three-hundred-pound blocks of ice were slid onto specially built bunkers under the car. Water ran over the ice and into pipes over which fans blew. The cooled air was channeled into the club car through ducts in the walls. When the railroad was electrified in 1930, the special cars were rebuilt. One of the subscription cars continued in operation until 1984.

A "Millionaire's Express" it was indeed. Allison Wright Post, in his *Recollections of Bernardsville*, describes the glittering scene at the first railroad station there in the years before 1905, when the automobile was not yet the common means of transportation. The railroad station he refers to is now the home of the *Bernardsville News*. It can be assumed that this particular scene took place before the line extended to Gladstone as reference is made to Peapack-Gladstone resident C. Ledyard Blair.

> *For some years before 1905, the number of owners of carriage and saddle horses, thoroughbreds of the finest kind, made Bernardsville remarkable. The sight on the arrival of trains at Bernardsville to meet the business men coming from New York did not fail to attract attention. Horses and carriages of all descriptions were here on a summer afternoon. The women met their husbands with their phaetons, a fringed canopy shading their flowered hats and bright gowns, and a groom standing at the heads of the horses. A spiked team of three horses, I well remember, of my father's driven to a wagonette, a carriage holding eight persons; Mr. Walter P. Bliss with his three beautiful horses*

Interior view of the old DL&W club car #3454, en route between Summit and Bernardsville. Photograph by Homer R. Hill, October 16, 1983.

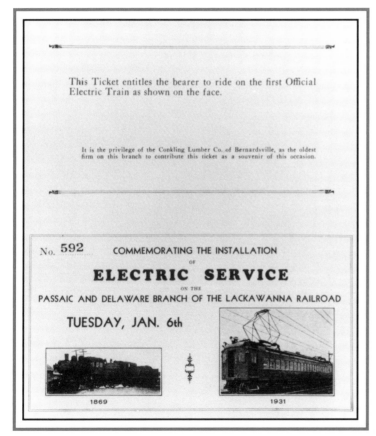

abreast; the tandems of Mr. Charles M. Chapin and Mr. J. Edward Davis driven by their owners; Miss Malvina Appleton in her phaeton and canopy with her pair of piebald ponies. Also the horses and carriages of the Messrs. C. Ledyard Blair, Edward T. H. Talmage, Frederic and Seymour Cromwell, Percy R. Pyne, Clarence B. Mitchell, Robert L. Stevens, Richard Stevens, Grant B. Schley, Richard V. Lindabury, Joseph Larocque, Charles Pfizer, George B. Post, Jr., Mrs. Archibald Alexander, Dean Sage, and many others.[1]

The first thirty years of the twentieth century saw an ever-growing commuter population in New Jersey. Along with this increase came related problems. Complaints about smoke and cinders, noise, and crowded conditions began to mount. A study was organized by J. M. Davis, president of the Delaware Lackawanna & Western, to find out how service and conditions might be improved. The outcome was a recommendation for a change to electric train service on the Morris & Essex division and the Montclair and Gladstone branches. A system of overhead power transmission with three-thousand-volt direct current was adopted—the first such system to be used in the United States. Multiple unit

A souvenir ticket commemorating the installation of electric service on the Passaic and Delaware Branch of the Lackawanna Railroad, 1931. From the Homer R. Hill collection.

Test train of new multiple unit motor cars passes between old ones, July 29, 1984. Photograph by Homer R. Hill.

Gladstone, November 10, 1961. Brake failure causes a DL&W train to run into house next to tracks. A prayer meeting had concluded shortly before the accident, so the house was empty. Photograph by Homer R. Hill.

The Gladstone train station, circa 1900. The building is listed on the State and National Registers of Historic Sites. From the Harold Chesson collection.

steel motor cars (MUS) were ordered from Chicago. On September 3, 1930, Thomas Alva Edison drove the first electric train from Hoboken to Montclair. On January 6, 1931, the first electric train arrived in Bernardsville. T. Leonard Hill of Gladstone was a passenger on that first ride. Homer Hill of Basking Ridge, an inveterate railroad buff, was also along for the ride. He was a wonderful source for this book of photographs, information, and anecdotes about the Gladstone branch and the Rockaway Valley railroads.

The new electric commuter cars featured rattan seats and an interior designed for safety, durability, and efficient maintenance. The choice proved to be a good one, as the "green" cars were in service until 1984.

The Delaware Lackawanna & Western Railroad merged with the Erie Railroad in 1960 and became the Erie Lackawanna, dubbed the "Weary Erie" by commuters, not necessarily with affection. The railbed and cars had descended into sad disrepair by the 1970s. In 1976 the Gladstone branch became part of the New Jersey Department of Transportation when Conrail was created and chose to maintain only the Summit and Millington branches.

In 1984 a new, more efficient system of high-voltage alternating current was put into use along with new Arrow III cars. The new system was installed after years of delay and discomfort for commuters and involved substantial railbed rebuilding. Today's ride is much improved. Homer Hill and Pea-

pack-Gladstone residents James Thomson, Leonard Hill, and Harold Chesson were among the railroad enthusiasts who rode the last of the MU cars. Hill is one of a few to have been a passenger on both the first electric run, in 1931, and the last, in 1984.

In 1984 the Gladstone train station was nominated to the New Jersey and National Registers of Historic Places. The station is believed to have been built in 1891 and is listed as being a "fine example of Queen Anne style" construction designed to suit the needs of a small community. The architect is unknown.

The Rock-a-Bye Baby

The story of the Rockaway Valley Railroad is fondly remembered by long-time residents and railroad enthusiasts. Although the line was short-lived and a financial failure, it was one of the more colorful episodes in New Jersey railroading history.

The Delaware and Lackawanna West line had reached Bernardsville in 1872, and there it languished for many years because of financial difficulties and ensuing construction delays. As the delays continued, petitions for railroad service to the Peapack area began to be heard. An article in the February 9, 1887, *Hunterdon Republican* tells of a meeting of local citizens:

> *The citizens of Peapack and vicinity who want a railroad, at a recent*

meeting appointed a committee to ascertain what amount of freight is being shipped to and from Peapack on wagons to Somerville, Chester, and Bernardsville, and report at an adjourned meeting. There is something over 100,000 bushels of lime per annum, and about 25% of it is shipped by railroad. The rest is hauled and used mostly by farmers. Sixty-thousand baskets of peaches were shipped last year. An iron mine is not worked at present for want of railroad facilities. The town has stone quarries and hat factories also. The citizens are willing to give a right of way and are hopeful that the Delaware and Lackawanna Railroad will extend its branch from Bernardsville, or that the Jersey Central will build a branch from Somerville or North Branch to town.[2]

In October of the same year John V. Mellick of Morristown came forward with plans to build the first part of a twenty-five mile line that would, according to the original official prospectus of 1888, start in Whitehouse, where there was a connection with the Jersey Central Line, continuing from there to New Germantown (later Oldwick), Pottersville, Peapack, Mendham, Morristown, and finally Montclair, where it would connect with the Greenwood Lake railroad. Mellick billed himself as a railroad man, but in truth his experience was limited to time spent as an inspector of railways for the Civil Engineering Corps in Illinois. The Erie Lackawanna projected costs of twenty-seven thousand dollars per mile to build a railroad to Mendham. Mellick, who proposed to spend fifteen thousand dollars per mile, was successful in securing subscriptions to build, and the project was soon under way.

The operation was financed by two peach-orchard owners. James N. Pidcock from Whitehouse invested ten thousand dollars and became the first president of the line. William W. Sutton of New Germantown, who invested five thousand, became vice-president. Pidcock and Mellick then proceeded to sell the local farmers on the idea and to persuade them to give the railroad right-of-way through their properties. In return the farmers were made stockholders in the enterprise. This was agreeable to most of the farmers, although some holdouts eventually found themselves surrounded by the railroad tracks. "One Pottersville farmer even allowed the railroad's right-of-way to proceed through his barn. The only hitch was that he had to come running out of his house or fields to open the barn doors every time one of the trains whistled to go through."[3]

The new railway was named the Rockaway Valley after a local Rockaway Creek and the proposed right-of-way through the valley to New Germantown.

By September 1888 the line to New Germantown was complete. It extended as far as Pottersville by June 1889, and by April 19, 1890, passenger and freight service was operating to Peapack, with three trips daily, except Sundays. Ironically, the long-delayed Delaware and Lackawanna line from Bernardsville reached Peapack six months later, but no connection between the two lines was ever considered to be practical. The terminus of the Rockaway Valley reached

Watnong, just north of Morristown, in 1892. The intended connection with the Lackawanna line in Morristown was never realized, as the tracks became mired in a swamp just short of their destination.

> *This did not discourage Pidcock and Mellick, who had great plans for the rearing of their "baby." They planned to extend the railroad from Whitehouse Station to Flemington where it would connect with the Pennsylvania in order to continue on to the Eastern Pennsylvania coal fields and then, of course, on to Chicago and San Francisco.*[4]

The Rockaway Valley Railroad was built with great haste. That, as well as Mellick's lack of experience and his attempts to hold costs to a bare minimum, resulted in a roadbed that was far below construction standards of the time. In those days the method used for laying a line consisted of building up a bed from six to twelve inches above ground level, laying the ties, then filling in around them with porous ballast for drainage. This was certainly not the method employed by Mellick. Instead, the ground was merely cleared of brush, some of the high and low spots were leveled, and the ties were laid on the ground with nothing but dirt thrown around them.

The railroad's course over an extremely uneven roadbed, through hilly terrain, and up and down many steep grades caused the cars to sway noticeably. Soon the line was affectionately dubbed the "Rock-a-Bye Baby" by passengers. What a ride it must have been!

> *The line was noted for its "roller coaster" grade; if the country rolled and dipped, so did the line. All the way from Oldwick to the Whippany River near the northerly terminal, there was a series of spectacular nose dives. Although the highest point was elevation 580 at Pitney Station, between Mendham and Brookside, the heaviest grade was found to be 4% between the Peapack trestle and the present Route 206. . . . One is amazed to stand at this spot today and wonder how it was possible to run a single engine up this hill, let alone haul cars.*[5]

The terminals were approximately twenty-four miles apart, and passenger trains took more than two hours to cover the entire distance; the slower freight trains took about three hours to complete the trip. The railroad at Peapack was located a half-mile west of the present Lackawanna station at Gladstone and about fifty feet higher, and although it was called the Peapack station, in actuality it missed what is now the community of Peapack altogether.[6]

The Peapack trestle was the longest wooden bridge of the line with a length of thirty spans or 250 feet. It was situated just behind what is now the home of Harold Chesson on Old Chester Road in Gladstone, which he has appropriately named "Trestle Brook." When the bridge was dismantled, some of the trestles were used by Garner Hill to build an addition to the family-owned feed mill.

The Rockaway Valley Railroad became a favorite line of tourists who enjoyed the beauty of the countryside, the many wooded areas, and rolling hills traversed by bubbling streams. Hundreds of people came from all over New Jersey on the

Central as far as Whitehouse Station. There they boarded the Rockaway and enjoyed a spectacular ride. A popular excursion was the ride from Peapack to Pottersville and a visit to Black River Falls. In his book *The Rock-a-Bye-Baby*, Thomas Tabor III includes a quote from the August 1, 1891, *Jerseyman*:

> *A ride over the new railroad from Peapack to White House, a distance of twelve miles is very interesting as the road opens up a beautifully rich section of the country, most abundantly blessed by nature both as to productive capacity and natural scenery. . . . From Peapack to Pottersville is a little over three miles, and the cars take you thru the suburbs of a real country village, but little known to people ten miles distant, which is richly endowed with natural advantages. It is situated on the Black River. At Pottersville the river passes through a most romantic and wild gorge, rushing and foaming.*[7]

The Rockaway Valley Railroad equipment consisted of a second-hand coach; used freight cars; two small steam locomotives, a second-hand one acquired from the Jersey Central Railroad named the "Peter Melick," and a newer one called the "Rachel" after a Gladstone woman who was the wife of James Rodenbaugh, one of the railroad's engineers. For a short time the line even boasted three locomotives. President Pidcock purchased a brand new "camel back" locomotive which was cheered enthusiastically on its first run at Whitehouse Station. However, the cheers were short-lived. The locomotive was too heavy for the tracks which buckled under its weight.

> *A few days later, to everyone's surprise, the "Prize Baby" mysteriously vanished.*
>
> *The mystery made headlines in the nation's newspapers. It was finally discovered that Pidcock, the president, had tried to turn his embarrassment into profit by having an engineer from his Georgia Railroad come up and "kidnap" the "baby" to Georgia one night. Needless to say the stockholders disapproved greatly of their president's high-handed action and threatened court charges. However Pidcock was soon able to evade criticism of the discontented stockholders.*[8]

People who reminisce about the Rock-A-Bye vividly recall the showers of soot and sparks that the locomotives spewed forth on their runs. Grass fires were frequent. Farmers would rush out with buckets of water to douse the flames in their fields. A Pottersville resident remembered "how those 'babies' would literally burn the bridges from under themselves," citing one night when an engine roared over a trestle bridge spewing sparks in its wake. By the time the train had passed over it, the bridge was engulfed in flames. During the line's short-lived heyday the engines burned up many of the stations along the route. The late Edith Tiger Canfield related that when she was a child, she and fellow mischief-makers greased the tracks with soap and vaseline, then watched with great glee as the engine failed to climb the grade and slid backward instead. After the Pottersville depot burned, the freight house was used for both freight and passenger service. The Gladstone station burned down, and

The Rockaway Valley Railroad station, Gladstone, 1900. William Vander Beek, agent. From the Harold Chesson collection.

William Vander Beek's coal-agency office was used as a depot from then on. Runaway cars and derailings were also common. In one incident the train was headed up the steep grade near Gladstone when a coupling broke, sending several freight cars and a crew careening backward down the hill. Unable to set the brakes, the crew members jumped for their lives. The freight cars crashed down in Gladstone. Luckily no one was killed.

The peach freight made up the greater part of the Rockaway's business. The railroad was a tremendous help to the farmers. It eliminated the overnight drives formerly required to reach the Newark Commerce Street Market by dawn. Instead buyers now came to the railroad to buy directly from the farmers, bidding on different farm loads. Peaches were hauled to the railroad in baskets with the names of the farms stenciled on the sides. A basket factory in Pottersville flourished for several years providing such containers. Sometimes as many as seventy carloads per day made the trip to Whitehouse from whence they were shipped on the Jersey Central to New York. It was common for a passenger coach to be sidelined for hours to make way for carloads laden with the highly perishable peaches. In Watnong the cargo was taken from the train and loaded onto wagons pulled by horse teams to Morristown and the connection there with the Delaware and Lackawanna Railroad.

Other products contributed to the line's freight business. Burnt lime from the quarries in the area was a major cargo.

Johnston tells us that on rainy days the lime would become saturated and boil in the freight cars. Millers made use of the railroad to haul grain, and the creameries shipped milk products. Coal was a significant source of freight business, second in volume to peaches. Pea coal was shoveled into the cars by hand. William Vander Beek of Gladstone handled a great deal of coal as he was the supplier to the lime kilns. He constructed a large six-pocket concrete coal dock for loading the cars. Unfortunately the railroad ceased operations and the docks were never used. The concrete docks still stand in the field behind the borough's water works.

The San José peach scale had reached a serious level in Hunterdon County by about 1900, and by 1905 most of the orchards in the area were ruined. This blight signaled the beginning of the end for the Rock-a-Bye Baby.

The Rockaway Valley began to decline and experience financial difficulties. Maintenance was shoddy, and equipment began to deteriorate. In November 1910 the Public Utilities Commission ordered the line to make major improvements and repairs to all switches, rails, and bridges and to add safety signals. By then the railroad was nearly bankrupt. Some half-hearted attempts at repairs were made, but they were not enough to satisfy the Public Utilities Commission. In April 1913 the line was ordered to begin major repairs by May 15 and complete them by August 15, 1913, or cease operations. The decision was made by the line to halt all train service in the fall. The last train over the "Rock-a-

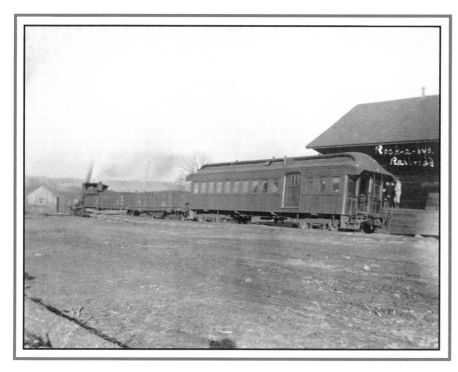

The Rock-a-Bye Railroad engine and cars, circa 1890. From the Daniel Van Doren collection, donated to the Peapack-Gladstone Library by Peter Ellis Van Doren.

Bye-Baby" was run on Saturday, October 13, 1913. The failure of the railroad meant failure for many of those dependent on its services. With no trains to service coal docks or milk platforms, many people lost their livelihood.

There is much mystery surrounding the demand that the New Jersey

and Pennsylvania railroad, operating between Whitehouse and Morristown, cease. . . .

But this road is doing more business than it ever has done before and has been using two trains most of the time. Property is being developed at various points along the road and business would be on a steady increase. But who is it says these things must cease! Why is it demanded that thousands of people who reside along this small, but convenient and valuable railroad, shall be deprived of their usual mails? Why is it demanded that hundreds of farms shall be left back to a distance of as many as eight miles from any shipping point or railroad station, and thus depreciate so in value? Why is it demanded that these hundreds of people shall be made to pay so much more for their coal, lumber, store goods, etc., that would necessitate carting so far and at such an additional expense? Why is it demanded that so many farmers be deprived of an outlet for the sale of milk and products of their dairies? Why is it demanded that every business man, every property holder, every resident along this 26 miles of road shall be damaged to an untold extent? Thousands are discussing it. Thousands are damaged and thousands are justly angered. All business men and shippers have petitioned against this closing.[9]

For the next few years several schemes to revitalize the railroad were proposed but never succeeded. Frank B. Allen was the final owner of the line and probably the only one ever to realize a profit when he abandoned attempts at revival and reportedly sold the tracks as scrap metal to France to aid the war effort.

Today one can still find sections of the old "Rock-a-Bye-Baby" roadbed. Conservation groups in the Mendham and Morristown area have purchased parts of it for preservation. There is an AT&T cable buried along the section of the roadbed that runs from Mendham to Gladstone. But for the most part it has been filled in or has given way to development. It is a fascinating story that prompts us to imagine what it may have been like in the days when the trains would stop if a would-be passenger waved a handkerchief and when special "picnic" trains ran "mechanical hayrides" through the picturesque countryside.

❧ Crossroads and Automobiles

Just as the extension of the Delaware and Lackawanna Railroad to Peapack-Gladstone was the major catalyst for many changes in the community before the turn of the century, so the introduction of the automobile and subsequent evolution of the county and interstate highway system created a climate for inevitable demographic and environmental development. Samuel Eliot Morison, in *The Oxford History of the American People*, refers to the years 1902–1939 as the era of "Great Change" and to the automobile as the "material key" to that change. According to Morison, the automobile was introduced into France about 1900 and was almost immediately accepted by the French people. For eight to ten years after it was first imported into America, the "horseless carriage" was mistrusted and ridiculed, dismissed as a gadget for the very wealthy. He points out that the primary reason for the slow success of the automobile in the United States was not cost or prejudice, but abominable road conditions.

In the early years of rural Somerset, communities developed where two roads intersected, the origins of these "roads" having been animal paths and Indian trails that traditionally followed the course of a river or stream. Thus, Lesser Crossroads (now Bedminster-Far Hills) and Larger Crossroads (near Lamington) came into being in the Colonial period, and we have seen reference to the Peapack Path in an earlier chapter. These early roads were nothing more than narrow, rutted paths, poorly maintained and often mired in mud. According to Snell's *History of Hunterdon and Somerset Counties*, the records of early roads in Bedminster Township were lost in a fire, but

> the highways from Bound Brook to Peapack and from Lamington to the "Great Road" appear to have been the earliest opened. In an old book of record in the county clerk's office we find that Sept. 18, 1744, a road was ordered opened which began "at a four-rod road that leads from Bound Brook betwixt the mountain at a black-oak tree standing at ye mouth of William McDaniel's lane"; it ran "down the hill by the salt ponds" and past McDaniels' Mills till it intersected Peapack Road.[10]

Snell goes on with his description:

> Herewith are extracts from early road records in Somerset County (Road Book A, No. 1, pages 1 and 25) October the second day, 1752. Whereas we Commissioners of the Road for the County of Somerset called by the inhabitants of Basking Ridge and Mine Brook to lay out a four-rod road from the house of Hendrick Smith to the Mill belonging to William Allen on Peapack Brook and we being six of us present upon the ground agree as followeth: Beginning where the Landing Road from Black River and the [Rocksiticus] crosses the mill [illegible]; thence upon a piece of low ground between John Clawson's house and the North Branch. Thence crossing said Branch to a Hickory Tree marked. Thence down the branch as near as the ground will allow to a Beach Tree marked by the Indian Wigwam. Thence along the side of the Branch to a little log bridge near to the widow Smith's house. Thence as the road now goes to the northeast side of the Saw Mill and still down the branch as near as the ground will allow good for a road to the corner of a turnip patch, and if the road be laid over the branch between Young Lowe and Teunas Mellick then to continue the same course down to the road and thence to the Mine Brook road before the said Smith's door, but if that road between said Young Lowe and Mellick is not allowed then it is to go as the path now goes to the north side of the turnip patch and so on to the said Mine Brook at the house of said Hendrick Smith before mentioned.
>
> Signed by us William Goves, William Boory, Robert Barklay, James Todd, Joris Middagh, Edward Barbor. Recorded the 4th day of October, 1752, R. L. Hooper, Clk.[11]

Snell also refers to an east-west road at Larger Crossroads laid out in 1745 along the line of the Major Daniel Axtell tract.[12]

The road system expanded in the nineteenth and early twentieth centuries, but road quality was little improved. As long as horses, wagons, and carriages remained the means of travel and transportation, dirt roads, riddled with potholes,

The Peapack Stage Coach in front of the post office, circa 1906. From the Daniel Van Doren collection, donated to the Peapack-Gladstone Library by Peter Ellis Van Doren.

were the accepted standard. With the appearance of automobiles, the deficiencies in the road systems became glaringly apparent. Passengers traveling by car could expect systematic delays caused by tire punctures; often several tire changes would be necessary during one outing, and spare tires were standard equipment. Dust and mud made linen dusters and goggles required apparel. Rough road conditions and deep

potholes often damaged the automobiles. Morison points out that in the early years, owners were forced to put their automobiles away for the winter because in rain or snow road conditions were impossible, and farmers, businessmen, and doctors kept horses and buggies for the times when automobile travel was impossible.

The first paving material used was macadam; in 1894, 39

miles of county roads were macadamized; by 1924, 80 miles had been macadamized, and 117 miles, including 90 miles of state highway were concrete. Tar was introduced as a road surface between 1921 and 1922.[13] Early in the century US 206 was State Highway 32; US 202, first paved in the 1920s, was State Highway 31.

As automobile traffic increased, so did the demand for better roads. The records of the Peapack-Gladstone town clerk in the early years of the twentieth century contain many references to road-improvement contracts. In August 1922 the *Weekly Exponent* carried an item noting that the unpaved road from Thomas Howard's and Oscar Smith's to the Delaware & Lackawanna Railroad was to be improved and named Holland Avenue.

The introduction of an automobile to Peapack-Gladstone appeared frequently as a newsworthy item in local publications. Hill family history has it that Garner Hill's Cadillac, purchased from Wiss Brothers in Morristown, was the first automobile in Peapack, and that when the battery needed charging, Mr. Hill took it to Bernardsville Power and Light Company. In 1912, the year the village incorporated as a twin borough, the *Weekly Exponent* reported "Postmaster Vorhees driving a natty new Ford; all night street lighting; and a new speed limit, not to exceed ten miles-per-hour."

In the 1800s a stagecoach run by John Stephens had traveled between Somerville and Peapack carrying mail, parcels, and passengers.[14] Charles Wyckoff started a stage line from Peapack to Somerville in 1848, which was taken over in 1909 by George R. Layton of Far Hills. In 1910 he converted the service to "Layton's Trackless Trolley." In 1913 he had expanded his business, and the *Exponent* reported: "At present time Mr. Layton owns five automobiles and is giving touring car service, making four regular trips each way, meeting trains at Far Hills, making direct connections with Peapack and Bernardsville. The mail and local work has been separated from the regular runs giving through service each way."[15] The same year it was reported that C. L. Blair had placed an auto hack in service at Blairsden.

It did not take long for local entrepreneurs to realize the profit potential of these early automobiles. William Jay Tiger was the first Ford dealer in New Jersey. Tiger family history has it that "Henry Ford always laid out the red carpet for William Tiger." He built the Tiger Building in 1923 as an automobile showroom. In 1930 he gave up selling Fords and began selling Chrysler products.

Garner Hill started a Chevrolet dealership in 1923, and Clayton Amerman started his automobile business in 1919, moving from the sale of Gates Half-Sole Tires and reconditioned batteries, to Star and Durant automobiles, to Graham and Paige trucks, and finally, in 1935, to the Dodge line (see "Commerce and Industry" below).

When the Delaware and Lackawanna Railroad extended the line to Peapack-Gladstone, the result was far-reaching. Wealthy newcomers built grand estates and changed the

The Reverend Harper and family in automobile, circa 1913. From the Canon R. J. Morrow collection.

demographics of a small rural community (see the next chapter). The county and interstate highway system developed gradually in Somerset County, but the ultimate effect of the expansion was to be far more profound than that of railroad expansion.

The Hudson Tube from New York opened in 1910, followed in 1927 by the Holland Tunnel, and in 1937 by the Lincoln Tunnel. The population of Somerset County increased dramatically in the twenties and thirties, probably a result of the new ease of access between New York City and New Jersey.

❧ Notes

1. Allison Wright Post, *Recollections of Bernardsville*, p. 35.
2. Thomas T. Tabor III, *The Rock-A-Bye Baby: A History of the Rockaway Valley Railroad*, p. 9.
3. *Bernardsville News*, July 20, 1950.
4. Ibid.
5. Howard E. Johnston, *The Rockaway Valley Railroad*, p. 6.
6. Tabor, *The Rock-a-Bye Baby*, p. 14.
7. Ibid.
8. *Bernardsville News*, July 20, 1950.
9. *Weekly Exponent*, October 17, 1913.
10. James P. Snell, *History of Hunterdon and Somerset Counties, New Jersey*, p. 708.
11. Ibid., p. 101.
12. Ibid., p. 713.
14. Stephanie A. McGrath, *Courier News*, May 21, 1988. Frederick Walter, *The Township of Bedminster*.
15. *Weekly Exponent*, May 2, 1913.

WOMEN'S CHRISTIAN TEMPERANCE UNION

The local chapter of the Women's Christian Temperance Union was very active during the first half of the twentieth century. Weekly meetings were held in private homes and reports published in the local paper.

On September 10, 1908, the *Whitehouse Weekly Review* reported that the WCTU held a "parlor" meeting at the home of Peter Tiger. The program for the evening:

Hymn: "Christ for the World"
Responsorial Reading: "Crusade Psalm"
"The Lord's Prayer"
Solo and Chorus: "Our Cause Is Gaining Ground"
Reading: "The Godmother of the WCTU"
Recitation: "An Angel in a Saloon"
Solo and Chorus: "We're Out for Prohibition"

On May 16, 1913, the *Weekly Exponent's* "WCTU Notes" included references to "The White Ribboners" and such phrases as "victory will surely come"; "the ultimate triumph of righteousness"; "the enemy"; "soon a child walking out in our town will see the closed doors of saloons and his impressionable mind shall drink in the great truth that his father or mother helped to close them because it was right to outlaw and destroy sin."

♣ The Grand Estates and the Resultant Changes

Introduction

*T*he industrial age created a new society of immensely affluent people whose wealth was acquired through ownership of railroads, utilities, coal mines, and banks. With the exception of the royal families of Europe or the dynasties of the Far East, rarely had such wealth rested in the hands of so few. New York City was the corporate and social headquarters of the new industrial moguls. The extension of the Delaware and Lackawanna line to Bernardsville, and then to

Curved double stairway in the main hall of Blairsden. From the Diana Villa collection.

Peapack and Gladstone, generated an influx of these moneyed families to the Somerset Hills. Attracted by the beauty of the countryside, they came in search of suitable properties on which to build estates where they could while away their leisure summer hours.

By the turn of the century the "Blue Hills" were dotted with vast estates, many of them opulently appointed architectural monuments. The "Summer People" led what seem in retrospect to have been idyllic lives, surrounded by elegance, their every need attended to. They entertained as lavishly at their country homes as they did in their New York brownstones. Their names read like a *Who's Who* of the wealthy and socially prominent people of that era.

> *Peapack and Gladstone are two of the neatest and most pleasant villages in the State. They have beautiful scenery which make them very popular for Summer boarders. The surrounding country is thickly populated and has many residences built by rich New Yorkers, who retire there in the summer to rest themselves and to enjoy the cool, healthful breezes of this vicinity. A lake has been built and the scenery improved so as to make it an ideal spot of beauty. Good roads and good walks; grade school; long distant and local telephone; a church at each place; large and well stocked stores and markets; two railroads, the Lackawanna and Rockaway Valley Railroad; a first-class mill; both towns are growing rapidly. Further information will be given or all inquiries answered by the "Exponent," Peapack, N.J.[1]*

That golden era of opulent life styles continues to fascinate

us, although many of the architectural treasures have since been converted to other uses. The architectural legacies remaining in Peapack-Gladstone include: Blairsden, the estate of C. Ledyard Blair; Natirar, the home built by Walter G. Ladd; James Cox Brady's Hamilton Farm; and the George R. Mosle estate.

Blairsden

The saga of "Blairsden" and the remarkable C. Ledyard Blair family is perhaps the most fascinating of all the stories that relate to the historical development of Peapack-Gladstone. Indeed it can be said that this magnificent mansion on the hill is the symbol of a rural borough's transition to the twentieth century.

A Financial Empire

C. Ledyard Blair was the grandson of John Insley Blair, a self-made millionaire who was born on a New Jersey farm in 1802 and quit school at the age of eleven to "get rich." At eighteen John I. Blair owned a general store near Gravel Hill (later named Blairstown). By the time he was just twenty-seven he operated a chain of five stores. In 1846 he joined the Scranton brothers and followed them to the anthracite fields of Pennsylvania. There he made a considerable fortune in coal. Before he was fifty years old he helped found the Delaware,

C. Ledyard Blair.
From the Diana Villa collection.

after D. C. Blair, by his father, when the Chicago and Northwestern Railroad was extended farther west. In 1905, when Blair & Co. was involved in the reorganization of the Western Pacific Railroad, a small town on the Nevada-California border was named Blairsden for the C. L. Blair estate in Peapack.[2]

Dewitt's son, Clinton Ledyard Blair, was born in 1867 and proceeded to carry on the family tradition of financial acumen. When he was a fifteen-year-old student he often made the trip from Belvidere, New Jersey, to the Lawrenceville School on horseback. "As it was about 80 miles, he would take two nights on the way, stopping at a farmhouse at the end of each day to ask for a room for himself and board for his horse and dog and himself."[3]

> *He graduated from Princeton University in 1890 and while in his senior year at the University joined his father and grandfather in founding Blair and Company at 1 Wall Street, New York City. The [banking] company participated in the financing of many large firms, including Republic Iron and Steel Company and Jones & McLaughlin Steel Company. Blair and Company at first was linked with the Gould railroad interests and during that period underwrote large bond issues for several major railroads. The firm was merged in 1920 with William Salomon & Company under the name of Blair and Company and [C. L.] Blair became chairman of the board. He also was a director of many railroads and other companies including the Sussex Railroad.[4]*

Lackawanna & Western Railroad. He went on to become the president of sixteen railroads, and in the mid-nineteenth century was known as "The Railroad King of the West." He was present at the joining of the Union Pacific tracks at Promontory Point, Utah, when the gold spike was hammered in 1869. His son, Dewitt Clinton, was named after Dewitt Clinton, the governor of New York, who was visiting the John Insley Blairs the night of their son's birth. D. C. Blair joined his father in business and later established Blair Academy in New Jersey. Clinton, Iowa, and Blair, Nebraska, were named

A Country Property

In 1897 Mr. and Mrs. C. L. Blair of 123 East 63rd Street, New York City, bought a beautiful 423-acre property known as the Mellick Farm in Peapack, where they proposed to build a spectacular country residence. The New York friends of the Blairs were dismayed, as they considered the site much too far from the city to be convenient. At that time the railroad extended only as far as Bernardsville. Horses and carriages were used to travel to and from the railroad stations in New York and Bernardsville. The "horseless carriage" was still a novelty, and travel by automobile was limited because of the rough dirt roads.

The Blairs selected the crown of the highest hill on the property as the site for their home. The grand vista it afforded was of gently rolling hills, wooded groves, and the Raritan River. Blair commissioned the firm of Carrere and Hastings to design the estate. The firm was prestigious, having designed the New York Public Library; it is credited with the first success of the Beaux-Arts Movement in American architecture. The firm also designed the Blair Building in New York City, constructed between 1902 and 1911. For the Blairs' Peapack estate the architects proposed a three-story house in the French chateau style with a facade of brick and limestone to be ornamented with graceful balustrades.

Taken from a portrait of
Mrs. C. Ledyard Blair,
by Jean Lawrence.
From the Diana Villa collection.

Construction of Blairsden

The building of Blairsden was hailed as a miracle of architectural planning and ingenious engineering. As the hilltop site was extremely steep, it was necessary to level it before a foundation could be built and construction begin. A single-track funicular railway with a miniature wood-burning engine was built to carry building materials to the site. Flat cars laden with limestone, brick, imported marbles, carved mahogany panels, and building materials of every kind traveled

The pasture once owned by the Smith family which became Ravine Lake when a dam was built on the Raritan River; the project was completed in 1899. From the Helen Smith collection.

up the north side of the hill from near the spot that would become Ravine Lake.

Ravine Lake was the brainchild of Blair and a group of prominent residents who formed an association and raised the necessary funds to build a dam on the Raritan River. The stones used in building the dam came from the New Jersey sources of Waterloo and German Valley. The cornerstone of the dam was laid October 1, 1898, by Marjory Blair, eldest daughter of the Blairs, and the first water ran over the dam in 1899, nearly three years before Blairsden was completed.[5]

The Blairs and their daughters, Marjory, Florence, Edith, and Marise, spent their time in Peapack during construction at what they called the White Cottage. This was the old Mellick farmhouse, now known as Windfall. After the house passed out of the Blair family, it was occupied for many years by the Percival Keith family, who made extensive alterations. Keith was noted for his work on the Manhattan Project, the research effort responsible for the development of the first

Windfall, the old Mellick farmhouse, also known as the White Cottage, as it looked in the early 1930s, before being altered by the Percival Keith family.

atomic bomb. In the 1990s the house was owned by the Ian McLaughlin family.

Mrs. Marise Campbell, the youngest child, was born on the day in 1899 that the last stone of the Ravine Lake dam was put into place. In an interview Mrs. Campbell said that from that day forward she was known as the "dam baby," having been so dubbed by Frank Tainter, the contracting engineer who designed the project. In the interview, the late Mrs. Edith Gambrill and Mrs. Campbell recalled those early summers spent at Peapack, in the White Cottage, telling of a favorite horse whose habit it was to stick its head into the cottage through an open main floor window; of the trip to and from the railroad stations in New York and Bernardsville in horse-drawn carriages; of their first automobile trips between New York and Peapack. The journeys lasted hours and were often interrupted more than once by punctures. The automobiles of the time carried several spare tires and had no windshields or tops.

The exquisite imported materials, meticulous details, and grand scale of the project required the work of skilled artisans and craftsmen, the majority of whom were stone masons culled from Italy's best by Blair to build his dream. Their expertise is obvious today when one examines the beautiful stonework legacy they created. The ornamental gate and entry to Blairsden were not completed until 1912, ten years after completion of the house. Some of the Italian craftsmen elected to remain in Peapack as permanent residents after their work was finished. Today their descendants are an integral part of the community in various professions and trades.

A Newark firm of masons, P. Vanderhoof and Sons, contracted to build the coach barns on the estate at a cost of thirty thousand dollars. Blair was an ardent horseman, as were so many of the wealthy people who came to the Somerset Hills at that time, and of course, they traveled by horse and carriage. Blair built a large coach barn and stables, a stable-master's house, and housing for other estate employees on the hill above the tennis court and rose garden. The site is now occupied by the Matheny School for Cerebral Palsied Children (see "The Schools" below). All of these buildings were constructed of the same beautiful rose-colored brick and limestone blocks employed in the design of the mansion. Horses and carriages entered through beautifully symmetrical limestone arches. Floors throughout were constructed of a variety of materials: glazed red brick terrazzo tile and yellow brick laid in a herringbone pattern. Interior walls were made of wooden tongue-in-groove wainscoting. Beautiful gabled eaves looked out from the second stories of the building. An elevator operated by giant pulleys and wires rose from the barn floor to the loft. Two of the Blairs' carriages were donated to the carriage museum at the Shelburne Village and Museum in Burlington, Vermont.

One can imagine the excitement such a grand project generated among the village residents. A constant parade of horse-drawn carts carrying construction materials and huge trees must have provided many happy hours for sidewalk superintendents. Each one of the maple trees at the front of the house was transported on specially constructed platforms pulled by twelve horses. Many of the small wooden bridges in Somerset County were damaged by these heavy loads and had to be replaced by Blair. An article in the *Somerville Messenger-Gazette* in 1954 reprinted an account of how Blair gathered rare boxwood trees for the estate:

> *On Sunday a number of heavy wagons loaded with boxwood trees passed through Main Street. Wagons similarly loaded have passed through town nearly every day during the past month and have excited the curiosity of a number of townspeople. Each wagon contains one diminutive tree set in a great box filled with earth that makes a heavy load for one team.*
>
> *These trees are carted to the estate of C. Ledyard Blair, near Peapack.*
>
> *Mr. Blair's latest investment in boxwood trees exceeds his great expenditure of last winter when he moved 100 mammoth trees by wagon 10 miles over mountain roads and transplanted them about his new residence.*
>
> *In front of Blairsden, as Mr. Blair's palatial residence is called, there is a picturesque basin or pond, which it is his intention to fringe with boxwood trees. The boxwood is the rarest tree found in New Jersey.*
>
> *A boxwood tree, which is said to grow only one inch a year, must have from 25 to 50 years' growth to be of the desired size, and several hundred of these are needed to go around the edge of the pool.*
>
> *In order to obtain these trees, agents of Mr. Blair are now canvassing the country for a distance of 50 miles around his residence, and are buying up boxwoods of the desired size wherever they can be found. The trees are frequently moved from the lawns of private residences where the owners have been induced to part with them for a generous price. The price paid for the trees represents only a small portion of their actual cost.* [6]

The Completed House and Grounds

The thirty-eight-room house was finally completed in 1902 at a cost of two million dollars. Carrere and Hasting's design for the interior is typical of the architectural syntax that they adhered to in most of their residential commissions after the mid-1890s. [7]

The interior details of the house and the provenance of some of the objects acquired by Blair were described in a pamphlet printed by the Sisters of St. John the Baptist, St. Joseph's Villa, who have owned the property since 1950 when it was converted to a retreat run by the order:

> *The three-story brick and limestone house was completed in 1902. Designed by Carrere and Hasting of New York, who were also architects for the New York Public Library, the main floor included a living room, now a Chapel, of which the doors and mantels were once*

Interior of Blairsden. Note the bronze front doors leading to the columned hallway. From the Diana Villa collection.

part of the Old Admiralty in London. A pair of exquisite crystal chandeliers adorn the sanctuary, and specially designed ceiling lights and wall sconces grace the main rooms throughout the residence. The dining room is decorated with elaborate plaster of Paris pilasters and the ceiling with inserts of old French and Italian oil paintings.[8] Other rooms off the main hall, which features in the center a broad semicircular stairway, complemented by a costly sterling silver and bronze chandelier hanging gracefully in the stairwell, include a walnut paneled library, once the music room; an oak panel morning room overlooking the terrace; and a room wainscoted in black enamel above which the wall is covered with hand-tooled leather, and a kitchen and pantry with floors of wooden bricks laid in herringbone pattern. A gallery surrounds the two-story pantry. Two elevators and a dumbwaiter are still in use. Entrance to the villa is through heavy bronze doors constructed with four by ten sheets of one-inch thick plate glass, each door weighing 1000 pounds.

The marble and limestone pilasters, mantels and the ornate plaster of Paris ceilings are reminiscent of the Italian Renaissance. Three Italian artisans were employed to assemble the marble work. There are twenty-five fireplaces throughout the building. The morning room opens to a tiled porch protected by a covered pergola which in the spring supports a beautiful wisteria vine. At the other end of the pergola, a high-ceilinged tea house completes the structure.

The pamphlet also describes the extraordinary grounds and landscaping:

The surrounding property, as meticulously planned as the house itself, was designed by landscape architect Henry Longfellow Greenleaf. On the south side of the chateau, there are two large terraces, running the length of the house and on the lower terrace was an orangerie where twenty-two bay trees stood on either side of the steps.[9] Below the orangerie, steps lead down to a long vista of the lake. The upper part consists of two flights of broad stone steps with several waterfall fountains and rhododendron plantings. Extending below are long sloping terraces and a walk with rounded stones in mosaic design. To give accent to the vista, Mr. Greenleaf designed a broad slope of lawn on both sides of the steps lined with tall cedar trees. In early spring the glorious blossoms of forsythia, magnolia, pink and white dogwood, enhance the surrounding green. A final touch of beauty to the entirety is the yearly return of song-birds to "Blairsden."[10]

A beautiful reflecting pool adorns the front entry of the chateau. The pool is flanked by busts of the Roman emperors which Blair purchased from the French government with the stipulation that they be returned rather than ever be resold or moved to another location. The late Mrs. Gambrill and Mrs. Campbell recalled the two graceful swans—Elsa and Lohengrin—that once floated with stately serenity on the pool.

Above the house, just below the stables, was a magnificent Italian garden famous for its fourteen hundred varieties of roses. The garden was Mrs. Blair's pride and joy. The flowers were planted on low, raised terraces flanked by pools of corresponding size. Above the rose beds was a tennis court

Terraced descent to
Ravine Lake from
Blairsden. From the
Diana Villa collection.

screened by climbing roses. In the winter the court was converted to a paddle court with platforms and canvas.

There is little information available regarding the interior furnishings of Blairsden. The contents of the estate were auctioned in 1950 by Parke-Bernet Galleries of New York. Listings and photographs in the sale catalogue give an indication of the treasures that once graced Blairsden. Included were paintings by Giovanni Battista Tiepolo (1696–1770); a Flemish Renaissance tapestry circa 1550; five Royal Gobelin tapestry panels; French and India carpets; a Steinway parlor grand piano; a Tiffany & Co. wrought sterling service; nine pages of silver and silver-plated items; and pages more of antiques and objets d'art. Also listed were Tuscan pottery oil jars and the twenty-two bay trees bought by Blair at the 1900 World Exhibition and so carefully protected and nourished for nearly fifty years.

An Enchanted Childhood

The late Mrs. Gambrill and Mrs. Campbell were kind enough to spend some time reminiscing about their early years at Blairsden. On that happy day in 1902 when it was at last time for the family to move to the house, the little girls were allowed to walk up the long drive pushing their doll carriages ahead of them.

The Blairs seem to have been not only loving, but fun-loving parents. In the winter months Mr. Blair arranged for a spectacular toboggan run to be built on the hill above the stables which descended at a steep incline to deposit the sledders onto the frozen lagoon in front of the house. For safety's sake a wall of hay bales was erected at the end of the course—perhaps so the sledders did not run right through the great front doors. One can imagine the stony visages of the Roman emperors as these antics unfolded. In the basement of the house there was a squash court and, what was then known as a "plunge," a deep indoor pool with no shallow end. There were excursions across Ravine Lake with estate employees to cut ice, which was then stored in straw in the ice house that had been carved into the hill under the funicular railway. Mrs. Gambrill recalled the "clock man" who came from New York every Thursday to wind all the clocks in the house.

The warm summer days were filled with happy activities, including stilt walking on the terrace walls! The Lake Club provided hours of water sports, including swimming lessons with Mr. Robinson and canoeing on the Raritan River below the dam. Mrs. Blair had a telephone line installed between the house and the lake. Mrs. Campbell remembers many telephone calls from her mother to the lifeguard when, games of splashing and dunking being in high gear, the message: "Tell Marise to stop all that screaming!" came down from the great house high above. Grand as the house and its contents may have been, it was not an overly formal environment. The

The four Blair daughters enjoy tea time at Blairsden with a faithful friend. From the Diana Villa collection.

children and their friends were welcome to return from horseback riding and lounge about the living room in their riding gear—muddy boots and all. Summer also brought picnic excursions to the seashore when all would rise very early to begin the long journey.

According to her daughters and granddaughters, Mrs. Blair was a wonderful mother, full of fun. The house was always full of guests. There were many costume parties, birthday parties, July Fourth parties, Easter egg hunts, and plays at Christmas.

Preparations for the Christmas season at Blairsden began weeks ahead when the third floor was converted into sewing rooms. There the maids began to assemble the family's costumes for the annual "Court of King Christmas." Costumes for this annual production were all white and featured such players as icicles, fairies, and snowflakes. Family and friends numbering thirty or more would gather for the Christmas feast after which the pageant would unfold. One memorable Christmas gift in particular was vividly recalled by Mrs. Campbell and Mrs. Gambrill. As the story unfolds, the children were told to assemble outdoors at the front of the house. From a distance came the sound of a trumpet, and soon a miniature pony cart came into sight, pulled by a new team of fourteen-hand ponies. Santa sat atop the cart blowing the Christmas horn. Mr. Blair had arranged to have the cart designed and crafted for the children. In other years

Santa "came down the chimney," having been secreted on a platform of bricks in the vast library fireplace before the children were shown into the room. He would emerge from his hiding place with his pack on his back to an audience of wide-eyed Blair daughters and their many cousins. When he departed "up the chimney," the children were quickly whisked into the next room to see him fly in his sleigh across Ravine Lake to the Mitchell cousins' home. Testimony from the Blair daughters indicates that they most certainly did see him fly away every year and that it is a vivid childhood recollection. The Gambrill daughters also recall that they know they heard him call "Ho-Ho-Ho" as he flew toward Blairsden from Vernon Manor in later years, and, most recently, the grandchildren are quite certain that they have seen him going toward Ravine Lake.

An Opulent Lifestyle

The Blairs led an active social life, dividing their time between their homes in Peapack, New York, Newport, and Bermuda. Blair had a small replica of Blairsden built in Deepdene, Smiths Parish, Bermuda. When the family traveled there each winter, the family horses were also shipped to the island.

Blair was an avid yachtsman and served as commodore of the New York Yacht Club in 1910. During that time his 240-foot yacht, *The Diana*, served as flagship. On the eve of the outbreak of World War I Blair voluntarily took the helm of the North German Lloyd liner *Kronprinzessin Cecilie* and piloted it safely into harbor at Bar Harbor, Maine. The liner had turned back west of Ireland, when the captain was informed of the imminence of war. The ship was carrying a full complement of passengers as well as a cargo of 10 million dollars in gold and 3.5 million dollars in silver. To evade British warships, the captain elected to sail to Maine instead of New York. Unfamiliar with the New England waters, he asked Blair to pilot the ship into the harbor. Blair, having memorized the charts of the Maine port from previous sailing experience there, successfully maneuvered the grand liner into port.

Blair was the founder and first president of the Somerset Hills Country Club, first organized at Ravine Lake in 1899, and he was instrumental in its move to its present Mine Mountain Road site in Bernardsville.

Blair was an ardent horseman. When automobile traffic increased after 1910, he pioneered the system of bridle paths throughout the Somerset Hills area. He was known as an expert four-in-hand driver and had many carriages in the days before automobiles. The Blair family traveled to church in Bernardsville in "the bus," a large enclosed carriage. The drive took an hour or longer each way, and the sermons were very long—no wonder that the children always cheered happily when they were snowed in on Sunday mornings.

Mrs. Gambrill claimed that riding inside "the bus" made her "seasick," so she was allowed to sit outside next to the driver. On rainy or very cold days she said she felt fine riding inside; her sisters were never allowed to ride on the box outside.

In 1909 Blair was named an escort for President Taft at his inaugural ball:

> *C. Ledyard Blair, of Peapack, was Saturday officially declared to be the handsomest man in New Jersey. Senators Kean and Briggs, at Washington, after canvassing the immense field, settled upon Mr. Blair and appointed him to represent New Jersey at the inaugural ball tendered to President Taft on the night of March 4. . . . The chairman of the inaugural ceremonies at Washington requested all Senators some time ago to select the handsomest man in their States, one man from each State, to form an escort of honor for the new President to the inaugural ball. Candidates by the score, or their friends, besieged the New Jersey Senators, but in this case influence did not count. After a process of elimination, the two Senators decided on Mr. Blair and so notified him.*[11]

The weddings of the four Blair daughters were grand social events. In the weeks before they took place the local paper dutifully kept the community up to date on the preparations. The editors of those days were prone to exaggeration, possibly wanting to make a good story better, perhaps in order to sell more papers. The September 19, 1913, *Weekly Exponent* reported that the Blairs had extended about three thousand invitations to the upcoming wedding of Marjory

Blair and William Clark; that preparations had been made to accommodate the five hundred automobiles expected; and that detectives had been guarding the house for some time because of the many wedding gifts arriving daily. The Blair descendants surmise that eight hundred invitations would be a more accurate estimate, and that it is doubtful that there were five hundred vehicles to be had in the area in those days. The wedding took place at Blairsden at four o'clock on the terrace where a temporary altar was erected. A special train conveyed guests from the Lackawanna terminal at Hoboken to Peapack, and returned after the reception.

Florence Blair married H. Rivington Pyne on June 16, 1916, in St. Bernard's church and had a large reception at Blairsden following the ceremony. Edith was married at Blairsden to Richard VanNest Gambrill on June 21, 1917. Marise was married to Pierpont Morgan Hamilton at Blairsden on September 11, 1919.

The End of a Grand Era

Mrs. Blair (née Jennings) died in New York City in 1931 after a long illness. C. L. Blair continued to spend summers at Blairsden, and in 1932 donated four acres to the borough, as an emergency relief garden. Borough residents contributed twenty-five bushels of seed potatoes, and the crop was handed out to the needy. In 1936 Blair married Harriet S. Browne Tailer. He died February 7, 1949, at the age of eighty-two.

Blairsden was sold at a public auction conducted by Parke-Bernet Galleries, Inc., New York, on June 10, 1950. The mansion, fifty acres, and the boathouse were purchased by the Sisters of St. John the Baptist, a Catholic order, with headquarters in White Plains, New York, for about sixty thousand dollars. The property is now operated as St. Joseph's Villa, a guest and retreat house for women. Liquidation of the estate involved the sale of nine separate buildings. In 1951 the Walter D. Matheny School purchased the stable group and adjacent cottages. Mrs. Edith Blair Gambrill had purchased most of the remaining Blair estate.

❧ Natirar

Kate Macy Ladd was a direct descendant of Thomas Macy who emigrated to America in 1635 from the parish of Chilmark near Salisbury, England. He was the original settler of Salisbury, Massachusetts, but in 1659 moved to Nantucket Island, where he engaged in the whaling business and was one of several men who purchased the island. His home still stands on the island as one of the finest examples of Colonial architecture. Josiah Macy, Jr., father of Kate, was born in New York City in 1838, a member of the eighth generation of the family in America and, like his ancestors, a Quaker. He was a prosperous businessman, a close personal friend and business associate of John D. Rockefeller. He died of typhoid at age thirty-seven.

Kate Macy was born in New York City on April 6, 1863.

The facade of Natirar. From the Borough Archives.

She met Walter Graeme Ladd, a young attorney from Brooklyn in 1881. They were married December 5, 1883, at the Macy home at 18 West 53rd Street, New York City. They returned from a brief honeymoon to their first home, a small apartment at 210 West 57th Street. Unfortunately, Mrs. Ladd became ill shortly thereafter, and from that time until her death, some sixty years later, she suffered from a variety of recurrent illnesses that made her an invalid most of her life. She would recover for brief periods, during which she was able to travel and function well enough to engage in vigorous outdoor activities, but these remissions were short-lived, lasting only a few months. She was constantly under the care of two eminent physicians, Dr. Weir Mitchell of Philadelphia and Dr. Ludwig Kast of New York City. Both of them influenced Mrs. Ladd in her life-long dedication to hospital services and medical care.

In the spring of 1905 the Ladds first came to Far Hills and purchased the Belcher property, known as Sunnybranch Farm, which the Belchers had purchased in 1895 from a Wyckoff family. The farm extended from the Far Hills train station to the Peapack hills. The Ladds lived in the Belcher house while a forty-room Tudor mansion was built. Set on a mile-long crest overlooking rolling hills, forests, and the North Branch of the Raritan River, the estate was called "Natirar" by the Ladds, the name being an anagram for Raritan. Originally the estate consisted of 128 acres, until Ladd increased his

holdings in 1913: he purchased the "Oppie Estate" from General Reeves and John Summons, after which "Natirar" straddled Far Hills, Bedminster, and Peapack. The brick and limestone mansion, designed by the G. Lowell architectural firm of Boston, featured a magnificent interior of richly paneled rooms with carved mantels over fireplaces, mullioned windows, terraces, and greenhouses. The coach barns were constructed in 1908.

Kate Macy Ladd commented in her diaries that the eight years following their move to "Natirar" were among the happiest in her entire life. Apparently she was relatively free from illness during that time and able to lead a vigorous life and participate in many different activities.

It was during that time that she started "Maple Cottage," a summer retreat and guest home for "professional and working women of refinement who were unable to pay for proper accommodations while convalescing from illness, recuperating from impaired health or otherwise in need of rest."[12] This cottage, one of several on the Ladd estate, was located on Peapack Road. In the early 1980s it was known as the "Sheptock" house, that being the name of a married couple living there, who increased their own family to great numbers when they adopted many underprivileged and handicapped children. The house was demolished in March 1990.

Maple Cottage was open from May 1 to October 15 each year for over thirty-five years, and during that time an

Maple Cottage, Peapack, N. J.

Postcard of Maple Cottage with ladies in residence on the porch, circa 1913. From the Harold Chesson collection.

average of about three hundred women a year were guests in the cottage for two weeks of convalescence and rest. Another dwelling on the estate, located southeast of Maple Cottage on Peapack Road, served as a library for the guests at Maple Cottage. At the bedside of each guest was a small book of poetry and inspirational verse compiled by Kate Macy Ladd, *Spring Blossoms from Maple Cottage*. The forward she wrote to the book reads:

> *Hope renewed, courage reborn, beauty unfolding anew its buds of life—such has seemed to me the meaning of Spring.*
>
> *After the silence of snow and the waiting wondering of winter sleep, branch and bird speak up again in their way of greeting the coming of Spring.*
>
> *With balm and breeze another feast of color and song and love prepares the glory of the Spirit of Life.*
>
> *To believe, to begin again, to hold fast to courage and purpose is the message with which these Spring-blossoms from Maple Cottage may greet its weary guests and comfort their parting.*—KML

The Ladds' philanthropic activities were broad and included various educational institutions for underprivileged youths; the Henry Street Settlement in New York City; the development of the Hospital Council of New York City; the donation of a residential building for the headquarters of the Visiting Nurse Association of Somerset Hills; the donation of the Infirmary of the New Jersey College for Women; an endowment for Somerset Hospital in Somerville, New Jersey;

the gift of large sums to the Bernardsville Library and Elizabeth General Hospital, Elizabeth, New Jersey.

Kate Macy Ladd made all her donations in the name of a relative or dear friend whom she wished to honor. It is appropriate that in W. G. Ladd's will he made provisions for the only charity that bore her name, the Kate Macy Ladd Fund and the Kate Macy Ladd Convalescent Home.

Walter Graeme Ladd, a vigorous man who enjoyed good health, developed pneumonia in the spring of 1933 and died a short time thereafter, on May 21. The Ladds had no children, and following the shock of his death she was primarily bedridden, except for brief periods when she would be taken out on the front terrace where she enjoyed the view of the river, the hills, and changing seasonal colors. After many years of suffering, Kate Macy Ladd died on August 27, 1945.

W. G. Ladd's will provided that after Kate Macy Ladd's death, the Kate Macy Ladd Fund would be incorporated under the laws of New York. Ladd left the entire residue of his estate in trust to the fund and directed that

> *said corporation shall establish and maintain on the estate where I now reside, known as "Natirar," in the Borough of Peapack and Gladstone, in the County of Somerset and State of New Jersey, a home in which deserving gentlewomen, who are compelled to depend upon their own exertions for support, shall be entertained without charge for periods of time while convalescing from illness, recuperating from impaired health, or otherwise in need of rest in such numbers and at such times as*

The paneled library of the
Kate Macy Ladd Convalescent
Home. From the Borough
Archives.

available accommodations and the income assigned by such Corporation to such trust will from time to time permit.

He further stated that his primary purpose in so declaring was "to insure the development and carrying on of the work which my beloved wife, Kate Macy Ladd, started in memory of her parents, Josiah Macy, Jr., and Caroline L. Macy . . . and which is now maintained and known as Maple Cottage."[13]

Ladd provided in his will that the trust must terminate no later than May 21, 1983, fifty years after his death. At that time the entire principal of the trust was to be distributed equally among the following remaindermen: New York University (successor by merger to New York Post Graduate Medical School and Hospital), John Hopkins Hospital, Tuskegee Institute, Hampton Institute, and the Berry Schools.

In accordance with W. G. Ladd's wishes, "Natirar" was converted to a fully staffed, forty-five-bed institution that cared for women between the ages of eighteen and sixty-nine recovering from surgery or illness for a two- to four-week period without charge. The first patient was accepted in 1949, and between then and 1953, 3,060 women were sheltered at the institution. In June 1979 a celebration was held marking the convalescent home's twenty-thousandth patient.

In 1982, as the expiration date of the trust drew near, a search was initiated for a buyer for "Natirar," and the property was placed on the market for $8.5 million. In March 1983, the sale of the estate to Hassan II, the king of Morocco,

for $7.5 million set a record for a home purchase in New Jersey.

The Ladd trustees continued to occupy the estate and operate the convalescent home until May 21, 1983. A pair of shattered champagne glasses are in a box in the archives of the Borough of Peapack and Gladstone and with them is the following note: "These glasses were used to offer a final toast at the Kate Macy Ladd Fund banquet on May 20, 1983. At the stroke of midnight, when the home officially closed, the glasses were tossed into the large fireplace in the mansion. At 12:01 A.M. the estate became the property of King Hassan II of Morocco."[14]

❧ *Hamilton Farm*

James Cox Brady's Hamilton Farm represented Brady's grand idealization of a gentleman's country property. The history of the farm that follows here is a condensed version of a pamphlet put out by Beneficial Finance Corporation.

The story of Hamilton Farm is a tale of great wealth and grand design.

At its zenith Hamilton Farm sprawled across 5,000 acres in the counties of Somerset, Morris, and Hunterdon. Here in the first decades of the 20th century James Cox Brady created a resplendent country estate and one of the largest working farms in New Jersey.

Hamilton Farm mirrored the expansive nature of its owner. Brady, a New York financier, was the grandson of an Irish immigrant and son of Anthony Nicholas Brady, who had made a fortune in utilities. Brady was known for his competitive spirit and keen desire to excel. His enterprises were on a sweeping scale and of great expense.

At the farm Brady established a way of life that the family could not have achieved in Ireland. Hamilton Farm was in the manner of the great country homes in England. It was as though Brady sought to exceed in scope and grandeur the lifestyle of the absentee English landlords who had caused his Irish forebears to lead such a wretched existence.

After the turn of the century when other wealthy New Yorkers were building palatial homes in the hills of Morris and Bernards, Brady looked west to the green fields and woodlands of Bedminster. He was attracted to the area through his friendship with Charles Pfizer, the pharmaceutical magnate, and his affiliation with the Essex Hunt.

Brady's first purchase was in 1911, a 180-acre farm adjoining the Pfizer estate, acquired for $100 per acre. He named the farm for his wife, Elizabeth Jane Hamilton Brady. He bought many other farms in the succeeding years. Ultimately Hamilton Farm reached into three counties, and embraced the headwaters of the North Branch of the Raritan River.

Construction at the farm began in 1911. The first building completed was the lodge, located along the main drive. It was used by the Brady family during the hunting season for brief visits to the farm.

The main house and the farm buildings were on a grand scale. The 2½ story clapboard house was on a knoll overlooking formal gardens and a green house. It was handsome and spacious. Not so elegant as the residences on Bernardsville mountain, for the Brady house was designed to be a home and not a castle.

Close by the house Brady built an athletic building, with a squash court, a 50-foot tiled pool, and indoor and outdoor tennis courts.

The farm buildings were screened from the residence by a stand of trees. The horse barn, bull barn and blacksmith shop were completed in 1913. Three years later the cow barn and horse stable were finished. Both are huge structures.

The farm became a vast operation. More than 4,000 acres were cultivated. Corn, wheat, oats, rye, and hay were harvested. Dairy and beef cattle, sheep, pigs, chickens, ducks, and geese were raised at Hamilton Farm.

One hundred or more men were regularly employed, exclusive of the staff in the main house or extra laborers hired on for construction. The farm manager and foreman earned more than $2 per day.

Management of the farm was under the careful eye of Fred Huyler, who held the job for 50 years. Huyler was the Peapack carpenter singled out by Brady to help him acquire the land, develop the farm, erect the houses, barns, stables, and kennels, and buy, breed, and exhibit the livestock, poultry, and dogs.

A tight chain of command from Brady through Huyler to various employees kept the farm running smoothly. Huyler, a showman at heart, spent much of his time on the road successfully exhibiting the Brady Herefords, Jersey cows, Dorset sheep, Duroc-Jersey swine, chickens, and German Shepherd dogs. Huyler became an international authority on training hounds and breeding chickens.

The Brady stock traveled to exhibitions and competitions by private train car. The animals were herded down the back farm drive directly to the Peapack station and loaded into specially outfitted cars. There was a festive air in the village when the parade of animals came to the station.

In 1921 the main house burned. On its foundation Brady built a larger residence, a Georgian brick mansion with 64 rooms, 11 fireplaces, two elevators, and a chapel with stained glass windows and an organ.

Hamilton Farm flourished during the 1920s. The stable was filled with Hackney ponies, hunters, Clydesdales, and Percheron draft horses. In the greenhouses grew nectarines, pineapples, melons, and every sort of vegetable and flower.

Homebred livestock was slaughtered and aged in the farm butcher shop. Milk, cream, and butter were produced at the creamery. The Bradys' New York City house and yacht were stocked with provisions from the farm.

The farm was in every way a showplace. The new main residence was furnished with the finest antiques, carpeting, and works of art. The grounds and gardens were planted with specimen trees, bushes, and flowering plants. Farm machinery and equipment were the newest and most sophisticated available. Every animal was an outstanding specimen of its breed. An animal photographer was employed to take posed pictures and portraits of the animals.

The influence of Hamilton Farm on the community was profound. Employment was provided for a generation of local people. Merchants prospered through endless orders for farm equipment and supplies. The lives of the people on the farm and in the neighboring villages were expanded by their proximity to such splendid abundance.

Then suddenly it was over. When Brady died of pneumonia in 1927, his heirs closed down the entire farm operation. The animals were sold. The farm was retained. Today most of Hamilton Farm is owned by the Brady family.[15]

James Cox Brady was born September 23, 1882, and died November 10, 1927. He was a trustee of the Union Central Trust Company in New York City, and a director of the Chrysler Motor Corporation, Brooklyn Edison, the Prudential Oil Corporation, and the Union Oil Corporation of California.

With his first wife, Elizabeth Jane Hamilton, who died in 1912, he had three children: Elizabeth Jane Hamilton Brady, James Cox Brady, Jr., and Ruth Brady. His second wife was Lady Victoria Mary Pery who died in 1918. Their children were Victoria Mary Pery Brady and Genevieve Brady. He married Helen McMahon in 1920.[16]

Brady, financially and socially prominent, was host to foreign and American society. His eldest daughter, Jane, was among eight American debutantes presented at the Court of St. James in England in 1925.

> *Last minute sessions with dressmakers, hair dressers and social promoters who imparted the secret of the required genuflection filled the anxious hours on the eve of what will be for many the thrill that comes once in a lifetime. . . . More than 100 British women, of course, are to be presented, but the eight Americans who won the coveted privilege through the maze of social requirements in their path feel their triumph keenly. . . . The Bradys have been in England about a month and are expected home soon after the introduction of Miss Brady to the court.*[17]

The wedding of Victoria Brady was an important social event:

> *Miss Victoria Mary Pery Brady was married Saturday afternoon to John Knox Cowperthwaite in a ceremony at Hamilton Farm, Gladstone. . . . Miss Brady is a daughter of the late James Cox Brady and a stepdaughter of Mrs. Charles Suydam Cutting, at whose residence the wedding took place, before a gathering of more than two-hundred members of Society. . . . The bride, a granddaughter of the Countess of Limerick, and a great granddaughter of the Earl of Limerick who was the Lord-in-Waiting to Queen Victoria, also is a granddaughter of the late Anthony N. Brady of Albany. She was escorted by her brother, James Cox Brady. Her gown of deep cream satin, was draped in front to the waist line, and had a long court train of rare old rose point lace. Her voluminous tulle veil, held in place with two diamond bands, extended to the end of the train. The lace train and the diamond bands are heirlooms and have been worn for generations, including [by] her mother, who was Lady Victoria Pery, a daughter of the fifth Earl of Limerick.*[18]

James Cox Brady was a devout Roman Catholic who donated large sums of money to the church. He was made Knight Commander of the Order of St. Gregory by Pope Pius XI. After his death, his widow, Mrs. Charles Suydam Cutting, commissioned St. Brigid Church in Peapack to be built in his memory (see "The Churches" below).

Hamilton Farm Equestrian Stables

One of the grandest monuments to the love of horses is the stable compound Brady built at Hamilton Farm, today the headquarters of the United States Equestrian Team. An ardent horseman, Brady regularly bought, bred, and sold prize stock; he once paid ten thousand dollars for King Largo, a great Shetland pony stallion. Brady spared no expense to create an equestrian showplace, not only for his prized Hackney ponies, but also for the Clydesdale and Percheron draft animals used to work his farm. Designed by architect William Weisenberger from New York City, and built by Thomas J. Steen Company, also from New York City, the stable complex was completed in 1916 at a cost of over $250,000. Unlike the main house, the barn, constructed of reinforced steel, concrete, and brick, was completely fireproof.

Special design features made the barn a world-famous showplace which has maintained its unique charm for more than seventy-five years. An arched center entrance leads into an octagonal foyer, walls are tiled, and the floors are of rust-colored terrazzo brick laid in a herringbone pattern, the same material employed in the corridors and harness rooms. To the left is a two-level stable that can accommodate fifty-four horses. Large gleaming brass globes top posts that make up the twelve-foot-square horse stalls, each equipped with a drain and floor plug. The floors of the stalls are covered with cork brick. Just opposite the foyer entrance is another set of huge double doors that leads to an oval sand exercise and training ring. The barn originally had sleeping rooms for ten men, an apartment for Fred Huyler, the stable manager, eight baths, and game rooms.

The trophy room on the second story was designed around a decorative plate glass floor, surrounded by ornate railings. Brady's guests would gather there to observe from above horses parading over a red carpet below. Hand-carved walnut trophy cabinets flank the room.

Brady brought two sculptors from Italy to craft three magnificent bronze weather vanes for his stables. At the center was a model of Brady's prize stallion Hamilton Model; flanking it were a tandem and a coach-and-four.

In 1917 Brady reduced the size of his stables, selling twenty horses and donating the proceeds to the American Red Cross's World War I efforts. In August 1942, during World War II, many years after Brady's death, the stables were converted to an emergency hospital facility for merchant marine seamen who had been torpedoed. The first civilian base hospital in the United States, "Hamilton Farm Base Hospital No. I" was staffed by nurses from Newark, Jersey City, and Montclair. The hospital was conceived, financed, and directed by Mrs. Charles Suydam Cutting, Brady's widow. The following article from the *Weekly Exponent* tells that story:

January 8, 1942

An emergency hospital is being set up by Mrs. Charles Suydam Cutting on her 5,000 acre estate, Hamilton Farm, as a volunteer contribution to the home defense program.

The project is unique in having been conceived, financed and directed by a single woman; in being the first such hospital to be constructed in America in war-time and probably the first hospital in the world to be set up in a coach barn.

When Mrs. Cutting first told metropolitan hospital authorities of her idea to transform her carriage house into a base hospital, she brought the physicians out to her estate. They needed only a brief look to become excited over the project.

"You didn't mention," the doctors said, "that it was a palace coach barn."

The "barn"—one-half of which is being made into the hospital with the other half being cleared in case additional room should be needed—consists of a main building 42 feet by 48 feet and two wings on each end, 42 by 112 feet. Built of concrete, brick and steel, the building is completely fireproof and relatively bombproof.

[The] primary purpose of the hospital will be to take care of overflow patients from institutions in this area, in the event of disaster or epidemic which might overtax their capacity. There will be no resident staff in the Hamilton Farm Defense Emergency Hospital, and its work will be directed entirely by the Defense Council physicians in this area. Nurses from agencies in this vicinity will be available as needed.

Patients will be bedded in one of the wings where 10 cubicles or small hospital rooms already have been constructed. The sterilizing and operating rooms are being set up in one of the sections opening into the central unit. The workroom of the Hamilton Farm Defense Unit, where Somerset Hills women do volunteer duty three days a week making hospital supplies and garments, occupies that section of the second floor directly over the main section of the building. Built balcony-fashion around a central oval of glass ceiling, the workroom was formerly the trophy room. The glass-front cabinets which run the entire circumference of the paneled room, formerly filled with bronze and silver, are now piled high with hospital garments and supplies.

Built during the first World War as a carriage house and stable, the building is amazingly adaptable for hospital use. Without having to use that section of the building which formerly housed the family's large stable of horses, there are more than enough good-sized rooms available in the carriage house for offices, consultation rooms, staff quarters, supply rooms and storage space, as well as almost unlimited expansion space. Ceilings for first floor rooms are 12 feet and they are nine feet in the second story.

Because much of the wall in the building is of glazed tile sterilization of the hospital quarters was a relatively simple matter. The walls first received several vigorous soap and water scrubbings and then were gone over with disinfectant. The floors—tiled on the first floor—also presented small problems for sterilization.

Although the architect who designed the building was obviously not thinking in terms of a potential hospital, he did an excellent job of providing staircases of regulation hospital width; of ordering the rounded corners where wall meets floor in all hospitals; of arranging space so that hospital routine can be carried out effectively and efficiently.

More than 15 workmen are now employed on the reconstruction work, which has ranged from blocking out a vast hospitable fireplace to make an operating room, to lining the room with a new plastic surface.

Evidence of the worth of the hospital in the opinion of officials is the fact that Mrs. Cutting has been able to purchase a large supply of equipment now subject to strict priorities by the government. Hospital equipment received to date includes wheel chairs, hospital beds, bedding and operating room apparatus. Bandages, garments and other hospital supplies are being prepared in the workroom.

Quarantine quarters will be available in the second story, where both room for patients with communicable diseases, staff quarters and separate kitchen and bathroom are available, cut off from the remainder of the building. The hay loft in the second floor wing, with its tremendous ceiling more than 16 feet high, could be utilized for additional bed space in the event of need. Mrs. Cutting is considering installing a heating and air-conditioning plant in this section.

In planning the hospital, Mrs. Cutting conferred with staff members of Post Graduate Hospital, New York City, and with local physicians, including Dr. C. R. Kay, who heads the defense medical unit for this area. Mrs. Cutting is a member of the Board of Trustees of Post Graduate Hospital.

Since the outbreak of the second World War, Mrs. Cutting has achieved recognition for her foresight and initiative in relief work. Among the several projects she has successfully engineered was the Hamilton Farms Cannery. Appropriately 36,000 quarts of vegetables were canned in a workroom she set up in the downstairs wing of the carriage house. The letter telling of the foods' arrival in an officers prison camp "somewhere in Germany," was probably the most satisfying communication ever received here.[19]

In 1943, the duke and duchess of Windsor visited the hospital at Hamilton Farm and spent the weekend with Mrs. C. Suydam Cutting.

The hospital closed its doors in 1947, the last of seven such facilities for seamen in the United States. It had served five thousand merchant marine seamen who were casualties of war at sea, having endured shipwrecks, torpedoing, and sea fatigue.

A second fire destroyed the rebuilt Hamilton Farm mansion in May 1978. This fire was more of a tragedy than the 1921 conflagration, in that it caused the death of nineteen-year-old Jane Moseley Crawford, a Brady relative staying in the house at the time.

From 1962 to 1978 the stables were leased by the United States Equestrian Team (USET) from Brady Securities and Realty Corporation. In 1978, Beneficial Management Corporation purchased 547 acres of Hamilton Farm and the rebuilt mansion, along with another 300 acres of Brady land on Route 206 in Peapack. The farm and stable were pur-

chased for use as a corporate conference center, the Route 206 property as the site of Beneficial's corporate headquarters. The chapter entitled "Commerce and Industry" elaborates on this architecturally noteworthy Palladian-style edifice.

After purchasing the property, Beneficial Management Corporation allowed the USET to continue using the stables. In December 1988, with Governor Thomas Kean observing, the company signed an agreement giving the United States Equestrian Team permanent rights to the stable, the indoor and outdoor riding rings, and a four-acre easement. The facility is ideal for equestrian training, clinics, and events, as it encompasses a cross-country course, the large sand ring, and an indoor arena that allows year-round activities. Chrystine Jones, a former member of the U.S. jumping squad and director of show jumping activities from 1981 to 1989, came east from Michigan to become the first official director of the facility. Equestrian activities sponsored by the USET include jumping, dressage, and driving squads; clinics for stewards and course designers; schooling sessions by prominent equestrian figures; training sessions for aspiring Olympeads. The compound now houses the Whitney Stone Memorial Hall and Library. Named after the team's late chairman, it is used for lectures and seminars requiring audiovisual equipment. The public is welcome, on given days, to visit the center.

James Cox Brady's famed equestrian showplace today stands as a grand legacy and a monument to his love of horses.

✸ *The Mosle Estate*

In 1906 George R. Mosle, a sugar merchant, made plans to build his home on a hilltop site straddling Morris and Somerset counties at Gladstone. The property he selected had been purchased from Elias Philhower in 1901 and comprised 620 acres 678 feet above sea level.

Grovesnor Atterbury, a Beaux Arts-trained architect and contemporary of Frank Lloyd Wright, was commissioned to design an estate worthy of the beautiful site. Atterbury was the architect of Forest Gardens in Queens, New York, an archetypal American middle-class community in its time. Working with him on the Forest Gardens project was Frederick Law Olmsted, the landscape architect of Central Park, who laid out a lavishly planted and flowing street plan. Atterbury's grand house projects, such as the Mosle estate, served to underwrite his abiding interest in designing more readily affordable housing. He developed the first practical precast concrete process and erected a precast plant on the Queens site.

For the Mosle estate, he created a three-story brick and stone mansion, gracefully proportioned and balanced in view of its grand dimensions—130 by 45 feet. The finished fireproof structure consisted of fifty rooms, ten maids' rooms, and ten baths. The house was surrounded by specially designed gardens and was approached via a long curved driveway winding up from the village below. At the time the road from Gladstone to the property was a private one, which Mosle lined with an alley of sugar maple trees that have grown to great size and beauty and are today a delight to travelers on Mosle Road. At one time the trees were tapped for sap to make maple syrup. A fireproof stone and steel garage on the estate is said to have been designed by the firm of Stanford White at a cost of one hundred thousand dollars. The structure was designed to accommodate seven cars, a workshop, and living quarters. Work on the garage had begun shortly before Stanford White was murdered by Harry Thaw, the deranged husband of White's former mistress.[20]

The estate included a working farm with dairy barns and outbuildings, which had belonged to Philhower, as had much of the land that is today the village of Gladstone. One of the original dairy barns has been converted into a spacious family residence through the addition of a middle floor and substantial alterations to the original loft and ground floor. Today ten of the original fifty cow stanchions remain in the basement of the residence presently owned by the Michael J. Farrell family.

Mosle himself remains an enigma. According to research

The Mosle mansion just after construction was completed, circa 1906. From the Reverend Paul Walther collection.

The intersection of Main Street in Gladstone, looking north, and "Mosle's Parkway," circa 1908. Mosle Road was a private drive to the estate when Mosle lived there. From the Norman Welsh collection.

done by Gladstone resident Allen Crossett, it is alleged that Mosle amassed his fortune importing sugar from Cuba to the United States. Crossett described Mosle's later misfortunes in a 1969 feature article written for the *Bernardsville News*:

> *Although it is not known for certain, it is believed by local historians that Mosle ran afoul of the law during the mid-1920s when one of his ships was sunk in a heavy gale off the coast of Florida, and the lives of at least three of the ship's crew were lost.*
>
> *When the tragedy was investigated by the federal government, it was discovered that the required import permits had not been obtained. In the legal action that followed, the Mosle fortune was dissolved. Mosle was forced to give up his home to meet pressing financial demands.*[21]

Crossett goes on to relate local rumors that Mosle, sensing the coming disaster, hid thousands of dollars throughout his home. No such fortune has ever been found.

The subsequent owner of the estate also encountered financial misfortunes. In 1924 Lillian D. Wetmore, wife of New York attorney J. D. Wetmore, purchased the estate from Wilkinson Bros. & Co., a New York paper-manufacturing firm, through a complicated financial transaction. In 1926 Mrs. Wetmore defaulted on the mortgage. This resulted in the repurchase of the property by the New York paper company at a special master's sale. The purchase price: $100,000! Mosle is said to have spent approximately $2,500,000 building the estate.

In 1926 the Sisters of St. John the Baptist, a Catholic order with headquarters in Rome, purchased some six hundred acres of the estate, the purchase including the mansion, the farm, and four houses. The Sisters are a religious order founded in Italy in 1878 by Father Alphonsus Fusco to shelter, feed, and educate the many poor children who wandered the streets there. They founded an orphanage on the Mosle property, which they called Villa O'Connor after Bishop O'Connor of Newark, who had invited members of the order to work with orphans in that city. The mansion became an administration building, with housing for the nuns and the girls. The huge stable was converted into a boys dormitory.

Just one year later a tragic fire struck the orphanage. Crossett's article continues:

> *After little more than a year of operation, on a freezing cold night in November of 1927, a fire turned the boy's building into a blazing inferno. During the day workmen had been busy trying to complete the installation of a new oil furnace.*
>
> *Coal had been used before, and a pile of glowing coals were removed from the old furnace and left to cool on the hard, dirt floor. It is believed that the fire started when leaking oil from the new furnace finally started to flow across the dirt floor, and eventually came in contact with the still-hot coals.*
>
> *The nuns, risking their own lives, ran repeatedly into the raging fire to save the boys. Most of the boys were brought to safety, but one little boy, shivering in the freezing cold, returned to the burning building to find warmth and was burned to death. Two others were never accounted for.*

The following morning was the darkest in the history of Mount St. John. The stables continued to smolder and the sisters were exhausted, especially those who had run into Gladstone in the middle of the night to find help. There was no telephone or other means of communication from the orphanage to the village.[22]

It is ironic that such a tragic fire should have occurred at the former estate of Mosle, who took great care to construct fireproof structures; and who himself played a major role in establishing the first Peapack-Gladstone Volunteer Fire Department.

With public and private aid, the Sisters were able to build a new boys' building in 1934. In 1937 state policies toward orphans changed, and as a result many of the Villa O'Connor children were placed in foster homes.

In 1938 St. John's School was founded as a private elementary school for boarding and day students, kindergarten through eighth grade. Two wings were added, the architecture and materials of which maintained the style of the Tudor mansion. The school expanded in 1949 to include a high school, and the name was changed to Mount Saint John Academy. A new chapel was blessed, and an academic building was dedicated in October 1950.

In the early 1970s the focus of the Mount changed again: the elementary education program was dropped, and the school became a preparatory school for young women.[23] Angels' Hall was built in 1975, and a gymnasium was added

before declining enrollment caused the school to close its doors in 1992.

❧ Vernon Manor

Edith Blair married Richard V. N. Gambrill in 1917. The couple chose to live in Peapack, and like the C. Ledyard Blairs, became noteworthy benefactors of the community. As we follow the development of the borough, we see that their generous gifts contributed immeasurably to many of the projects initiated after incorporation (see, for example, "First Aid and Rescue Squad" in "Community Services" below).

In 1927 the Gambrills purchased a house and two hundred acres in Peapack (known in the 1800s as the Apgar farm and in the 1900s as the Riker farm) from John Sloane, who then built his estate on Liberty Corner Road, now the headquarters of the United States Golf Association. Sloane allegedly had complained to Gambrill about the noise made by the Lackawanna Railroad steam engines, and Gambrill then offered to buy his Peapack property. The white clapboard house on the property, dating from 1900, became a rebuilding project for the Gambrills, during which time they lived in the "White Cottage" on the Blair estate and in a cottage on Holland Road past the Essex Hunt Club.

The Gambrills contracted with the noted architect James C. Mackenzie, who designed Vernon Manor for them, a

Vernon Manor, front facade. Note decorative garlands and busts of the four seasons in niches. From the Diana Villa collection.

stately brick Georgian mansion of twenty-four rooms set on two hundred acres. His plan included a facade ornamented by four niches which contained stone busts representing each of the four seasons. A U-shaped stable complex around a central courtyard contained a carriage house, sixteen wood-paneled stalls, a sleigh room, storage rooms, and a five-room groom's apartment. The stable complex also encompassed a Georgian six-room house for a head groom, a five-stall stable for mares and foals, a greenhouse, a frame house, and a garage. The Gambrills continued to operate the former Riker dairy farm. Two houses and the barns of that old farm still stand on the property located at 4 Main Street, just south of the borough municipal building.

The entrance to the estate was located on the east side of Main Street, a site now occupied by Amerman's automobile lot. Long-time residents recall sledding down the estate drive-way and across Main Street on long-ago winter days. Mrs. Diana Villa, daughter of the Gambrills, remembered skating down the drive at hair-raising speed on trips to bring up the milk, the long climb back up the drive while balancing the milk jugs being considerably less fun. The Gambrills were partial to the color yellow, so many of the wooden structures associated with Vernon Manor were painted that color; some of them are distinguished by the same hue today. The house at 15 Willow Avenue was the residence of Mrs. Gambrill's chauffeur, and 25 Willow Avenue was also part of the estate.

Ellen Shipman, a landscape architect, designed all the outdoor property. There were stone and grass terraces, and dwarf boxwood hedges bordered all the garden beds. The plan included a playhouse, which was used for tea parties by the Gambrill daughters and subsequently by nine grandchildren.

Richard V. N. Gambrill was a noted sportsman. During World War II he served as master of the Essex Fox Hounds. Over the course of his life, he drove four-in-hand, pair, and tandem teams to many events, including shows at Madison Square Garden. His coach, the Defiance, formerly C. L. Blair's, appeared annually at the Far Hills Races. Gambrill was also a yachtsman, and in the late thirties his M Boat, the *Carolina*, raced against the J Boats off Newport, Rhode Island. From 1915 to 1952 he perpetuated the ancient sport of hunting hare with his private pack of beagles. The sport, practiced in the Somerset Hills since 1888, involves hunting hare cross-country, on foot, following a pack of hounds. The Tewksbury Foot Bassets were successors to Gambrill's private pack. In *Recollections of Bernardsville*, written in 1941, Allison Wright Post related the following:

> It was my brother, George, who took the initiative in forming a pack of beagles which later under his ownership, when the joint kennels of my father and Mr. Drayton were given up, became the well-known Somerset Beagles. The origin of that pack of beagles was a purchase of a few beagles, two of them named Punch and Judy, from Mr. Pottinger Dorsey of Frederick, Maryland.

The Vernon-Somerset Beagles. Richard V. N. Gambrill, master, center; Edith Blair Gambrill, whip, right. From the Diana Villa collection.

After many years when my brother George found it difficult to continue running with the beagles, and he always liked to handle his pack himself as far as possible, he fortunately arranged with Mr. Richard V. N. Gambrill of Peapack, New Jersey, to take over his beagles and consolidate them with his own pack; and as a result Mr. Gambrill's present pack at Peapack is known as the Vernon Somerset Beagles.[24]

Headstones located in the woods on the hill opposite the municipal building on School Street bear the names of the Gambrills' horses: Ben Johnson, 1943; Navarino, 1930–1943; Calico, 1942; Thornby, 1939; California, 1934; Daisy, 1929; and Nancy, 1928. The favorite family dogs interred there are Teeny, 1938; Ben, 1933; and Eric, 1930.

Gambrill continued to add to the property: between 1933 and 1938 he bought about eighty-five acres from C. L. Blair, which included the farm group and the quarry pond. In 1949 Mrs. Gambrill bought approximately one hundred acres from her father's estate, which included land between High-land Avenue and Blair Drive (abutting the farm group) and the woods bordering Ravine Lake. She gave acreage along the river to the Lake Club as a bird sanctuary.

Richard V. N. Gambrill died in 1952. Between 1967 and 1972 Edith Blair Gambrill sold most of her property to her daughters, retaining ten acres around the new home that she built for herself on Willow Avenue in 1969, where she lived until her death in 1988. Vernon Manor itself, with forty acres, was sold in 1969. In 1979 Mrs. Gambrill's daughter Diana

The Richard V. N. Gambrill family in its sleigh at the front entrance of Vernon Manor, 1943. Richard V. N. Gambrill and Edith Blair Gambrill in the front, daughters Diana, left rear, and Ann, right, with faithful friend between them. From the Diana Villa collection.

transferred one-half of her property to a partnership of her children.

Around 1949 the Gambrills donated land on Main Street to the community so that the eight-room brick school could be enlarged. In 1949 they donated the land on St. Luke's Avenue as the site for the First Aid and Rescue Squad building. The Rectory of St. Luke's was moved to Gambrill property in 1965 when Anne's Chapel was built, and in 1986 Mrs. Gambrill gave additional land to the rectory.

Mrs. Gambrill was a member of St. Luke's parish to which she donated the carillon bells in memory of her husband. The altar was given by her in memory of her mother-in-law. During World War II she was active in the American Red Cross as a nurse's aid in Somerville. She also had various English children residing at Vernon Manor to escape the bombing in London. Mrs. Gambrill was an active birder and conservationist, and traveled often with her great friend, the noted ornithologist and author Roger Tory Peterson, to Asia, Africa, and Europe. She was a director of the National Audubon Society and at her death donated her large library of birds, animals, and horticulture to the New Jersey Audubon Society. She had been a president of the Garden Club of Somerset Hills, and a dedicated member of the Visiting Nurse Association.

Two of the Blair carriages and all of the Gambrill carriages donated by Mrs. Gambrill are on view at the Carriage Museum at Historic Shelburne Village and Museum in Burlington, Vermont. These carriages were made by Brewster of England.

❧ *The Equestrians*

Many of the prominent families who chose to live in the Somerset Hills did so because the area was eminently suited to their abiding passion for all things equestrian. "Hamilton Farm" talks about the stable complex that is now the home of the USET; this section describes some of the other local equestrian activities, in particular hunting.

A network of bridal paths was developed under the auspices of the Somerset Hills Bridal Paths Association, and in 1917 the first of the main lines, two that traversed the C. Ledyard Blair and Grant B. Schley estates, were completed. The line that extended through Blairsden proceeded to Ravine Lake and thence to the Raritan River and on through the Somerset Hills Country Club. Eventually the Somerset Hills were thoroughly criss-crossed by scenic trails for equestrians. The equestrian tradition has continued through the decades, and many of the bridal trails are still open to Somerset Hills riders. However, development and the subsequent break-up of vast estates into suburban parcels have taken a distinct toll on the number of trails available to local equestrians.

Not just trail riding, but hunting and polo were also pursued in the Somerset Hills. Polo was introduced to the area in the early 1900s and grew in popularity, becoming quite fashionable during the 1930s. A July 21, 1932, article in the *Bernardsville News* made note of a match played by the "Peapack Blues." The team played matches every weekend, and the players mentioned include A. Fowler, A. Wadley, B. Johnson, and F. Johnson.

❧ *Essex Hunt*

On, to Mount Paul, through its Chestnut Cover
Up its rough slope to the top and over,
Then what a picture greets our eyes,
One's heart beats faster in glad surprise

There, stretched out to the South in view
The Peapack Valley and hills of blue—
A valley of grass and a line to follow,
Toward Gladstone and Peapack in their hollow,
A line to gallop and jump at speed,
A line to test the worth of your steed.[25]

The story of the Essex Hunt begins in Montclair, New Jersey, where it was established at the Essex Country Club in 1870. It was originally a drag hunt, in which a scent trail was created the day before the hunt by dragging over the land the scent of the fox, or of anise-seed oil, which the hounds will follow. Long recognized as one of the major hunts in the eastern states, the Essex Hunt is mentioned in early accounts of hunting in this country. As the Montclair area began to develop and the population to increase, the need to find a less densely settled site for the hunt became apparent, and the Essex Country Club sought to unburden itself of the expenses and responsibilities of the hunt.

In 1891 Charles Pfizer bought the hounds, horses, and equipment of the Essex Hunt. Pfizer and his brother, Emile, were the heirs to the vast Pfizer chemical fortune, and their grandfather is said to have been the founder of the Essex Hunt in Montclair. Charles was an avid sportsman who devoted his life to fox hunting, and the records of the Essex Hunt are replete with stories of his sportsmanship and hospitality. He was master of the Essex Hunt from 1891 until 1912. Once he owned the hunt, it was possible for non-members to participate, something that had not happened when it was owned by a private country club. Many hunters came from the Morristown area, where the pack had hunted for several seasons. Charles Pfizer lived in Bernardsville, then known as Vealtown, and in 1892 the pack was temporarily located there at "Seney Cottage" near his home.

Just off Old Chester Road in Gladstone is an established neighborhood of comfortable houses on Brook Hollow, Farm Cottage, and Pfizer roads. In the late 1890s Pfizer acquired a two-hundred-acre farm and established his Upper and Lower Kennels there. The Upper Kennels, located at the

ESSEX FOX HOUNDS.
A. F. Hyde, M. F. H. G. Brice, Huntsman.
Season, 1917 — 1918.

The Essex Fox Hounds, 1917–1918 season. A. F. Hyde, master of fox hounds; G. Brice, huntsman. Photograph courtesy of the Essex Hunt Club via Mrs. Ann Winston.

A temporary "hospital" to house victims of the influenza epidemic during World War I was built on the Charles Pfizer estate near the far end of what is now Brook Hollow Drive in Gladstone. Left to right: Mayor John Bodine; Rev. John M. Harper, rector of St. Luke's Episcopal Church; and Eldridge M. Ward, who was in charge of the plumbing installation. From the Thomas Ward collection.

corner of what is now Pottersville Road and Route 206, were used only for fox hunting. The Lower Kennels, situated at the Old Chester Road location, were used only for drag hunting. Pfizer remodeled the old farmhouse into a clubhouse and converted the large farm barns into stables and kennels. It is said that before the clubhouse was available, hunters traveling to the area would change into their sports clothes on the train. Polo games were also played at the Lower Kennel location. Pfizer added on to the farmhouse an area where he could entertain his fellow huntsmen handsomely. These days are described by F. W. Jones in *Recollections of the Essex Hunt:*

> *Subsequently, Mr. Pfizer built the big oak room with vaulted ceiling, gallery, and an enormous stone chimney. There his hunting friends enjoyed his hospitality for many years. The hunt dinners every Saturday night and holidays in the "big room" were not easily forgotten occasions. Ladies from Bernardsville and Morristown, who followed the hunt on wheels, were often present. [Ladies did not join in the hunt until 1910.] Pink dress coats were in order, and the Master and Secretary turned out in black satin knee breeches.*[26]

Jones goes on to describe the colorful attire worn by the hunters:

> *The hunt field livery at that time was scarlet full frock coat with orange velvet claw collar and initial buttons. The evening coat was pink with claret velvet collar and orange facings and script initial buttons. These detailed specifications were posted on a bulletin board in the main hall, together with the fixture card and other notices pertaining to the hunt.*

> *The majority of the men in the field wore mufti, but one could wear what one chose. However, if you chose scarlet, you must turn yourself out correctly in every detail, even down to your boot tops which were Belgravian brown—no pink tops—they were for coachmen.*[27]

After 1909, Charles Pfizer could no longer continue his financial support of the hunt. He turned over the hunting privileges to interested members, and a new club was incorporated under the name of the Essex Fox Hounds on February 10, 1913. The stated purpose of the club was "to encourage riding and other country sports." Witnesses who signed the documents of incorporation were numbered among the financially and socially prominent of the time: William C. Commann, Seymour L. Cromwell, George D. Dutton, Arthur A. Fowler, Ogden H. Hammond, Fred W. Jones, William A. Larned, Joseph Larocque, George Meserve, Clarence B. Mitchell, Benjamin Nicoll, Charles Pfizer, Percy R. Pyne, W. S. Richardson, Kenneth B. Schley, Arthur Turnbull, Arthur Whitney, and Richard H. Williams, Jr. Other members of the hunt who took an active part were James Cox Brady, Oliver D. Filley, Harold Fowler, Richard V. N. Gambrill, R. Stuyvesant Pierrepont, Richard Whitney, and Owen Winston.

From that time forward the hunt was maintained financially by the members' annual dues. A. F. Hyde was named master of the hunt, and George Brice was recruited from Maryland and brought to the club as huntsman.

The clubhouse burned to the ground in 1912 and was not rebuilt. The large old stone barn was converted to an apartment and the former stable remodeled into a single-family home. When Pfizer died in 1928, the property passed into the hands of his brother, Emile, who built a house on the northern edge of the property that was once used as the polo field. For many years it was the property of Dr. Bernard Sugermann.

The Essex Fox Hounds moved to its present location when it leased, with an option to buy, what was then the Miller farm. Kennels were built, and the Miller house was converted into a clubhouse. The drag hunt was abandoned completely for live fox hunting, and the Upper Kennel site was sold by Pfizer to James Cox Brady. Hyde's stables at Larger Crossroads became prominent as the home of forty to fifty hunters.

Emile Pfizer died in 1929 at his Bernardsville estate, "Yademos" (Someday spelled backward), the estate built by George I. Seney for his son Robert in 1881. A special train left the station at Hoboken at 9:15 to bring mourners from New York to the funeral services held at St. Luke's Episcopal Church in Peapack, rites performed by Reverend Harper. "He was renowned for his generosity and hospitality. He mounted most of his friends for the hunting and carried all the expenses of the hunt during his mastership. His home was always full of guests, and his hunt breakfasts will long be remembered by all his numerous friends."[28]

Since the hunters pursued the fox through the lands of the local farmers, the hunt's relationship with the local farmers was carefully nurtured, as can be seen from the following letter to local farmers:

&   *A Letter to the Landlords of the Hunting District*

All are welcome to hunt with the pack at any time and the Secretary will be glad to send regular notices of the meets to any one who cares to have them.

Mr. Brice, the huntsman, will be pleased if any one hearing of foxes in their neighborhood will report the same to him. He will bring the hounds at the first opportunity, and we believe we can give you better sport by running your fox with the hounds than if he is killed in any other way.

Any time we start a fox on a man's place, the Hunt will give him $5.00, and will pay $10 to any landholder on whose place a fox is killed by the hounds.

If any damage is done to fences, fields or poultry, it should be reported at once to Mr. Brice, at the club, and it will receive prompt and fair attention.

The members of the hunt are constantly warned against riding over crops, leaving bars down and gates open, or stampeding cattle. If these rules are neglected, kindly report to the officers of the hunt.

The hunt has no desire to ride over the property of any one who does not wish us to do so. But we intend to show every consideration for the feelings and property of landholders, and we hope to conduct the hunting in such a way that we will be welcome everywhere.

Any farmers having hay, grain, straw or live stock to sell should

Richard V. N. Gambrill works his coach and four. From a painting signed Voss, 1934. From the Diana Villa collection.

report the same to Mr. Brice. Members will buy as much as possible from those over whose land we hunt.

    The club will be glad to furnish post and rail panels wherever landholders are willing to have them placed in wired fields.

    George Brice, Huntsman.

    Dr. A. S. Knight, Chairman, Landholders' Committee.

    Barney Schley, Wm. A. Larned, Masters of Hounds.

    Arthur Fowler, Secretary.

    November, 1913[29]

Under Hyde's direction the countryside was developed for hunting; most of the farmers were persuaded to replace the prevalent wire fencing with post and rail, and before long the hunt encompassed thirty square miles of rolling hills and "paneled" farms. The farmers were encouraged to breed and sell prospective hunters. Jim Brennan, the stud groom, made Uncas Chief, the hunt's stallion, available free of charge to farmers interested in breeding stock. The annual Far Hills Horse Show at the time held well-attended breeding classes. Soon area residents bred one to two mares a year and began raising their own horses. An annual "Farmers' Day" had been inaugurated by Pfizer in 1910. F. Jones quotes the notes of J. C. Wilmerding, club secretary:

❧   *Farmers' Day—February 11, 1910*

    A glorious day overhead brought to Pottersville at the hour appointed (1:00 P.M.) a large gathering of farmers invited by the members of the Hunt for a day of sport and good fellowship. They were greeted by the

Essex men (being a stag affair—no ladies) and afterwards enjoyed the hospitality in the form of a hearty luncheon, music and singing by the Black Diamond Quartet. A liberal supply of liquor and cigars furthering good feeling and cheer, they brought on an exhibition of marksmanship for trophies donated by the Hunt (a young bull, a turkey and a pig).[30]

That first annual "Farmers' Day Race Meeting," hosted by the hunt club in honor of the farmers on whose land they hunted, drew three hundred local men. The day evolved through the years to include luncheon and the running of a steeplechase, the first race traditionally being the "Farmers' Race." The club established another tradition with the first running of the New Jersey Hunt Cup on Saturday, October 23, 1915; it continues as one of the oldest steeplechases run in the United States. In 1916 the races were moved to the "Fro-Heim," the Far Hills estate of Grant Schley, which had fairgrounds and ample stables. It continues there today, held each year on the last Saturday of October, as a benefit for the Somerset Medical Center. The property, renamed Moorland Farms, is now owned by AT&T. The Essex Fox Hounds Steeple Chase is attended by upward of thirty thousand people each year, many of whom come from miles away to enjoy the races and sumptuous, or simple, picnics in the beautiful rolling hills of Somerset.

The language of a hunt may be confusing to those not familiar with the sport. The "field" is all of the riders on a given day; the field is always headed by a "master of fox hounds," who is a member of the hunt; the "pack" consists of thirty-six hounds, or eighteen couples; the "huntsman" and the "whippers-in" are employed by the hunt to manage the pack during a hunt.

The Essex Fox Hounds has continued through the decades as a private pack of hounds owned by subscribers. The hunts are run from different members' land on given days. The official hunt season runs from November through February and is comprised of three hunts a week: Saturdays, Mondays, and Wednesdays. The fox is not killed in the United States, as it is in England. Some members of the field wear the pink hunting jackets so beautifully represented in paintings and prints that deal with the sport of fox hunting. Others are attired in plain black jackets. Jacqueline Kennedy Onassis is an accomplished horsewoman and member of the Essex Fox Hounds.

Some sense of the intensity with which horse enthusiasts followed the Essex Hunt can be garnered from the following excerpts from an article that appeared in 1930 during the time Kenneth Schley served as master of the hounds.

"A great variety of country. Hilly with plenty of cover and fair amount of grass. Fences all post and rail. Foxes are hunted."

Thus Baily's Hunting directory, that lexicon of fox-hunting, that Webster of fox-chasing. But these short sentences describe Essex only as completely as a preface describes the book. . . . You must have hunted with the Essex yourself to know those patent qualifications which have given the hunt the great name it has. . . . Essex is a hunt for horsemen and houndsmen, sportsmen who like to see hounds work and feel horses jump, who want a run for their money, and a stiff run.

Suppose you are going down to Peapack for a week's hunting. . . . From the bleak chilly city you will motor through those peculiarly unprepossessing suburbs which surround New York until the large scent of the country fills your nostrils, and you observe on either hand the four-rail fences typical of the Essex country, sturdy and formidable. Your pulse quickens as you see shining thoroughbreds, with coats of silk and muscles of steel, being exercised by grooms in brick-red breeches in the big, yellow-brown fields.

At length you reach the clubhouse, which is more than a clubhouse, comprising a large house with a ballroom wing, hunt stables, garage, farriers' shop and stalls for temporary stabling. . . . Through a romantic low arch you enter a court with members' and Hunt servants' tackrooms, cleaning rooms, boiler room and so on, and beyond that are the stalls for the Hunt horses. . . .

Your next voyage of discovery is to the kennels, whose architecture is the last word in kennel construction. Floors and walls are of concrete, there are wooden sleeping benches raised ten inches above the floor and bedded with straw. . . . The drainage, lighting and ventilation are a joy to those who know a dog's Paradise must be on earth. . . .

You hear about the mid-winter Hunt Balls, and about the two-day race meet that takes place in the fall. . . . Next day you rise tingling with anticipation. . . . Who can describe the romance and the picturesque quality of a meet of hounds? . . . It takes a horse of considerable foot and one with ability to jump the country if you want to be up in a big run, because the field is so big. . . . You remark to a neighbor on a stalwart gray that the country seems to be very carefully panelled. He agrees and adds that it's also full of foxes and the hounds seldom draw blank.[31]

A less enthusiastic picture was painted by E. B. White.

❧   *The Fox of Peapack*
    A Ballad of Somerset County

The fox of Peapack left his earth
    And trailed his brush across New Jersey,
Absorbed in apple-fall and mirth,
    And feeling very loud and nirsey.

The leaf was brown beneath his paw,
    The sky was cloud-besirk and frowsy,
The fox of Peapack clicked his jaw
    And noticed he was feeling lousy.

Down wind he took his bushy way
    To buy his vixen wife a trinket,
And as he skirted Peapack Bay
    He stopped, at intervals, to drink it.

Forgetting what he'd gone to get,
    And falling in with thieves and planters,

He bought his wife a table set,
    A Mason jar, and two decanters.

Well pleased withal, he started back
    Through fen and weir and Lincoln highway,
Quite anxious to avoid the pack
    That hunt in every Peapack byway.

Upon the funniest fen of all,
    With Peapack still a mile aborning,
He heard the scarlet hunter call
    And knew it must be Thursday morning.

He smelled the hound, he smelled the horse,
    He smelled the Peapack store and steeple,
And lastly, as a matter of course,
    He also smelled the Peapack people.

Determined that he wouldn't let
    His Mason jar be confiscated,
He calmly burned the table set
    And watched the hunters while he waited.

Amused, he hung around a while
    At fifty or a hundred paces
To analyze the hunters' guile
    And note the curious Peapack faces.

He then went home, athwart with life,

To wash and do a little fixin',
"I'm back from town," he told his wife.
  "I see you are," replied the vixen.

They ate a bit of sobel stew
  And read a page or so from Genesis,
They carried out a threat or two
  And certain harmless little menaces.

"What did you bring me?" asked his spouse,
  Who spoke in genitives and datives.
"I brought you something for the house
  "And news about the Peapack natives."

He showed his wife the Mason jar,
  Concealing it with quips and banter,
And managed, in the end, to mar
  The scene by breaking one decanter.

"I saw the hunt today," he said,
  "I saw the people plainly, honey;
"I saw the M.F.H. in red,
  "And listen, dear, it's pretty funny.

"I smelled the hound, I smelled the horse,
  "I smelled the Peapack store and steeple,
"And lastly, as a matter of course,
  "I also smelled the Peapack people."

They talked it over in a pet,
  The fox's voice grew loud and mannish:
"I now regard the hunting set
  "As disagreeable and clannish.

"There's this about it," said the fox,
  Dropping his wife a graceful curtsy,
"It seems to me a paradox
  "When rural folks go hurtsy-turtsy.

"I like the country here about,
  "The Peapack store, the Peapack steeple,
"But now it's time you found it out:
  "I do not like the Peapack people."

"That settles it," the vixen said,
  "Get down our satchel and our wee pack,
"We'll put the Mason jar in bed
  "And get the devil out of Peapack."

Next day they went. They left their earth
  And trailed their brushes 'cross New Jersey
Absorbed in apple-fall and mirth,
  And acting very loud and nirsey.[32]

According to Valerie Barnes, Mr. White never actually visited Peapack. Rather, he was intrigued by the name Peapack, which he heard from acquaintances who rode to hounds here.[33]

The original daily log of the Essex Hunt, kept from the 1890s, disappeared about 1935,[34] but a hunting journal can be found in the manuscript collection of the New Jersey Historical Society.

❧ *A Drag with the Old Essex by Somerset*
    Dedicated "to that good sportsman, Charles Pfizer MFH, and all the
    members of the Essex Hunt who rode so gallantly in the old drag."

"A drag with the Essex"
My Word! What a thrill
It gives to us old ones
To think of it still.

The country was open
The galloping fast,
The fences upstanding,
Pace held till the last.

Charles Pfizer, the Master,
Showed sport that was fine
The better, the faster,
The stiffer the line.

His stables were ample
And full of the best;
All leppers and stayers
And fit for the test

"Open House!" was his motto,
The kennels were gay;
After hunting, a dinner
And a bed, if you'd stay.

Mrs. Pfizer as hostess,
With Lulu, Nineteen,
Was gracious and charming,
And ruled like a queen.

So here's to Charles Pfizer,
And the days we recall,
The father of hunting
Where Essex holds thrall![35]

❧ The Changing Population

Immigrants from Europe began arriving in the Somerset Hills area just before the turn of the century when the large estates were being built. They came to work as stone masons and general laborers, gardeners and landscapers, and builders of the expanding railroads. The legacy of their craftsmanship survives and is visible today: the exquisite stone walls that wind up Blair Drive; brick and terrazzo floors laid in intricate patterns at the United States Equestrian Team stables at Hamilton Farm and the coach barns at the Matheny School; the stone dam at Ravine Lake; and the limestone and marble details that embellish the facades of the grand houses.

Daisy Cooper is a daughter of Patrick Cooper and Bridget Giardino, who raised a family of six children here after emigrating from Italy. She and her brother Michael were the only two born in the United States. Their brother Tony worked as a water boy at the Blairsden construction, and Daisy recalls a shed on the property that was used to house the laborers. The family built a house at 72 Mendham Road in 1908 and took in boarders to supplement their income and to help other immigrants who came to make a new life for themselves here. The second floor of the house served as a dormitory lined with bunks for as many as fifteen boarders. For many years the family operated Coopers' Market (now known as Gladstone Market) on Main Street.

It was common practice for one member of an Italian family to emigrate to the United States, and, once established, to secure employment for other family members and friends and send for them. The DeLucas, parents of three young men, Michael, Patsy, and Dick (all under the age of twenty-one), wrote to Bridget Cooper from Italy asking that she look after the boys in the United States. She agreed and they arrived to seek employment and to board at the Cooper home. The three men have remained here as businessmen in various capacities. Michael DeLuca was an owner of the Peapack Hotel.

Anthony DeSesso came to the United States in 1894 through Ellis Island from a small village in Italy near Naples. He was just sixteen. He worked at first in the Virginia coal mines, then migrated to this area because of a family friend in Morristown. Here he worked as a stone mason on the Blair and Mosle estates, eventually giving up the trade because of his fear of heights. In those days stone masons earned $1.00 to $1.25 per day, which was considered by the immigrants as a good wage. He sent for Rose M. Scinto, his future wife, in 1902, and she joined him here. In 1907 he built his home at 70 Mendham Road. They had six children, Jennie, Bennie, Angelo, Rossie, John, and George. George DeSesso is the local pharmacist and owner of Debus Drug Store.

Several houses in the community served as boardinghouses for newly arrived immigrants. A group of row houses across Peapack Brook served as multifamily dwellings, and the house at 143 Main Street was a boardinghouse run by the Morelli family. Angel Bolio came from Italy to Peapack with his mother. He began as a railroad worker and eventually accumulated several properties on Main Street. At one time he ran an Italian grocery store at the corner of Highland Avenue.

The immigrants, especially the Italian Roman Catholics, encountered deep-seated prejudice within the community. The Ku Klux Klan was openly active in Somerset County until the 1950s, and older residents recall a series of cross-burnings, one atop the limestone quarry hill, opposite St.

Brigid Roman Catholic Church. Parents were concerned for the safety of their children who were taunted with ethnic and religious slurs on their trips to and from school. On March 20, 1924, a large Klan march took place in Peapack. Jim Brennan, an employee at Hamilton Farm, drove "his black Model T Ford into the middle of a torch-light procession of white-robed KKK, who were proceeding up the main street of Peapack four abreast" and was subsequently arrested by local police.[36]

In 1925 a local newspaper reported that a Peapack minister had been reinstated by the KKK after a five-month suspension. And in 1942, the following item was reprinted:

April 9, 1936

An announcement of the Easter Sunrise Service conducted by the Ku Klux Klan on the grounds of the Owannamassie Club on Highway 31 (now 206) in Pluckemin starting at sunrise, 5:26 A.M., the service will be conducted by the officials of the Klan wearing regalia. A trombone quartet will lead the assemblage in the singing of well-known hymns of the Church and other selections.

Grand Dragon William I. Morgaan of Long Branch, the New Jersey head of the Klan, will have among his guests the Grand Dragons of eight neighboring states, accompanied by delegations of Klanspeople from their respective realms. Last Easter over 5,000 gathered at Pluckemin, where one of two New Jersey Klan services was held. This year there will be just the one service, and an attendance of over 10,000 is anticipated.[37]

Today many local businesses and residences bear the names of the Italian families who are descended from those first immigrants who came here seeking better lives. They worked hard and prospered in their adopted land, and their children have become a vital part of our community, as volunteers, public servants, professionals, and business people. The war memorials in Liberty Park testify to their service in the United States military when called upon by their country.

❧ The Naming of Gladstone

When the Delaware and Lackawanna Railroad extended its line from Bernardsville to Peapack in 1890, a post office was established at the upper end of the village in what we know today as Gladstone. The new village acquired its name through the actions of William Hillard, a local judge and farm owner. An admirer of the Honorable William E. Gladstone, prime minister of Great Britain at the time, Hillard wrote to Gladstone asking permission to use his name.

The Hillard property subsequently became St. Bernard's School (now Gill St. Bernard's; see "The Schools" below). The Reverend Thomas A. Conover, the first headmaster of the school, wrote an account of the proceedings.

When in the year 1900, I came, with Mrs. Conover, to Gladstone and occupied the homestead of the Hillard family, I learned that when the people living in the northern end of Peapack wished to have a post office

The "GladPackers" baseball team, circa 1913. From the Reverend Paul Walther collection.

nearer than the one in Peapack, they learned that it was necessary for them to make application to become another town. When the question of what the name of the new town should be, someone suggested calling it after the Hon. W. E. Gladstone, then Prime Minister of Great Britain, and Mr. Hillard, I was informed, was requested to write Mr.

Gladstone asking for permission to use his name and he received a courteous reply giving this permission. Just a few weeks ago I wrote to Mr. Gladstone's old home in Hawarden and asked if a member of the family there would be good enough to send a photograph of Mr. Gladstone for the library at St. Bernard's School because the School *now occupies the old home of the Hillard family. I have just received a very courteous letter from Mr. Gladstone's grandson, enclosing a photograph and an autograph of his grandfather, and these I am placing in the library of St. Bernard's School. We should be very happy to have any people of Gladstone or others interested visit the School and see this photograph and letter.*[38]

A. C. Gladstone's letter follows:

Broadlane

Hawarden, Chester

Dear Sir:

I was very much interested to have your letter, as I had no knowledge that there was a place called Gladstone. I am a grandson of Mr. Gladstone—(as the family always call him)—being the eldest son of his second son Stephen. I inherited the Hawarden estate when my cousin William was killed in 1915.

Hawarden Castle is now used for a war purpose and for censorship reason[s] I had better not say more. This house is within 50 yards of it and is of a modest size, but sufficient for present circumstances.

I enclose a photograph of Mr. Gladstone, which being old and somewhat faded, I am rather ashamed of, but it is the only one to hand at the moment. You will see that it was taken in France, and probably I think after his retirement in 1894 when he was 85. I know, however, that this photograph was selected by one of his sons as an excellent likeness of him at the time. I also enclose a specimen of his signature which you will see comes from another photograph.

I am interested in your pamphlets and to hear of your link with the English Schools. If any of your boys serving ever get to Hawarden I would be delighted to show them round.

I hope you will send me a line of acknowledgment so that I am [to] know that the photograph has reached you safely.

I earnestly pray that this appalling war may have one good outcome—in drawing our respective countries close to one another in the future.

Yours faithfully

A. C. Gladstone[39]

William E. Gladstone was a fascinating figure and a sponsor of reform in Great Britain. He oversaw the Endowed School Bill, the Habitual Criminal Bill, the Ballot Bill, the Elementary Education Act, the University Tests Bill, the Ecclesiastical Titles Act, the Trades Union Bill, and the Affirmation Bill and supported Home Rule in the Irish question. A great admirer of the United States, Gladstone called the American constitution "the most remarkable work ever struck off at a given time by the brain and purpose of man" and thought the United States Senate "the most remarkable of all the inventions of modern politics." He was a great orator and a prolific writer on many subjects, including economics and ecclesiastical, historical, political, artistic, literary, and practical subjects. An accomplished pianist, he was fond of Scottish ballads.[40]

Evidently the namesake of the new post office was not

revered by everyone. Mr. L. Van Doren wished to send the first telegram on the day the new service opened. On hearing that the town was to be called Gladstone he promptly tore up his telegram and threw it away.

❧ *Incorporation*

In 1912 Peapack, on the threshold of incorporation, was adjusting to the changes we associate with the turn of the century. The headlines of that year included the significant political news of the nomination of the governor of New Jersey, Woodrow Wilson, as the Democratic party's presidential candidate. Local news items spoke of a new speed limit, not to exceed ten miles per hour; the formation of an electric lighting commission; excellent skating at Todd's Quarry; Ed McKinstry having adopted acetylene gas as an illuminant; the "Pea-Glad" versus "Laddies" (Ladd estate employees) baseball game; typhoid, diphtheria, and measles.

For a light-hearted overview of the commercial, civic, and social scene near the time of incorporation, here is a spoof from a local paper:

❧ *"Jersey Devil" Visits (?) Peapack*
So Says the New York Journal, So We Go for an Interview
Editor Evening Journal:

Dear Sir—The following may be of some value as a news item:

The devil that created so much excitement in Jersey reappeared last night in Peapack, and this morning tracks were found leading to a cave in a lime stone quarry.

The cave was explored in the morning by five mechanics working near by, and unmistakable signs of an animal were found. The tracks were peculiar, not unlike those of a pony in shape, but they were cloven.

Among the inhabitants who saw the devil are such responsible people as John Stevens, Town Constable; Hagar Mayberry the barber, and Dan Sallivan, a pupular [sic] young man from New York.

If any doubts exist as to the truth of this story, they can be verified by calling up the Howard House on [the] phone.

Respectfully Yours,

John Hays [41]

The above appeared in the New York Evening Journal a few evenings ago. Immediately upon securing such strong (?) evidence, as the above named person, who never lived here, we hastily grabbed our camera and started in search of the "beast" for a photo and interview. We hardly expected him to pass by without stopping here, for one traveling throughout the state misses fully one-half the sights if they do not stop in our vicinity. Just before searching for this "devil" we interviewed the parties mentioned in the Journal. Constable Stevens informed us that he had not seen the "devil" mentioned, but he had at different times arrested "Jersey Devils." Berber Mayberry said he occasionally saw one go speeding through town in an automobile. We still went further and inquired of others. Merchant McKinstry said that he had the name of one on his books; Esquire Charles Wikoff said he would give him more than thirty days if brought before him; Wm. VanDerbeek said he could make it warm for him with his coal; Charles Berner is willing to bet considerable that one of his English pheasant will give him a hard fight; Oscar Vliet says he would like to meet him in the road when his auto was at full speed; E. C. Lamerson said he would like to have his help in ice; G.F. Hill & Co., are willing to race him with several [of] their good livery horses; Ellis Tiger Co. would like to sell him lumber for a new house if he intended to remain here; Flomerfelt & Huyler would give a right figure on the contract; W. L. Ballantine would take care of the plumbing; John Hulick offers to bet that several of our bowlers can beat him; L. Huber says if he ever tasted his baking he would have no other; Schefcik claims he can convince him he has the most up-to-date drug store for many miles; J. M. Allen would like him to exhibit in Allen's Auditorium; D. H. Van Doren says from the tracks he does not think him properly shod; H. N. Miller & Co., think they could give him right figures on grain while here; Postmaster Van Arsdale has no notice to forward his mail elsewhere; Thomas Howard will wager he can wing him in one shot; Ludlow Bros. invites him to inspect their fine factory.

We finally started for the interview with the noted traveler. He met us at the mouth of the cave and greeted us kindly. We were fortunate enough to secure the first photograph he has ever posed for, giving us exclusive rights, and we shall prosecute all infringers. The "old fellow" had a great story to tell. He admitted that many of the newspaper reports were true and that he had been in various parts of New York,

Pennsylvania and New Jersey all in the same minute. When asked if it was true that he could spit fire 40 feet he said the best he had ever done was 39 feet 11 ¾ inches. He acknowled [sic] having just devoured 3 houses, 6 lots and considerable lime stone rock. He stated that he like [sic] this section but thought the people we [sic] too good for him here. So he soon expects to move to—well, where ever he appears next.[42]

Industrial and technical developments had brought railroads, electricity, the telephone, the automobile, and, as a result, population growth to a rural community. A new service economy had developed to accommodate these changes, giving rise to a series of commercial ventures. Churches and schools were organized, as were a women's club, a library, the fire department, the First Aid Squad, and the police department.

The advantages of incorporating as a borough became increasingly obvious. The need for such community services as electric lighting, water hydrants and reservoirs, telephone lines, a constable, and road building, maintenance, and repairs imposed new financial burdens on the taxpayers. They objected to paying high taxes for the many miles of rural roads in Bedminster Township not serving the immediate needs of the twin villages. Incorporation as a separate borough seemed to be the solution to the local problems, and in 1912 Peapack-Gladstone elected to secede from Bedminster Township and form a new borough.

On March 4, Assemblyman A. G. Anderson introduced to

The first telephone exchange was located in the house on the northeast corner of Main Street and Willow Avenue. From the Reverend Paul Walther collection.

the New Jersey legislature Bill 483 calling for the incorpora-tion of the Borough of Peapack and Gladstone. The bill was approved by the state legislature and signed by Governor Woodrow Wilson. Colorful reports of the subsequent events are recorded in the *Bernardsville News* and the *Weekly Exponent,* which was published in Peapack and sold for three cents per copy or one dollar per year.

The *Exponent* editors endorsed the idea of incorporation but were not as enthusiastic about other legislative proceed-ings. In an April issue pertaining to the session in Trenton appear the following comments:

> *It has been a session of no great importance in any respect: like many of its predecessors. It has been remarkable mainly for its threshing over of old straw, fussing over trifles and tinkering former legislation. Much of the new stuff ground out is crude and ill-considered and will need to be tinkered and patched up in its turn. It is ever thus.*[43]

The editors had a more positive attitude about Bill 483, calling it "a good piece of work," and went on to say

> *and Assemblyman Anderson for whom we predict a bright future has ably seconded Somerset's more experienced legislator (Mr. Smalley) in dealing with every measure "touchin upon an' appertainen' to" the best interests of County and State. Both were found on the right side of every question that came up and they were the introducers of a number of most important bills, as may be noted by a glance over the Legislative proceedings from day to day. . . . Mr. Anderson successfully "fathered" the Peapack-Gladstone Borough Bill.*[44]

It is interesting to note how some other legislative business introduced at the same session in Trenton fared: "Equal suffrage was lost in the House, as previously in the Senate."[45] Among bills passed were:

> ✦ *Fixing a premium of 50 cents each on ground hogs.*
> ✦ *The Stickel automobile reciprocity bill, which opens up to foreign motor car traffic, the costly roads of the State.*
> ✦ *The Woman's ten-hours-a-day bill.*[46]

The *Bernardsville News* continued to follow events.

> *The people of Peapack and Gladstone voted for a borough on Tuesday, 136 to 17. Congratulations!*[47]

> *Borough of Peapack and Gladstone is far too long and clumsy for use in these days of hurry and hustle. Make it "Pea-Glad" or, better still, "Glad-Pea." Brevity is the soul of wit. . . . The new borough is nothing if not ambitious. It is disposed to try its wings at once and acquire its own water supply and, in time, establish an electric light plant. That's the sort of a community for a live man to live in with people who have a mind to do things, and not take it out in talking about doing them.*[48]

> *The new Borough of Pea-Glad boasts of 4,000 acres. Well, one would expect as much when Far Hills could do almost as well by incorporating but one estate. By the way, the new borough is without officials as yet.*[49]

An election was held on June 18, and John Bodine was the successful candidate, becoming the first mayor of Peapack and Gladstone. Councilmen elected were N. T. Ballentine, M. C. Smalley, G. F. Hill, W. C. Horton, F. Huyler, and D. H. Van Doren.

The first Borough Council of newly incorporated Peapack-Gladstone, 1912. Left to right, standing: Fred Huyler, manager, Hamilton Farm; Nicholas Ballentine, merchant; W. C. Horton, insurance agent; Daniel Van Doren, blacksmith. Left to right, seated: Garner F. Hill, merchant, borough clerk; Frank Ludlow, merchant; Mayor John Bodine, builder; Dr. M. Smalley, physician. From the T. Leonard Hill collection.

The business of managing the new borough was under way. Funding was a fundamental concern in the early stages of incorporation. The June 7 edition of the *Bernardsville News* reports: "Local talent presented a very clever little playlet in Allen's Hall a few nights since for the benefit of the Pea-Glad incorporation expense fund." The first annual report of the borough included expenditures for printing advance election notices, tickets, and notices of incorporation, as well as one pair of handcuffs.

Progress reports continued to appear throughout that summer and fall:

> "The Pea-Glad" Lockup will have two (2) cells. Quite enough. It costs only one dollar for a revolver permit. . . . The parsonage of the Reformed Church at Peapack is now lighted by electricity. . . . The new Pea-Glad Borough officers do not permit motorists, wheelmen or others to despise their authority. Toe the mark's the word. . . . An ordinance forbidding bicycles on the borough sidewalks and requiring that they carry lights has been adopted. . . . A board of health has been created. . . . A new walk in front of the public school building.[50]

And finally, in October:

> Little and newly incorporated "Pea-Glad" can now manage her own affairs right here at home: and she's doing it well. Big, bumptious, conceited Bernardsville is still under Township government and is overrun with hawkers, street vendors, cheap shows and other outside barbarians who lug off its money and leave the home dealers to pay the taxes.[51]

Citizens of the new community voiced their opinions as well. The following letters from the "Communicated" column of the *Weekly Exponent* one year later, are indicative of the problems inherent in the process of incorporating a new borough.

> I, as a citizen cannot see any improvement or betterment of our town since becoming a borough. We have borough limit signs at all points, stating that the automobile law will be enforced. These signs cost $50.00 or $60.00 and of what consequence are they? Every day autos run through our main thoroughfare at the rate of 25 to 35 miles an hour and often times, much faster. And right in the center of our borough we have a very dangerous corner, nearly at right angle. At one side lumber is piled ten feet high and on the other side the weeds are now five feet high, preventing approaching cars from seeing one another, and not a sign is shown to "slow down" "sound your horn" or "danger, go slow." What would be the consequence if an accident happened there? Why not use an ounce of prevention at the right time, before a serious accident, which may mean the cost of life? If we have an automobile law, why not enforce it?
>
> I cannot see what our Borough Council is doing. We have trees along our street with limbs hanging over the center of the street, catching wagon tops and tearing grain and hay from loads that pass, making our streets look like a barnyard. Briers and weeds grow along our sidewalks, catching and soiling the apparel of pedestrians as they pass. We wanted or expected an improvement of our town, and I fail to see the first sign of any. The only improvement I have learned of was that Main St. has

been surveyed for the purpose of having the street widened. That is alright when the time comes but we are not ready for that yet.

> *A Citizen*
> *August 8th, 1913*[52]

Next week, the rebuttal:

Mr. Editor:

In reply to "A Citizen's" communication in last week's issue (I) will say I must take exception to the part stating the Borough officials have as yet done nothing. The work of a new borough is naturally slow. It is first necessary to make ordinances that will stand law and then to pass them. These ordinances are necessary to have laws that will cover many nuisances if they exist or arise. The Council has made many good laws, such as ordinances against Sunday closing, loitering and indecent language, dogs running at large, establishing a grade for both walks and streets and many others. A jail has been purchased and order maintained, two marshals employed, sidewalks improved, excellent Board of Education and Board of Health and many other things we would not have had we not become a borough. And there are many improvements in sight that will be accomplished gradually. The macadam road is a county road and can not be governed by the borough. Several things stated by "A Citizen" are true and undoubtedly will be eliminated in time. And I think in years to come "A Citizen" will rejoice many times that we had become a Borough.

> *Borough Admirer*
> *August 15, 1913*[53]

On June 6, 1987, the citizens of Peapack-Gladstone celebrated the seventy-fifth anniversary of their town's incorporation with a day of celebration described here in the "Prologue."

❧ Notes

1. *Weekly Exponent*, May 15, 1903.
2. Marise Campbell's recollections, Blair Family Collection of Diana Villa, Peapack, New Jersey.
3. Ibid.
4. *Bernardsville News*, February 10, 1949.
5. *Fascinating Blairsden*, a pamphlet printed by the Sisters of St. John the Baptist, St. Joseph's Villa.
6. As quoted in the *Bernardsville News*, January 7, 1954, in an article commemorating the fiftieth anniversary of the construction of Blairsden.
7. "Decorative detail on the walls in the limestone hall and 54' by 25' drawing room was minimal. The two stone fireplaces in the living room define seating areas, but ionic volutes barely protrude from the wall plane." *Antiques Magazine*, August 1976.
8. The first floor of the house was redecorated in 1912, at which time the ceiling in the dining room was installed. It is believed to have been taken from an old house in England, and one of the panels is attributed to Angelica Kaufman.
9. The bay trees were purchased by Blair at the Columbia Exposition. These trees were in large tubs and were stored over the winter in a special room constructed under the terrace and ceremonially brought out each year when weather permitted.
10. *Fascinating Blairsden*.

11. *Weekly Exponent*, February 12, 1909.
12. From a booklet prepared by the staff of the Kate Macy Ladd Convalescent Home. The information in this booklet was gathered from items in Mrs. Ladd's diaries and from obituaries of family members.
13. Ibid.
14. Archives of the Borough of Peapack-Gladstone.
15. *The Story of Hamilton Farm*.
16. L. E. and A. L. DeForest, *James Cox Brady and His Ancestry*.
17. *Bernardsville News*, May 21, 1925.
18. Ibid., June 18, 1936.
19. *Peapack-Gladstone Exponent*, January 8, 1942.
20. *Macmillan Encyclopedia of Architects*.
21. *Bernardsville News*, October 2, 1969.
22. Ibid.
23. Mount Saint John Academy sixtieth-anniversary booklet.
24. Allison Wright Post, *Recollections of Bernardsville*, p. 47.
25. "A Drag with the Old Essex" by Somerset, in Frederick W. Jones, *Recollections of the Essex Hunt*, p. 30.
26. Ibid., p. 25.
27. Ibid.
28. *Morristown Topics*, October 10, 1929.
29. *Weekly Exponent*, November 21, 1913.
30. Jones, *Recollections of the Essex Hunt*, p. 33.
31. The article, "The Essex Fox Hounds" by Octavia Throop, is in the Peapack-Gladstone local history file in the Morristown Library. The name of the magazine in which it appeared was not noted on the copy, but the words "Atlantic and Pacific" appear under a photograph.
32. First published in the *New Yorker*, December 7, 1929. Reprinted in E. B. White, *The Fox of Peapack and Other Poems*.
33. Valerie Barnes, *The Strange and Mysterious Past in the Somerset Hills Area*.
34. For a detailed history of the Essex Hunt see Jones, *Recollections of the Essex Hunt*, which covers the period from 1870 to 1912, and *Early Times*, by James S. Jones (son of Frederick), which covers the years from 1913 to 1935.
35. "A Drag with the Old Essex," p. 123.
36. *Bernardsville News*, March 30, 1972, article on the history of the Klan in Somerset County.
37. *Peapack-Gladstone Exponent*, January 8, 1942.
38. Ibid., March 19, 1943.
39. Ibid.
40. Art Derson, *Historical Sketch of the Gladstone Methodist Episcopal Church and a Short Biography of William Evart Gladstone*.
41. *Weekly Exponent*, February 12, 1909.
42. Ibid.
43. *Bernardsville News*, April 5, 1912.
44. Ibid.
45. Ibid.
46. Ibid.
47. Ibid., April 26, 1912.
48. Ibid., May 10, 1912.
49. Ibid., May 24, 1912.
50. Ibid., August 9, 1912.
51. Ibid., October 25, 1912.
52. *Weekly Exponent*, August 8, 1913.
53. Ibid., August 15, 1913.

Old Stone Blacksmith Shop built by a stone mason named Jackson for Frederick Van Doren in 1836. A frame house to the left of the structure, circa 1800, was occupied by Alfred Bryan, who wrote the words to the popular song "Peg O' My Heart," in 1913. The two structures were joined to form a single residence in 1972 according to a design by noted architect J. Robert Hillier of Princeton. Drawing courtesy of Peter Smith.

OLD BLACKSMITH SHOP   CIRCA 1800

PETER SMITH

Commerce and Industry

Blacksmiths

Blacksmiths were an integral part of the rural economy that evolved as more farms developed in the Peapack area. According to Snell, William Logan, father of Captain John Logan, was the first blacksmith in Peapack, and Peter Van Doren erected another blacksmith shop about 1814. The old stone blacksmith shop still standing at 4 Jackson Avenue in Gladstone was built in 1836 by a stone mason named Jackson, in the employ of Ferdinand Van Doren. It is a fine example of early masonry, and, according to Snell, the first blacksmith there was a man named Cole. The 1850 map in the *Atlas of Somerset County* shows William Van Ness's black-smith shop on the northwest corner of Broad Street (now Main Street) and Branch Road (now Willow Avenue). On that same 1850 map, P. R. Pelly is listed as a blacksmith and harness maker, and a blacksmith and tin shop were indicated on the southwest corner of Broad Street, opposite what is now Highland Avenue. And according to the Somerville *Unionist Gazette* of March 3, 1898, a man named Hardgrave had been a blacksmith in Upper Peapack for several years.

In July 1949 John C. Turner, a Somerville dentist, purchased the Peapack Blacksmith Shop at 138 Main Street from Daniel Van Doren. Dr. Turner bought the enterprise in order to save it, as he considered it one of the oldest county landmarks and one of the few working smithies remaining in New Jersey. Daniel Van Doren had run the smithy for forty years, having bought it in 1908 from William Quimby of Somerville. The blacksmith shop is thought by local residents to date from 1899, but the name of the original smith is unknown. When Dr. Turner bought it, the shop was heated by an old pitch stove which burned pine needles, a duplicate of which, Dr. Turner discovered, was located in a smithy in Williamsburg, Virginia.

> The shop was set up in 1899, and is one of the oldest as well as one of the few left in the state. Originally the blacksmith worked on the first floor of the three-story structure, carriages were manufactured on the second floor, and painted on the third. Now the two upper stories are used as apartments.

"Bill" Amerman, "young-timer" still in his 40's has been running the shop for the past five years and he'll continue in this capacity, working with George Happe of Liberty Corner, who qualifies for the old-timer class. As a matter of fact, he retired some time ago after working a quarter-century in the local shop, but when he heard of Dr. Turner's semi-expansion program, he showed up readily for a job. And at this point he's back at the old forge regaining his stride fast, with his tools arranged on the floor in his own special fashion. All black-smiths have their own particular arrangement for tools. First glance might indicate that they're just thrown there, but each implement has its own special spot. Future plans also call for the hiring of an apprentice.

Dr. Turner is hoping that the spot will prove itself a mecca for what few smiths are left in this area. He wants them to feel free to drop in any time just to talk old times and make suggestions on how the job of the moment should be handled.

As well as shoeing horses, and repair jobs, the "new" shop will feature ornamental work and welding. In contrast to the all-over quaintness of the place is the shiny '49 truck which Dr. Turner has purchased for deliveries. Mr. Amerman goes on calls as far as 25 miles away, carrying an assortment of horseshoes made up in the shop. He takes his shoeing equipment with him to the stables.

It stands to reason that the office, the truck and the electrically operated equipment represent a far cry from Longfellow's classic lines, but very little of the quaint appeal of the shop itself is affected. Only thing lacking is a chestnut tree out front. The maple tree standing there will have to do.[1]

&   *The Limestone Quarry*

The excavation and processing of limestone were for many years a major industry in Peapack-Gladstone. One of the remarkable landmarks in Peapack is the old stone kiln on the east side of Main Street. The structure, a pristine and imposing example of industrial masonry, is all that remains of what was once a thriving limestone business known as Todd's Quarry. The facility, which was operational well before the turn of the century, included a quarry and limestone-processing facilities, and the map of Peapack in the 1850 *Atlas of Somerset County* indicates a lime quarry at that site.

Commercial production of lime for fertilizer did not begin locally until after the revolutionary war. Lime burning started at Peapack as early as 1794, but did not become extensive until 1830. Lime was used to make mortar, but its most extensive use was in agriculture. The 1880 *Atlas of Somerset County* counted six perpetual lime kilns and nine set kilns in Peapack that produced two hundred bushels of unslaked lime annually.

The Peapack bed of limestone extended in length about fourteen miles, running in part into Morris County, and varied in breadth from an eighth to a quarter of a mile. The stone belongs to the magnesium limestone family and is nearly a true dolomite because of the large amounts of magnesium it contains. In New Jersey it occurs in a long narrow series of parallel belts extending from the northeast to the southwest. In general the stone is fine-grained, but assumes a subcrystalline form at some places. Quartz crystals may be found within the beds. A layer of shale occurs between some of the beds. In color the limestone varies from a dull red to red to gray. Stone from the reddish and drab-colored beds was used to make water lime in the building of the Morris Canal.[2]

Percy Terry, a long-time resident of Peapack, was employed at Todd's Quarry (along with his uncle and grandfather) from about 1917 to 1919. He has described the methods of mining and processing used at the quarry in those years. Workers descended into the pits or caves via a long ladder. At the base of the tunnel was a running stream. Ropes were used as guides to prevent miners from becoming confused and losing their way in the mazelike formation. The miners used pickaxes to take the raw stone from the quarry. Two grades of lime were produced on the site: pulverized and dehydrated. Pulverized lime was produced by putting the raw stone through a crusher and then through a grinder, after which it was packed into fifty-pound bags. A two-wheel cart drawn by horses was used to transport the loads of stone from the quarry to the crusher.

Dehydrated lime production was a more involved process. Eight- to ten-inch chunks of stone were taken from the quarry to the kilns for burning. (The stone structures seen on Main Street are what remain of the ovens.) A kiln was about fifty feet deep. One layer of wood was used as kindling to start the fires. Next, a fine coal called rice coal was added, then a layer of lime. Consecutive layers of coal and lime filled the kilns. The burned limestone was then put through a crusher and taken by a conveyor up to a large vat where it was "slaked." The slaking process employed a water bath and a blade in the vat which rotated and pulverized the lime.

The limestone quarry was owned by the Dr. Edwin Perry family for many years and leased to various operators. Phillip Todd leased the site for fifteen years and finally purchased it from Perry in 1899. The February 2, 1912, edition of the *Weekly Exponent* noted "excellent skating at Todd's Quarry."

By 1950 the Peapack limestone quarry was considered one of the most prosperous quarries in the state. It was by then almost completely mechanized and therefore employed only about six men. A new fifteen-thousand-dollar processing plant that allowed the facility to put out one hundred tons of limestone each day was built that year alongside the quarry. The company also sold building stone and top soil. The plant manager then was Elmer Hess.

The presence of the lime beds and their operation have contributed some moments of excitement, even disaster, to the community. In 1932 the *Peapack-Gladstone Exponent* reported that a man was killed while working in the lime quarry at the intersection of Gladstone and Mendham roads, when shale from a ten-foot pit caved in on him. New veins of limestone were blasted open at the quarries with dynamite.

Paul Kelmer exploring the cavern discovered at the lime quarry on Main Street in 1958. Photograph by the Kelmers. From the Irene Aspell Collection.

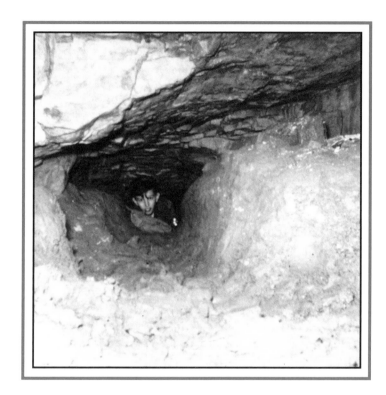

In 1958 a new cavern was discovered at the lime quarry on Main Street. Paul Kelmer and his son, Paul Jr. (visible in the cave), took this photograph while exploring the cavern. From the Irene Aspell Collection.

Mrs. Ruth Thomson (née Hill) recalls that when she was a child living on Prospect Street, a whistle would signal that blasting was about to begin, and the workmen would shout for all to clear the area and go indoors. The lime beds have contributed building "headaches," as natural sink holes occur within the beds. At times areas of ground thought to be solid have collapsed into old hollow veins beneath. One such cave-in of major proportions occurred behind the Peapack-Gladstone Bank building in the early 1960s.

The discovery of a large cave in the quarries prompted the following feature article in the January 9, 1902, edition of the *Newark Evening News*. The author has chosen to quote it in its entirety because of its colorful description of the cave and the excitement the cave's discovery generated among local residents and tourists.

❧ *Peapack Cavern Appropriately Called Watkins Glen*

Gladstone, N.J. Jan. 9.—The recently discovered cave in the lime quarry owned and operated by Phillip Todd at Peapack, the third to be discovered under the Peapack Mountain, has become the center of attraction about the usually quiet hamlet of Peapack, and it is now the fad among the wealthy residents in the vicinity to organize exploring parties and at the risk of damaged suits and gowns visit the strange formation of nature under the mountain.

Although the cave was discovered but a week ago, 1,200 curiosity seekers have visited the place, and it has been dismantled of all the stalactites that made it a place of beauty. The owner has been forced

A rare view of the entire lime kiln on Main Street, date not known. From the Norman Welsh collection.

to prohibit visitors from entering the cave with crowbars, sledge hammers and drills, but his warning came too late for now the main channels of the cave contain but little of their former beauty.

Although the fact that there was a hole under the mountain was known to the workers in the lime quarry for nearly a year, it was not explored until Monday, December 30th and a Newark man was the first to enter. William Garvel of Newark, and Robert Cortwright of Peapack, employees of the Todd quarry, decided to find out how far back the "hole" extended, and after enlarging the entrance with picks and bars entered and found that the "hole" was a series of tunnels branching out and running through a wide area.

CARRYING AWAY SOUVENIRS

After reporting their find to the owner of the quarry the explorers talked it over at the village store, and as a result the news was spread so far and wide that the cave has since been visited by geologists, mineralogists and curiosity seekers from all the surrounding country: and from the appearance of the cave each visitor has taken out as a souvenir many pounds of rock.

A walk of an eighth of a mile from the railroad station at Peapack brings one to the foot of the Ledyard Blair Hill, as it is known in the vicinity, and a winding road leads to the lime quarries at its base. The only indication of a cave is a small opening just wide enough for a small man to crawl through, and one enters the main corridor of the cavern.

Before entering the cavern it is necessary to dress in overalls and waterproof garments, and so large has been the demand that the local merchants are entirely sold out and in anticipation of a continued flow of sightseers have ordered large quantities by express. Provided with a lantern, candles and a guide, a small boy, whose teacher has excused him from school temporarily to reveal the glories of the Peapack mountain, you are pushed and hauled into a narrow passage, the sides of which glisten with the reflected rays of your lantern. After entering the cave you are able to stand upright and walk over broken stone through a tunnel about a hundred yards in length under a vaulted dome.

At the end of the main tunnel a crude ladder has been built from fence rails and after a scramble of twenty feet an upper corridor is reached where two persons can walk abreast for a short distance. Branching off from this tunnel is another, leading about due west, but containing no interesting features. It extends about sixty feet.

WHEN A MISSTEP WOULD BE FATAL

At the end of the first upper corridor one finds himself in a circular room large enough to accommodate ten people and here the cave takes an arched formation, the roof being nearly thirty feet high. Another improvised ladder and another scramble leads to what is the third story of the cave. To explore this a steady hand and sure foot are required for the difficulties before encountered are slight compared with the ones before you. Crawling like a snake, the highest part of the cave is reached and it comes to an abrupt end. On the right is a large gap leading to a deep well, and a misstep would be fatal. You can count twenty slowly from the time a pebble leaves your hand until it strikes the water. How deep the well is no one knows as no measurements have been taken.

Opposite the well is an opening in the rock not large enough to pass through but giving a view of the chamber beyond, probably twenty feet square. The roof is circular and hung with stalactites that glisten in the light. This is the largest room thus far discovered in the cavern. The entire cave is gothic in formation, and no architect ever designed the roof of a building in more graceful lines. The formation of the cavern gives the impression that in past ages the mountain had been rent in twain and fallen together again, leaving a passageway varying in width from two to six feet at its base, a veritable underground Watkins Glen.

WALLS OF CRYSTAL, RED-VEINED

Most of the rock on the roof of the tunnels is brown in color and brittle, and the blasting in the lime quarries outside has undoubtedly shattered it and caused it to fall in many places. The formation on the side walls is entirely different and has the appearance of a crystal substance that in past years has dripped and hardened. Veins in the rock stand out blood red in the light, and the picturesque effect is emphasized by the setting of white crystals.

The appearance of the second upper chamber is weird in the extreme. As you enter with a lantern or miner's lamp the stalactites flash from the dome as though suspended in air, while the sides of the cavern glow with a mellow red light. Before you is a formation of reddish crystals, shaped like a pulpit, and above that what looks like a frozen waterfall.

The temperature of the cave is even and the atmosphere fresh. Apparently a current of fresh air circulates toward the opening. The blaze of a match or uncovered flame will always point toward the mouth of the cavern, indicating an opening or crevice yet undiscovered, probably on the other side of the mountain.

LIMESTONE SUPPLY INEXHAUSTIBLE

For many years the limestone quarry on Ledyard Blair hill has been one of the landmarks of Peapack. For years it was owned by the Perry family and rented to persons who desire to operate it. The present owner has worked the lime quarries for fifteen years and three years ago purchased the farm on which they are located from Dr. Edwin Perry. The lime produced is used primarily as fertilizer by the neighboring farmers about Peapack and Gladstone. The opening of the new cave has proven that the supply is practicably inexhaustible, for it is apparent that the entire mountain is of limestone formation.

The operatives in the Todd quarries are of the opinion that the avenues of the cavern thus far explored, are but the entrances to a much larger cave under the brow of the mountain, and this belief is shared by the residents of Peapack and Gladstone. While the finding of the new cavern has brought a quiet country village into prominence and made famous its owner, it is doubtful if he appreciates the honor, for work in his lime quarries is retarded and his employees lose much time giving information to visitors who incidentally earn amounts weekly equal to their wages for the loan of suits, lanterns and other articles necessary to cave explorers.[3]

In November 1958, another natural limestone cavern was discovered at the Peapack-Gladstone quarry. The discovery must have been rather dramatic as six hundred tons of rock disappeared into a hole opened by the explosives. A description of the cave appeared in a publication of the New Jersey State Geological Survey:

The cave is entered through a small hole about 15 feet deep in the middle section of the cave. This room is about 40 feet long and eight feet wide. East of the entrance and parallel to the entrance room, a fissure passage connects with a filled sink. There are two pits leading to the water table and a natural bridge in this passage.

To the west of the entrance room is a large room over 50 feet long and 30 feet wide. The floor is very uneven and slippery; behind breakdown in one corner is a deep pool and there is a dome pit in the ceiling. At the northern end of the room a small hole called the "peephole" was enlarged and access was gained to a small rough-walled upper level.

The cave is closed at the present time and no permission to enter it has been given for many years.[4]

Dr. Helgi Johnson, a professor of geology at Rutgers University, in reference to the cave discovered in 1958, was quoted in the *Newark Evening News* as saying that underground lime "streams" exist in the area. "The only difference between an underground 'stream' and a cave is that the cave doesn't have water in it," Dr. Johnson said.

In 1992 the old kilns and quarry were owned by The Peapack Partners whose controversial plan to develop the property for townhouses and private homes was turned down by the borough planning board. Entrances to the caves have been closed by grading and are now inaccessible. Trespassing on the site is prohibited.

❧ Other Local Businesses

Gravity Water Company

The "Gravity Water Company" was an ingenious scheme developed in 1910 by four Peapack men—Theodore S. Hill, S. G. Bloodgood, David B. Melick, and George R. Layton— to bring water from a Chester reservoir to Peapack-Gladstone. The corporation was formed when the men acquired a 170-acre tract that included water sources. Officially titled the Somerset Water Company, the company was known as the Gravity Water Company because no pumping stations were used; rather, the water route employed a system of gate valves through which water at a higher elevation flowed naturally to sites at lower elevations. The reservoir, actually an ancient millpond, was located on the Peapack Brook, about 3.5 miles north of Gladstone at an elevation of 600 feet. The brooks supplying the reservoir were entirely spring fed. They rose about 1.25 miles north of the pond at an elevation of 870 feet. The volume of discharge at the pond was six hundred gallons per minute, and the water route, which used a six-inch supply line, was the most direct possible. Water flowed from the reservoir to Peapack-Gladstone (elevation 245 feet), on to Bedminster (elevation 180 feet), then to Far Hills (elevation 160 feet), and eventually as far as the Sloane estate on Liberty Corner Road. The system was completed at a cost of fifty thousand dollars. Income was based on a

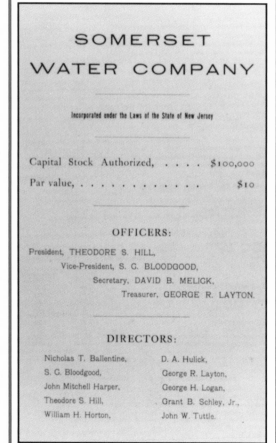

SOMERSET
WATER COMPANY

Incorporated under the Laws of the State of New Jersey

Capital Stock Authorized, ... $100,000

Par value, ... $10

OFFICERS:

President, THEODORE S. HILL,
Vice-President, S. G. BLOODGOOD,
Secretary, DAVID B. MELICK,
Treasurer, GEORGE R. LAYTON.

DIRECTORS:

Nicholas T. Ballentine,   D. A. Hulick,
S. G. Bloodgood,   George R. Layton,
John Mitchell Harper,   George H. Logan,
Theodore S. Hill,   Grant B. Schley, Jr.,
William H. Horton,   John W. Tuttle.

Prospectus announcing the formation of the Somerset Water Company in 1910. From the T. Leonard Hill collection.

charge of fifteen dollars per household and twenty-five dollars per fire hydrant. The system remained in place until 1983 when the borough sold the reservoir and arranged for water to be supplied through the Elizabethtown Water Company. The water supply has been fluoridated since 1955.

The Peapack-Gladstone Bank

The Peapack-Gladstone Trust Company was organized September 21, 1921, by Garner F. Hill and Ellis Tiger with an original capitalization of thirty thousand dollars. The first officers were Ellis Tiger, president; W. D. Vander Beek; E. C. Willets, vice president; and R. P. Williamson, cashier. Edith Tiger Canfield, daughter of Ellis Tiger, was the first to receive a bank passbook and proudly used "Passbook #1" all her life.

The bank was first located on the southeast corner of Main Street and Lackawanna Avenue in a duplex building. The commercial space on the right side of that building was occupied by Hill's Hardware Store. In 1958 the bank built a handsome brick colonial-style structure at the intersection of Mendham Road and Main Street, which was enlarged in 1983 to accommodate the growing need for office space.

Peapack-Gladstone Bank reported assets of $230,505,000 and total deposits of $211,353,000 as of June 30, 1992. Net income per share was $3.17 on earnings of $1,605,000. A new

The founders of the Peapack-Gladstone Trust Company, established in 1921: Garner F. Hill, left, and Ellis Tiger, right. Photographs courtesy of T. Leonard Hill from the Peapack-Gladstone Bank.

facility in the Village at Bedminster in Pluckemin marked its first anniversary in December 1989. Other bank branches are located in Far Hills, Bernardsville, Long Valley, Mendham, Pottersville, and Califon. T. Leonard Hill was elected chairman of the board late in 1989. Frank A. Kissel succeeded the late George M. Jenkins as president in mid-1989.

Wm. Vaness building — J. M. Allen's, Peapack, N. J.

A copy of a postcard dated 1909 with a view of Main Street. William Vaness building on the left, J. M. Allen's store on the right. The store sign reads "The Valley Pharmacy." From the George DeSesso collection.

Allen's Auditorium, Borough of Peapack, Gladstone, N. J.

MOVING-PICTURES
EVERY SATURDAY NIGHT

Postcard of Allen's Auditorium dated 1913. From the George DeSesso collection.

Main Street

The small shopping area on Main Street in Peapack has seen many commercial ventures come and go. The name Allen was consistently associated with the original buildings erected there in the mid-1800s; these included a general store and auditorium. A deed dated December 28, 1865, conveyed "about ³⁶/₁₀₀ acre" of property from Morris Lance and wife to Theodore Allen for the sum of $2,000. The parcel was described as follows: "Beginning at the second half of a post and rail fence on the E side of Peapack Brook, from the brook and in the line of a lot of land conveyed by John Jeroleman and wife to David Apgar dated AD 1836, thence N 74 ½ E one chain and eighty four links in the Peapack Road."[5]

A deed dated March 13, 1868, conveyed property from John W. Demun and wife to Theodore Allen, for the sum of $4,250: bounded by the "SE Corner garden part of said Allen's lot next the mill race. S to John Jeroleman's corner, to a butterball tree on the W side of Peapack Brook to a butternut sapling marked and standing on the W bank of the millrace."[6]

In 1903 the *Weekly Exponent* reported that John M. Allen's new store was nearly finished, and a later issue announced that "Finnigan's Fortune" was to be presented by Ravine Lodge, 274 I.O.O.F., on an April evening with dancing to Ludlow's Orchestra after the play. In December 1909 a disastrous fire struck John Allen's Main Street buildings.

Commercial ventures mentioned in the newspaper account of the fire included the drugstore of Joseph F. Schefcik, Allen's general store and auditorium, the harness shop of William Van Ness, and a barber shop owned by Phillip Todd. Allen apparently rebounded quickly from his loss. Construction of the new auditorium was begun in late October 1911, and on February 2, 1912, the *Exponent* reported Allen's new auditorium would open February 9, when the Peapack Fire Company would present a play. "The new edifice is large, comfortable and neat. Druggist Courter has painted all the new sets." Entertainment continued to be on the agenda, as reported March 6, 1914, in an announcement in the *Exponent*: "We beg to announce the reorganization of Ludlow's Orchestra under the name of 'The Valley Orchestra,' which will be composed of first-class talent only, from Newark, New York, and this borough."

Amerman's

Clayton Amerman started his business on April 12, 1919, upon his return from World War 1, in what is now the Peapack Post Office. His business began as a salesroom for Gates Half-Sole Tires; he also rebuilt batteries. In 1920 he acquired the franchise for Star and Durant automobiles, and his brother Vernon became service manager. In 1923 he moved to Amerman's present location, formerly Allen's store and auditorium, where he sold home appliances and Gra-

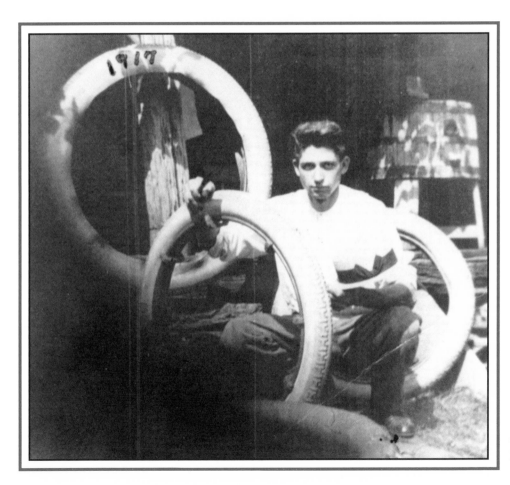

Clayton Amerman, 1917.
From the John Amerman collection.

ham and Paige trucks. He acquired the Dodge franchise in 1935, and the business still operates in the same building under his son John, who took over on Clayton's death. In 1990 Amerman celebrated the company's fifty-fifth anniversary as a Dodge dealer.

Clayton Amerman continued to operate the auditorium where local residents enjoyed summer theater, silent movies, and, finally, talking pictures. Long-time residents fondly remember that Sid Aldridge, who lived in the borough until his death in 1993, played the piano during the silent movies, and, as one long-time resident reminisced: "He played the same three songs for every picture."

Progress intervened:

> *All-talking moving pictures will be shown in Amerman's Auditorium on Saturday afternoon and evening. There will be nine reels of comedies, starring Slim Summerville, George Sidney, Charles Murray and others. Besides all this, Johnny Hinds and his Marionettes will appear in person. A fine big program.*[7]

> *Clayton Amerman will open his auditorium next Saturday to talking moving pictures. Mr. Amerman has been working some time upon the installation of a large and good sounding machine, has the walls draped, and is now prepared to give excellent pictures with both sight and sound. The opening will be on Saturday and the picture secured for this opening is "Attorney for the Defense." This feature will be followed by a comedy and "Mickey Mouse." The stars of the feature*

are Evelyn Brent, Constance Summings [sic], Donald Dilloway, Bradley Page, Dorothy Peterson and Clarence Muse. The price for the matinee will be 15 cents and 25 cents and evening 25 cents and 35 cents.[8]

Other early offerings included *When Knighthood Was in Flower* and *The Rain Came.* Alas, it all ended in 1940, when, after a fire severely damaged the auditorium, Amerman closed the theater and refurbished the space for an expanded auto showroom and parts department. He remained an entrepreneur and was the first in the area to acquire a television set; this remarkable advance, local papers announced, could be seen in his showroom.

The Local Drugstore

The local drugstore is an institution in most small towns, and Debus Pharmacy in Peapack is no exception. Presently owned by George DeSesso, the establishment dates from 1901. An advertisement in the February 12, 1909, issue of the *Weekly Exponent* declares Schefcik's Drug Store to be "headquarters for Valentines Lace, fancy and mechanical Valentines, all new, from 1¢ to $2.00." Or, customers were invited to "select any two pieces of sheet music every time you buy a bottle of Bromo seltzer." And here is yet another product offered:

> *The modern way of smoking meat with "Liquid Extract of Smoke" is followed by most of the best farmers and large meat dealers. A wholesome, safe and labor-saving method. Avoids possibility of fire and*

smokehouse thefts. At Schefcik's Drug Store you can procure the most reliable smoke on the market, in quart bottles.[9]

The founder of the establishment is not known, but Mr. Schefcik was the proprietor in 1909 and Mr. Courter in 1912.[10] In 1913 the drugstore was involved in an unusual event, as can be seen from the following news item:

⚬ *Some Flies*

The fly contest conducted by Druggist E. F. Courter for Mrs. C. L. Blair in which $25.00 in prizes was offered for the one killing the most flies came to a close on November 1, and the following were the winners and the numbers of their victims:

Dayton Allen, 51,500; Charles Henry Tiger, 42,575; Dorothy Johnson, 23,550; Patsy Copperi, 12,220; Frank Johnson, 10,400; Dominick Trullo, 7,450; Dumont Huyler, 6,335; Myrtle Alpaugh, 4,545; Victor Crater, 4,375; Violet Philhower, 3,800; Adelaide Davis, 3,750; Herbert Chesson, 2,925; Grace Dalrymple, 2,825; Lester Smalley, 2,600; Ronald Hill, 1,200; Harold Horton, 1,000; Mildred Cortwright, 940; Kenneth Ballentine, 900; Vera Miller, 800; Rosalind Harper, 350; [total] 184,040.[11]

Typhoid fever was a particular problem in those days; was the great fly contest an effort to make citizens aware of the fact that the disease was transmitted by insects?

The drugstore was taken over by H. Louis Debus in 1926.[12]

With a real professional touch the pharmacy features the compounding of prescriptives and family recipes and holds the favor of the general public and the approval of the medical fraternity as a result of its work.

. . . Founded thirty-five years ago, the establishment came under the present management a decade ago.

Mr. Debus was graduated from Rutgers College of Pharmacy and is a member of the university's alumni. . . .

The soda fountain dispenses Breyers' ice cream and various light foods and beverages, while Mr. Debus has a license for selling beer and liquors while featuring Bellow's wines.[13]

George DeSesso, present owner of the drugstore, earned a bachelor's degree in pharmacy from Rutgers in 1933 at age nineteen. He was too young to take the state boards, the age requirement being twenty-one, so he did postgraduate work at Rutgers while he apprenticed under Debus. Debus died in 1936, and DeSesso ran the store for Debus's widow during the Depression years. He bought the store in 1947.

The Gladstone Hotel

The Andrew Rarick farmhouse, which dates from about 1840, was acquired by the Vliet family in the 1930s and renamed the Gladstone Hotel. (The Vliet family owned the original tavern and inn that were once run by W. A. Mellick. This building is still standing at 291 Main Street, and is now a two-family home.) The local hunters brought deer to Mr. Vliet to be butchered. The next owner of the building was the Elks' Club; then Arthur Would turned it into the Willow Tree Inn. The David Karner family bought the property in 1974, remodeled it, and opened it as the Brass Penny. The layout

The Gladstone Hotel, 291 Main Street, circa 1930. Built in the 1840s as a farmhouse by Andrew Rarick, the building has housed several restaurants over the years. From the Ruth Thomson collection.

Main Street, Gladstone, looking north, circa 1912. Note the ice cream shop on left and Gladstone Hotel in background behind tree. From the Norman Welsh collection.

of the building when the Karners bought it consisted of a room to the right, which is a small dining room now, and the long bar in a narrow room to the left of the entry. The Karners added the large dining room to the left of the bar. The papier-mâché horse that stood on the porch was acquired in 1982 by Karner, Sr. for $1,250. It is over one hundred years old and was a saddle mannequin for a saddlemaker. Its previous owner dubbed it Norman's Castle, he being a Norman Woolley, from Maplewood, and an owner of the Castle Ice Cream Company of Irvington. At one time a ghost named Fred was a co-inhabitant of the building, but he is no longer active. In 1989 the building was purchased and extensively renovated by Kim Chatfield and re-opened as an American grill called Chatfield's.

Howard House

Howard House was built circa 1902 by Thomas Howard. His brother William owned the Bedminster Inn. Thomas sold Howard House and later ran the Bedminster Inn for his brother.

In 1907 Michael DeLuca, Sr., an Italian immigrant, bought the structure. For many years it was owned and operated as a family hotel and tavern, known variously as Howard House and the Peapack Hotel, by DeLuca and his three sons, Victor, Joseph, and Michael.

It was a popular gathering place for local inhabitants and a traditional yearly stopover for hunters. Howard House boasted one of the first color television sets in the area and sponsored a local baseball team, the Hotel Keglers. On Sunday afternoons participants in sports car rallies would gather in the parking lot, often the final destination of the rallies.

Over the years, the motto of the Hotel Peapack was "Ring and We'll Bring"—on Friday nights telephone orders were taken for Victor's special pizza.

On October 15, 1968, Mr. DeLuca, Sr., closed the doors for the last time. The structure was bought by Komline-Sanderson Engineering Company and stood vacant until 1975 when it was demolished.

Dominick's

This building on Lackawanna Avenue was once next to the firehouse on Main Street. At that time it had a wooden walkway entrance with rose arbors on each side and was used as a kindergarten. It was next occupied by an upholsterer and caner and then became John Belton's general store, offering men's shoes and belts, women's pocketbooks, hosiery and corsets, fabric and sewing necessities, and penny candy.

In 1926 the building was moved to the site where Scott Chevrolet had been, and the double front doors were added. W. C. Horton Insurance Agency offices were on one side, with Trimmer & Fenner, an electricians' shop, on the other.

PEAPACK HOTEL, BAR AND GRILL,
PEAPACK N.J.   TEL. PEAPACK 99.

Peapack Hotel (Howard House), built circa 1902 by Thomas Howard. Operated as a hotel and tavern until 1968 when it was bought by Komline-Sanderson Engineering Company. It stood vacant until 1975 when it was demolished. From the T. Leonard Hill collection.

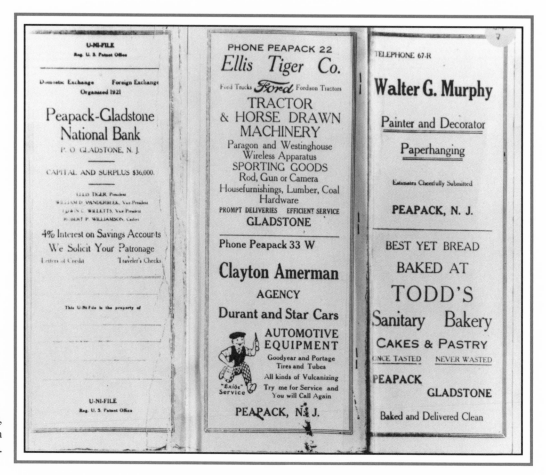

Advertisements for local businesses, circa 1930. From the John Amerman collection.

Miss Ann Ballentine, then Horton's secretary, recalled frequently waiting on customers of the electricians. She remembers keeping the stove going.

The building was then moved to its present site, where it was first a showroom for Frigidaire, then an office. It is remembered by many as the little white store.

A Small Town

The commercial enterprises that have continued in the borough through the years contribute to the special small-town character of Peapack-Gladstone. What would Main Street and the surrounding area be without Bob's Flower Shop, the Copper Kettle, the Gladstone Market, Glad-pack Sunoco, the elegant "thoroughbred" automobiles at the Stable, Telesco's Barber Shop and Salon, or the culinary delights of Ristorante Trattoria Toscana and Rudolfo's Ristorante?

❧ The Beneficial Management Corporation Headquarters

In 1982 Beneficial Management Corporation moved to its palatial new headquarters on a 150-acre setting in Peapack-Gladstone. The project was planned and initiated by Beneficial Corporation Chairman Finn Caspersen, who took over leadership of the corporation in 1976 at the age of thirty-five.

Under Caspersen's chairmanship Beneficial expanded and prospered and eventually outgrew its Morristown headquarters. In 1978 architect J. Robert Hillier of Princeton was hired to design a one-million-square-foot corporate complex that would symbolize Beneficial's status in the world of finance.

The location chosen for the new headquarters, just off I-287 near Route 206, reflects forces similar to those that earlier created rural villages. Just as villages developed where two or more roads crossed, so in the second half of the twentieth century we find that intersecting superhighways have spawned corporate complexes. Corporations have been migrating to the Somerset Hills, their buildings replacing the opulent mansions tycoons built on large acreages when the century was new. Colossal corporate monuments, housing developments, and shopping centers have also been created, and once again the demographics of a rural community are undergoing irreversible changes.

Humanize the workplace and harmonize with the nearby villages was the challenge presented to the Hillier Group. Beneficial wanted its facility to be built of brick and on a domestic scale and was predisposed to a multiple-building campus plan.

To realize the "corporate village" theme, each building houses both corporate and support activities. The arches and colonnades recall the sixteenth-century work of Andrea Palladio. Hillier has been quoted as saying that "buildings

Beneficial Management Headquarters, Route 206, Peapack. Photograph courtesy of Beneficial Management Corporation, Corporate and Community Affairs.

from that period struck me as the most comfortable, the most pleasant to live and work in, just what Finn Caspersen wanted."[14] However, the clean lines, window treatment, access to natural light, and atrium lobby lend a distinctly modern flavor.

The high visibility of the site demanded special treatment. All 1,250 employee cars are housed beneath the complex in two brick-faced garages hidden by plantings and garden walls. The dominant materials are brick, cast stone (used for columns and trim), bronze, glass, granite, and cobblestone pavers, and the exterior courtyards and plaza are landscaped to reinforce the individuality of each building.

The eleven buildings are linked by arcades at the main plaza level and by skylit tunnels in the parking levels below. The focal point of the village is the eighty-eight-foot campanile—a clock tower concealing a water-storage tank. Seen from a distance in the pastoral landscape, the tower produces the effect of an Italian hill town. Also located in the tower are security television cameras linked to the main control room, the command center for overall security and monitoring of the support system. Access to the site is controlled by a security gatehouse and television surveillance.

The interiors use an open-office design, and because one long and one short wall of each building are kept free of offices, pleasant views and natural light are available to everyone.[15]

Financier C. Ledyard Blair came to Peapack at the end of the nineteenth century and erected a palatial brick and limestone estate derivative of a French chateau. We have discussed the demographic changes within the community brought about by the estate builders: the move from a rural to a service and entrepreneurial community; the increase in population; the changes in the ethnic make-up of the population; and Blair's role as a benefactor of the community. Blairsden can be seen as an icon of change: Peapack-Gladstone, a remote pastoral village, moved toward the twentieth century. We can draw similar conclusions when discussing the Beneficial Finance Corporation's move to the borough. The changes wrought by the influx of corporations relocating to our community are more and more evident: an increasing number of residents who require housing, services, transportation; concerns about the environment; traffic congestion; and Beneficial's financial role in the community, as a benefactor, and the largest contributor of tax dollars.

❧ *Notes*

1. *Somerset Messenger Gazette*, July 1949.
2. James P. Snell, *History of Hunterdon and Somerset Counties, New Jersey.*
3. The article was found in a file at the New Jersey Historical Society, Newark.
4. Richard F. Dalton, *Caves of New Jersey*, p. 18.

5. Deed Book R 3 70, p. 363.
6. Deed Book X 3, p. 237.
7. *Peapack-Gladstone Exponent*, September 29, 1932.
8. Ibid., February 2, 1932.
9. Ibid.
10. Ibid.
11. *Weekly Exponent*, November 14, 1913.
12. *Peapack-Gladstone Exponent*, February 12, 1936.
13. Ibid.
14. Newark *Sunday Star-Ledger*, September 12, 1982.
15. Most of the material in this section is excerpted from a description supplied by The Hillier Group, Princeton, New Jersey.

PROHIBITION AND APPLE JACK

During the 1930s the newspapers reported on local innkeepers having been arrested in raids for serving apple liquor or beer during prohibition, and the discovery of a still in nearby woods.

After the repeal of prohibition, the same local innkeepers took the steps needed to serve their thirsty patrons legally. In May 1936 the *Weekly Exponent* reported that the following establishments had been granted liquor licenses:

Harold Vliet of the Gladstone Hotel
Michael DeLuca of the Peapack Hotel
H. Louis Debus
The Essex Fox Hounds

Community Services

The Post Offices

Upper Peapack

Through the influence of William Van Doren, the first post office in Upper Peapack was established on March 5, 1823, on the second floor of what is known as the Old Trimble house, at 8 Jackson Avenue; access to it was via an outside staircase. Until that time the mail had been delivered elsewhere: to New Brunswick first and later to Somerville. Van Doren, the first postmaster, had a thriving farm in Upper Peapack, as well as a general store located in his house. Elias

Post Office
Gladstone, N.J.

The early post office in Upper Peapack on Jackson Avenue, the small one-story structure to the right of the two-story house. It was torn down when the Stone Blacksmith Shop was renovated in the 1970s. From the Reverend Paul Walther collection.

Post Office & Dept. Store, Pea Pack N.J.

A postcard featuring the Van Arsdale and Ballentine building at 87 Main Street, a general store and post office in Lower Peapack. The two gentlemen on the porch are probably the proprietors, Ballentine and Van Arsdale, who operated the establishment between 1915 and 1936. From the Reverend Paul Walther collection.

Lawrence, who died in 1853, succeeded Van Doren as postmaster; Lawrence was followed by Amos Foster, who held the position in 1881, according to Snell. The post office moved to Lower Peapack in the late 1800s when George Van Arsdale took over as postmaster. It moved from the Ballentine building to the Main Street location it now occupies around 1940.

Lower Peapack

The post office in Lower Peapack was first housed in the brick building at 87 Main Street now known as the Ballentine Building. The building was originally constructed for the First Christian Church, founded by John Jeroleman and Austin Craig in 1838,[1] but the congregation dwindled, and in 1868 the building was sold to Peter Z. Smith. Smith converted it into a store with living quarters in the rear, where he lived until 1874.

The building continued as a general store. George Van Arsdale, postmaster in the late 1880s, was the storekeeper for many years, with Nicholas T. Ballentine as his associate. (Van Arsdale built the house next door, at 89 Main Street, in 1897;[2] this building was purchased by Dr. Kay in 1913; in 1990 it housed a restaurant.) Ballentine succeeded Van Arsdale as postmaster, and with his brother, Lewis Ballentine, conducted business at 87 Main Street from 1915 to 1936, delivering groceries in a horse-drawn wagon. Long-time residents recall the general store's cracker barrels and cheese under a glass.

Remson Howard was Peapack postmaster in 1936, and it was probably in that year that the post office moved to its present location in the business district on Main Street.

In later years the Ballentine Building housed a series of businesses, including D'Apolito Brothers Tailor Shop. For many years now it has been leased by tenants as office space.

Gladstone

In 1912 William Vorhees was named postmaster in Gladstone, and from 1914 to 1934 Fred P. Crater served as Gladstone postmaster. The post office was first located in a small (fifteen-foot square) building on Jackson Avenue. That building was razed in 1970, when the old blacksmith shop was renovated and joined to a small house nearby. In 1921 the post office moved to a new building on Main Street constructed by Crater, where it still does business today.

❧ The Fire Department

The history of the Volunteer Fire Department is the story of men and women who have served the community with admirable dedication.

In 1980 the Borough of Peapack and Gladstone Fire Department observed its seventy-fifth anniversary, and as part of the celebration *Our First Seventy-five Years, 1905–1980*, a booklet that traced the development of Company Number

Early equipment of the Peapack Valley Fire Company #1, including a gasoline-operated pump on a horse-drawn chassis, circa 1905. From the T. Leonard Hill collection.

Demonstration of equipment by the Peapack Valley Fire Department at the annual carnival, circa 1905. Note carousel in background. From the Reverend Paul Walther collection.

The carousel at the annual carnival sponsored by the Peapack Valley Fire Department, circa 1905. From the Reverend Paul Walther collection.

Annual carnival sponsored by the Peapack Valley Fire Department held on the property next to what is now the Bailey Funeral Home on Main Street. Group at left engaged in pitching game. Ladies' dresses suggest photo is circa 1905. From the Reverend Paul Walther collection.

1, was printed. Here are the introductory paragraphs from that booklet:

Fire—when properly harnessed—is one of the greatest forces ever put to the service of mankind. Fire—out of control—can hardly be exceeded in its destructive violence. America's physical expansion has been paralleled by the growth of groups of men pledged to the protection of our country's material wealth from the ravages of fire. The individuals composing these groups are our nation's volunteer firemen.

In the early months of the year 1905, the residents of the towns of Peapack and Gladstone, then a part of the Township of Bedminster, undertook in earnest the organization of a fire company to protect their homes and holdings. One of the driving forces behind the movement,

Rev. John M. Harper, offered the use of St. Luke's Hall as a meeting place, and it was there that organizational plans were effected.

On August 1, 1905, "The Peapack Valley Fire Company" was officially proclaimed and incorporated, ten trustees affixing their names to the company's charter, and the Certificate of Incorporation was registered with the State of New Jersey. The following individuals were elected as officers to guide the newly organized fire company: Chief, J. S. Kessler; Foreman, Frank H. Ludlow; 1st Asst. Foreman, William L. Trimmer; Chief Engineer, John J. Draney; 2nd Asst. Foreman, Fred Huyler; Asst. Engineer, George B. Smith; Secretary, Thomas Finn, Sr.; Treasurer, George R. Mosle.[3]

The first fire-fighting equipment consisted of a gasoline-operated pump mounted on a horse-drawn chassis, two hand-drawn hose reels, and one thousand feet of hose. The total cost of the new equipment was not to exceed two thousand dollars. In those early days the fire alarm was sounded by a steam whistle on a locomotive in the yards of the Delaware Lackawanna & Western Railroad in Gladstone. Calls to report fires in Gladstone were made to the Ellis Tiger Company. Ludlow's Hub Factory took calls for fire emergencies in Peapack. The horse-drawn apparatus was housed in a barn belonging to Chandler W. Riker. After the fire whistle sounded, the first man who arrived at the barn hitched his team of horses to the equipment. The owner received three dollars for each use of his team, an amount raised to five dollars in 1907. During the twenties and thirties

calls were received by the G. F. Hills at their home, and they sounded the fire whistle from there.

During its first two years the fire company continued to meet in St. Luke's Hall. In 1907 a plot of ground on which to erect a firehouse was purchased from William Van Ness for $650.00. Included in that purchase was a small building housing a marble-work business. This building served as a meeting place and headquarters until 1912, when a new building was added to the front of it. That first firehouse stands at 207 Main Street and is the property of C. H. Fox, a dealer in modern and rare antique firearms.

Plans and specifications for a new fire headquarters were received in November, 1911. Bids were to be received and construction started as soon as possible. A bid of $3,500.00 submitted by Mr. John Bodine was accepted. The Fire House on Main Street was erected in accordance with approved plans and specifications and dedicated in 1912. Electrical wiring and fixtures in the building were installed by Mr. Andrew Boyle, a member of the fire company, free of charge. Furniture and other furnishings—including six porcelain cuspidors!—were supplied for the meeting room.[4]

The incorporation of Peapack-Gladstone as a borough in 1912 dictated that some changes would take place within the fire department. The new firehouse was an early meeting place for the first Borough Council in 1912. For an annual rental fee of twenty-five dollars the borough was granted use of the meeting room and a two-cell "lock-up" in the base-

Peapack Valley Fire
Company #1 second
firehouse, 1913. From
the Norman Welsh
collection.

ment. It was not until 1920 that the fire company became subject to municipal control. In that year the company consented to a local ordinance that made the fire department an arm of the local government. "Clean-up Day" was initiated in 1921 as a fire-prevention measure. The department was fully integrated into local government on May 5, 1925, when the firehouse and the land on which it stood were deeded to the borough. The name "Peapack Valley Fire Company" was abandoned in 1931, and the designation "Borough of Peapack and Gladstone Fire Department, Company No. 1" was adopted. After the company came under municipal control in 1920, members were paid three dollars for each fire call answered. In 1933, in order to reduce the local budget during the Depression, some monetary concessions were asked of the department. Members agreed to forego any compensation for fire service, and officers who received an annual salary agreed to a 50 percent pay reduction. On the return of prosperity, firemen continued to serve without compensation.

In 1976 the Borough of Peapack and Gladstone approved plans for a new firehouse. The architectural firm of Giles and Hoagland was selected to design the building, which was to be located on Dewey Avenue in Gladstone. For several years the site for a new firehouse had been a source of contention within the borough. In 1972, a bitter dispute was waged over a Liberty Park location, advocated by the fire department.

That location was rejected in a general referendum. Another site was rejected in 1974, and the firemen responded by staging a two-month work slowdown. The matter having been resolved, work was begun on the new structure. Plans called for a staged development whereby the upper level, which would house a meeting room and spaces to be developed for other uses as the need arose, would be finished at a later date. The new firehouse was dedicated in 1980.

Fire-fighting apparatus has changed considerably from the days of the horse-drawn gasoline-engine pumper and the hand-drawn hose reels. The Peapack-Gladstone volunteer forces have continually improved equipment in keeping with advances in technology. As the borough expanded after incorporation, so too did the fire department and its needs. A synopsis of purchases and innovations that have occurred within the department follows:

❧ In 1914 a new Packard chassis was purchased and equipped.

❧ In 1916 an additional method of fire fighting was introduced within the borough when chemical tanks were purchased and mounted on a chassis.

❧ In 1925 the borough accepted delivery on a Mack 500-gpm pumper equipped with auxiliary chemical tanks.

❧ A new American-LaFrance truck, equipped with a 750-gpm pump, booster tank, and reel, carrying a load of more than 1,200 feet of 2½ inch hose was purchased in 1937.

❧ In 1958 a new Oren 750-gpm pumper was delivered to the borough.

❧ Next, a Hahn 750-gpm pumper was purchased by the borough.

❧ A four-wheel-drive Dodge "brush truck" was purchased and put into service in 1970 to fight brush fires.

❧ In 1979 the new Hammerly fire truck equipped with a 1,250-gpm diesel pumper was purchased.

The communication systems within a fire department are vital to the efficiency of the overall operation. The Peapack Valley Fire Company began with a primitive system of telephone calls and locomotive whistles to summon fire fighters to a conflagration. Improvements followed as technology advanced.

❧ In 1914 a new and more efficient code of fire signals was designed in cooperation with the New Jersey Bell Telephone Company, and the purchase and installation of a fire siren was considered.

❧ In 1921 recommendations were made to the borough regarding an improved fire alarm system that called for the use of claxons.

❧ By 1959 the first two-way radio communication equipment was introduced to the fire department when one sixty-watt mobile unit and two portable units were installed in the Oren.

❧ The year 1963 saw the installation of a mobile radio unit

from the police department in the LaFrance pumper, allowing for communications between the Oren and LaFrance during fire-fighting operations, and a radio base station was installed in the fire station.

❧ In 1967 it was decided to update the alarm system with the more modern "Plectron" or home receivers activated by an answering service.

❧ A radio was installed in the fire chief's private vehicle in 1972 to enable him to respond directly to a call and direct the company before the trucks actually arrived on the scene.

❧ In 1975 scanner-type radio receivers were installed in all fire trucks to enable communication between the police and neighboring fire departments on different radio frequencies.

One of the original hand-drawn hose carts was purchased by St. Bernard's School in 1916 for $12.50. After it became obsolete as fire equipment, it was used for some years on the school's farm to carry spools of barbed wire. In 1954 St. Bernard's School made a gift of the hose cart to the fire department. It was fully restored by a group of the firemen under the supervision of Ex-Chief Frank Johnston. Since that time it has been displayed with pride in any number of local parades.

During the two World Wars, members of the fire department were called upon for special services. With the entry of the United States into World War I in 1917, the fire company members resolved to act as an emergency organization at the

This photograph, taken about 1918 during the parade following the end of World War I, is a southern view of Main Street, Peapack. On the right can be seen the foot bridges over the millrace, which ran from what is now Liberty Park to the H.N. Miller gristmill at 108 Main Street. From the Thomas Ward collection.

call of the mayor. Twenty-eight members were sworn in by the borough clerk as special marshals of the borough. In further support of the war effort, a substantial portion of all funds in the company's treasury was invested in Liberty Bonds and War Savings Bonds. Proceeds from the Firemen's Ball in 1917 were donated to the American Red Cross. A service flag was purchased and displayed to commemorate those members entering military service.

During World War II fire department personnel played a major role in the civil defense program. As more and more members were called away to serve in the armed forces, the town youth was organized into a corps of fire reserves, and able-bodied "old-timers" were called on to participate in defense council activities. Two new sirens were installed as air raid signals. Members reported at regular intervals to the Merchant Marine Hospital on the Brady estate to assist in the rehabilitation of patients confined there. War bonds were purchased, and a service flag was maintained. Lloyd Crater, a member of the fire department, lost his life while in service in the North Atlantic.

Volunteer firemen must function as an efficient team. To make this possible, members share hours of training, and at times they must face physical danger. The camaraderie that the members of the Peapack-Gladstone Fire Department have traditionally shared has given rise to a number of social developments within the organization. In 1911 the company was accepted as a member of the New Jersey State Firemen's Association, a move that produced the formation of the Peapack Valley Firemen's Relief Association. That organization provides financial and physical assistance to local firemen in need of such help. In their declining years members of the ranks are eligible for entrance into the Firemen's Home in Boonton, New Jersey. On the death of a fireman, his relatives receive a financial benefit from the association as well. The wives of the firemen organized a Ladies Auxiliary in April 1913. That organization was traditionally active in fund-raising affairs, such as dances, carnivals, and plays, and today continues to sponsor annual pancake breakfasts.

In 1908, during the term of Chief William L. Trimmer, the Peapack Valley Fire Company accepted an invitation to participate in a parade in Newark, New Jersey:

> *A band was hired; the fire equipment was spotlessly cleaned and polished. Same was moved to Newark by railroad flat car. There a team which had been hired was hooked up to the apparatus, and the company proudly moved along Broad Street. Despite red flannel-lined dress uniforms on the hottest day of the year our old-timers report a good time on the part of all those present.*[5]

Another social highlight that marked the department's early days was the Firemen's Field Day, held on Labor Day, 1914 at the Far Hills Fair Grounds. "First honors in the 'Tug-of-War' contest were taken that day by a team composed of Messrs. James Carson, Charles E. Meyers, Oscar J. Smith,

Jr., Daniel M. Todd, and William D. Vander Beek. Each of the members of this team came away the proud possessor of a silver cup for his efforts."[6]

Other early social occasions of note included the Annual Firemen's Night at the Basking Ridge Firemen's Carnival 1929, when the company was awarded first prize of twenty-five dollars in gold for having a 100 percent turnout of members; the first Somerset County Firemen's Field Day held at the Far Hills Fair Grounds on Labor Day, 1929; and in 1971 participation in a parade in Trenton, New Jersey, celebrating the 250th anniversary of the founding of that city.

No history of any fire department is complete without tales of notable conflagrations. The details of the disasters that have occurred in Peapack-Gladstone have been faithfully recorded by the fire company. Let us look at a few of the more spectacular fires, fires that have altered the complexion of the borough. It is appropriate to hear about fires from firemen, so the following reports are quoted from the Peapack-Gladstone seventy-fifth-anniversary booklet.[7]

> *Mr. William L. Trimmer was chief at our first fire when a barn was struck by lightning on the property of the late Peter Apgar (now Fred S. Condit) in Gladstone.*
>
> *A panel of fence was ordered removed so that the engine could be taken through the field to the nearby stream. Soft ground was encountered; the engine went hub-deep in mud and was finally pulled free the following day. The barn? It burned to the ground.*

> *Chief Fred Huyler and his firemen on Sunday morning, December 5, 1909, experienced the most "disastrous" fire in the company's history when the "John Allen Fire" occurred. It started in the drug store of the late Joseph F. Schefcik (now Debus Drugs) and before being finally extinguished had wiped out an entire block. Consumed in the wake of the flames were an auditorium and general store owned by Mr. Allen; structures belonging to Mr. Alvah C. Moke and Mr. Andrew Ballentine; a building owned by Mr. William Wilson; the harness shop of Mr. William Van Ness with its landmark—the white wooden horse; and a barber shop and dwelling owned by Mr. Phillip Todd.*
>
> *Naturally our local fire company was unable to cope with such a conflagration alone. They needed a lot of assistance—quickly. Our good neighbors responded at once, and soon there were on the scene fire companies from Far Hills, Mendham, Bernardsville, Basking Ridge, and Morristown. Through their combined efforts, the homes of many of our residents were saved from destruction.*
>
> *A mill race ran immediately in front of the line of buildings and shops which were afire and was the source of water for fighting the several blazes. Again the seriousness of the situation was tempered with a lighter side. It is recalled by several towns-people present at the time how two of our firemen, Mr. Daniel M. Todd and Mr. Tay Handville, were handling a hose line on the roof of one of the buildings. They signaled for more water. As the pressure was increased at the pumper, the hose began to snake to the point that they lost their footing and their hold on the hose line and a short time later were fished from the mill race none the worse, fortunately, for their experience. Not quite so*

fortunate were two firemen from one of the assisting companies who were injured by a falling chimney.

Neighbors in the immediate area whose dwellings had not been affected by the fire opened their homes to those who had suffered loss or damage. Hot drinks and food, bedding and wearing apparel were furnished to those whose possessions had been laid waste by the fire.

On January 15, 1940, a fire was fought at Amerman's Auditorium which all too vividly recalled the Allen fire on the same site back in December, 1909. Fortunately this fire did not reach the destructive proportions the earlier conflagration reached. It was confined to the Amerman property, but some estimate of its possibilities could be drawn from the blistered paint on the adjoining Allen property.

July 20, 1945, marked another eventful date for the company. It was then that Cleaveland Laboratories, Inc., at a site near Peapack Station, suffered extensive fire damage. For several days electrical storms had hovered over and around the entire Peapack valley. On the evening of July 20 at about 9:00 P.M., while our local firemen were at a meeting in the firehouse, the alarm sounded. The Cleaveland properties had been struck by lightning and were ablaze. Fire spread quickly through the stores of solvents, coatings, and fabrics being processed in the plant. Drums of solvent, super-heated and ruptured by the flames, lent to the already serious situation. The high-voltage electric lines of the D. L. & W. RR., adjacent to the fire, added to the other hazards present. Contact was made with the railroad's power dispatcher, and the lines

were de-energized. Meanwhile, our own hose lines had been laid and charged: Union Hook and Ladder Company of Far Hills was called on for assistance and had moved in. The combined efforts of the two companies were not enough in the face of the intense flames and the headway they had gained. All efforts went then where the fire had originated. Other buildings were wet down to prevent their igniting; hose streams were played on outside stores of solvents and chemicals to keep drums from heating and bursting. It was well along towards dawn when danger from further outbreak of fire was eliminated. As a further precaution a fire guard remained on duty throughout the next day.

In January, 1954, after several years of comparative quiet and lack of fires of a serious nature, a most destructive fire struck at the Somerset County Barns in Peapack. The fire had made considerable headway when the alarm sounded about 3:45 A.M. on January 19. By the time the company arrived, a good portion of one wing of the L-shaped structure was already in flames. A wooden frame structure without fire walls, considerable amounts of gasoline feeding the flames, intense heat and exploding auxiliary gasoline supplies, near-freezing temperature— all these factors seriously hampered the firemen in their efforts to overcome the blaze. Each time it appeared that they had turned the tide, the firemen were forced to fall back in the face of a new wall of flame from another exploding gasoline tank or drum. It was a tired company of firemen that finally "picked up" at about 7:00 A.M. More than 2000 feet of hose had been laid. Ladders, ropes, pike poles, axes, smoke masks, and other equipment had to be gathered up. The scene at the still-

smoldering fire was not a pleasant one. The entire structure was leveled. Most equipment and rolling stock which it had housed were a total loss. It had been a losing battle in the face of overpowering odds.

At 10:00 P.M., August 8, 1971, the company was called to the Reformed Church in Gladstone which is one of the oldest buildings in the area. Fire had started in the kitchen and was spreading to the balcony area directly over the kitchen. Heat was so intense in the chapel that, although no fire was visible, the tapestries hanging from the windows were igniting. The fire was contained to the kitchen where fire damage was extensive. However, with the fine team effort of all firemen involved, heat and smoke damage to the rest of the building was slight. The fire was brought under control within two hours.

At 9:45 P.M., February 5, 1972, the two pumpers and Powerwagon responded to an alarm at the Tiger Lumber Yard.[8] On arrival the fire was raging out of control. Pottersville, Far Hills and Bernardsville Fire Departments were immediately summoned for back-up. Because of pre-planning over the previous years at this site each department was strategically set up without hesitation or confusion. The result was the saving of the Arthur Alpaugh home located only six feet from the burning lumber storage sheds. Buildings located directly to the rear were also protected. Small sheds across the street suffered minor damage from intense heat. The blustery winds scattered burning embers over the area, but were extinguished by using the Powerwagon to roam freely wherever needed. One ember lodged against the 3rd floor dormer window on the

then Tiger Hardware Store.[9] It was spotted immediately and extinguished by the Bernardsville Fire Department without any damage. While the lumber shed was a total loss, all surrounding buildings were well protected. Men and equipment from the department remained on the scene throughout the night and on into the next morning until the fire was declared out.

At 4:00 A.M., May 22, 1978, the alarm was sounded to respond to the Crawford residence on Hamilton Farms for what could be described as one of the most spectacular, yet tragic fires in this area over the past twenty-five years. It was also a clear illustration of firematic teamwork at its fullest when the occasion becomes necessary. At one point there were no less than 175 firemen and first-aiders directly involved at the fire scene, displaying frustration from being unable to stop the ensuing enemy, fright from the crumbling walls and roof, and above all sorrow at the tragic loss that was appearing before them. Companies from Peapack-Gladstone, Far Hills-Bedminster, Pottersville, Chester and Bernardsville all teamed together as one to fight the insurmountable odds. Twenty-seven hours would pass before our company could officially clear the scene and go home.[10]

At 11:50 P.M., July 19, 1979, the department responded to the G.F. Hill and Co. feed mill in Gladstone.[11] On arrival the south and west side of this four-tiered structure was found fully involved with fire spreading from the ground level to the roof. Companies from Far Hills, Pottersville and Bernardsville were called in to back up and contain this

One of Peapack-Gladstone's worst fires, which destroyed the Tiger lumberyard February 5, 1972. Photograph by George Tiger. From the Mary Tiger collection.

spectacular blaze. No one was injured but the fire was not brought under control until approximately 4:00 A.M., nearly twelve hours after it had started.[12]

The Borough of Peapack and Gladstone Fire Department continues to develop and provide volunteer services to the community. Between 1987 and 1988 fire calls increased 60 percent; from January to October of 1989 the firemen contributed more than twenty-one hundred man-hours of volunteer services to the borough.

♣ The First Aid and Rescue Squad

The First Aid and Rescue Squad embodies the sense of community responsibility that has always sustained the Borough of Peapack and Gladstone. In the autumn of 1934, twelve members of the Borough of Peapack and Gladstone Fire Department attended a first-aid training course in Somerville. Subsequently, the First Aid and Rescue Squad was formed in January 1935 "to render such services to the public as will lessen suffering and help to preserve life,"[13] the squad's purpose as stated in the Certificate of Incorporation, dated February 11, 1935.

Charter members of the squad were Walter C. Atkinson, Harold W. Chesson, W. Dudley Chesson, Claude M. Crater, Frank Hamler, T. Leonard Hill, A. Merle Hoffman, Harold Horton, Frank F. Johnston, Theodore Smalley, Elias H. Sutton, and Edward J. Zimmerman, Sr.

The squad's beginning was modest indeed, as it had no mobile equipment at all, and the inventory of available emergency equipment was meager, consisting of a portable first-aid kit and a pair of blankets. In September 1935, a Packard sedan was presented to the squad by R. Stuyvesant Pierrepont. Extensive modifications were made to the body. Rescue, salvage, and first-aid equipment were mounted, and the combination ambulance–emergency truck was readied for operations. Flood lights and a generator were added as standard equipment in October 1936. This rescue truck continued in service as an auxiliary piece of equipment until December 1949. A list of equipment carried in the Packard in those early days was found among the 1936 minutes of the squad meetings and is reprinted here.

♣ *First Aid Equipment*
1 pair driver's mittens
1 accident report book
3 large heat pads
6 small heat pads
2 towels
9 triangle bandages
2 police whistles
1 Flash bulb

2 3C bulbs 6–8

paper cups

2 ice bags

2 First Aid books

1 Schedule of Antidotes

hose for pumping tires

2 pair sun glasses

1 piece muslin

1 bottle Picric acid

1 bottle vinegar

1 bottle olive oil

1 bottle H_2O

1 CO_2

2 stretchers

1 large piece of canvas

2 helmets

4 blankets

2 rubber covering for stretchers

1 First Aid Kit complete

2 smoke masks

wooden splints

2 Thomas Splints

1 axe

1 wire cutters

1 Pike pole

4 crow bars

1 horse blanket

1 H. H. Inhalator

2 coats (rubber)

2 pr. rubber boots

6 hats (rubber)

2 clubs

1 canvas bucket

1 rope

1 hook

1 Hay hook

1 20Ft. ladder

2 electric torches

1 set flares

1 set tire chains

1 flood light

1 motor (Gen.)

6 Union-All suits

1 can gas

1 Carpenters light

The minutes also describe a decision to purchase "one blanket from Globe Sales and Mfg. Company weight 3½ pounds, 62x82 for $2.50."[14]

In 1936 Central telephone exchange had two numbers listed to call in case of emergency: "Peapack 15" (Hill's), or "Peapack 154" (Chesson's). First Aid and Rescue Squad members were summoned then by the siren sounding once.

First Aid and Rescue
Squad equipment on
display at the
ceremony dedicating
the squad's building,
May 24, 1953.

First Aid and Rescue
Squad at the
ceremony dedicating
the squad's building,
May 24, 1953.

Captain Hill was head driver, and F. Johnston second driver.

The early minutes from squad meetings include reports of the first calls made by the squad. December 13, 1935: Lieutenant Chesson reported that the squad had been called to St. Bernard's School to administer first aid to one of the school's football players who had suffered a broken leg. The minutes of August 14, 1936, tell of a call on July 9 to hunt for a man reported missing from the Blair estate, and again for a World War I veteran who had run away from the home at Millington.

During the year 1937 the minutes tell of two fatal automobile accidents; three hospital cases (automobile); one general alarm; two blood transfusions; and eleven fire calls.

In 1940 the need for a new custom-built ambulance came under discussion. At a special meeting on August 15, Somerset Hills Post No. 216 of the American Legion made it known that it would like to present an ambulance to the squad. Formal presentation of the LaSalle ambulance followed in March 1941.

As the squad grew in members and in emergency rescue and first-aid activities, the need for larger quarters became pressing. Several building sites were considered, as were plans for the type of structure needed. Once again the generosity of the community was manifested through several important grants. Early in the summer of 1949, a plot on St. Luke's Avenue was secured, the gift of Richard V. N. Gambrill. Building plans were accelerated and became a reality with a generous monetary grant by Mrs. Reginald B. Rives, in memory of her father, the architect Whitney Warren. Plans and specifications were drawn and donated by the architect James C. Mackenzie. Ground was broken and construction started in August 1952; January 1953 marked completion. The new building was dedicated at a public ceremony on Sunday, May 24, 1953.

The community needs for emergency services increased through the years as the population of the borough grew. Compare the number of emergency calls answered in the 1960 annual report with those for the year 1937 mentioned above.

&   *Annual Report of the Peapack-Gladstone First-Aid & Rescue Squad   Inc. for the Year of 1960*

The year of 1960 finds that the local Squad has again had a very busy year. According to a report submitted by the Squad secretary Percy Terry, the Ambulance traveled 3,814 miles and 530 man hours were used in the calls.

Included in the calls were 60 transportation of patients from their homes to hospitals, also there were 25 accident calls, 16 heart attacks, 5 oxygen cases, and 16 miscellaneous calls such as horse shows, parade etc. making a total amount of calls for the year of 122.

The following contributions received were most helpful in helping us to cover our operating expenses:

Borough of Peapack-Gladstone —————	*$ 350.00*
Somerset County —————	*$ 200.00*
Donations —————	*$ 595.00*

Tag Day Receipts ———————————— *$3065.54*

The following members were elected to office for the year of 1961:

> *Captain & President Clyde Manning Sr.*
>
> *First Lt. Edwin VanArsdale*
>
> *Second Lt. Benjamin Card*
>
> *Treasurer Fred Kuhmichel*
>
> *Secretary Percy Terry*
>
> *Trustee Patrick McCrory, LeRoy Sullivan, Gordon Dickinson.*
>
> *Delegates, Fred Kuhmichel, Francis Kelly, Rita Card.*
>
> *Alternates, Richard Deans, Raymond Manning, Dorothy Monahan.*

At this time we would like to extend our sincere thanks to all our many friends for their contributions and donations to our Squad.

Since its modest beginning in 1935, the squad has made great strides. It has continued to grow and keep abreast of the latest emergency procedures, progressing from its original first-aid kit and blankets to a highly mobile, fully equipped and trained unit. In 1990 the inventory of emergency equipment included two modern ambulances and a four-wheel-drive utility vehicle. Squad personnel is entirely volunteer, each member undergoing a 110-hour emergency training course and a CPR course in order to qualify. Funding is supplied by public and private donations.

In 1989 the squad responded to 203 calls and volunteered over 450 man-hours, all with but one goal, as initiated by the first volunteer First Aid and Rescue Squad in 1935, to "lessen suffering and help to preserve life."[15]

❧ *The Police Department*

When Peapack-Gladstone incorporated as a borough, it became necessary to establish a separate law-enforcement agency. Provisions were made for a two-cell borough lock-up, and two marshals were employed. Martin Huyler became the first marshal of the new twin borough, and the borough's First Annual Report shows the purchase of one pair of handcuffs.

Here is the ordinance establishing the new department:

> ❧ *An Ordinance to Establish, Equip and Regulate a Police Department in the Borough of Peapack & Gladstone and Adopt Rules for Its Government.*
>
> *Be it ordained, by the common council of the Borough of Peapack & Gladstone.*
>
> *1. The Police committee of the Common Council, with the Borough Marshall shall constitute the Police Department of the Borough of Peapack & Gladstone.*
>
> *2. The Marshall shall receive no pay or compensation for his services as Policeman, except when actually employed as hereinafter provided, and when no[t] actually employed shall receive such salary as the Council shall determine from time to time.*
>
> *3. The power to direct the employment of the Marshals in Police*

First officers of the Peapack-Gladstone Police Department, 1938. Left to right: Winfield Morris, police officer; Amzie B. Hoffman, chairman of police committee for Borough Council, auxiliary policeman; Frank J. Gallo, police officer. From the Ruth Thomson collection.

Service from time to time shall be vested in the Police Committee, the Chairman of which committee for the time being shall be the Chief of Police and shall serve without compensation.

Passed, April 12, 1921 Approved and passed, April 12, 1921 F. H. Ludlow, Clerk. John Bodine, Mayor

Whereas the original ordinance, pertaining to the establishment and equipment and regulation of a Police Department in the Borough is missing, said Ordinance was approved and passed, by former Mayor John Bodine, April 12th 1921 and recorded as a passed Ordinance by F. H. Ludlow, Borough Clerk, April 12th 1921

And whereas, The former Borough Clerk (Mr. Ludlow) has in his possession a copy of said Ordinance as passed and approved, April 12th 1921.

Therefore be it resolved: That the above copy of Ordinance be recognized as the Original Ordinance, as passed and approved April 12th, 1921, and that the Mayor & Clerk be requested to affix their signatures to same, and copy of this resolution be attached to copy of the Ordinance as presented.[16]

The police blotter of the late 1920s and the 1930s includes numerous entries regarding traveling peddlers plying their wares without proper licenses. Entries included warnings to

In 1983 the municipal offices and police department relocated to the newly renovated municipal building in the former elementary school on Main Street.

When the municipal offices were relocated in 1983, the building that had housed them at 12 Prospect Avenue was restored to a single-family home; seen here being removed is the prefabricated structure used by the police. From the Canon R. J. Morrow collection.

New York Clothiers, Fish Man, A Man Selling Goats, A Woman Selling Wax Flowers, and numerous Vegetable Men.

Perhaps the most colorful period in the history of Peapack-Gladstone law enforcement occurred in 1968 when Jacqueline Kennedy Onassis first came to our borough. Hordes of press personnel relentlessly followed her about, and there are many newspaper accounts of incidents that took place that year, including the arrest of a suspicious looking character out walking at night who was detained until the Secret Service could identify him. One particularly persistent French *paparazzo* followed Mrs. Onassis constantly, using a telephoto lens to spy on her at picnics, near her residence, and even photographing her through the Debus Drugstore window. One Sunday he tried to photograph her at church and was arrested. A compromise was reached: no trespassing charges would be filed if he promised never to take pictures of the Kennedys in Peapack again.[17]

A particularly difficult period for the police department followed the death in 1986 of long-time Police Chief Charles Bocchino. An often bitter dispute continued for several years over the proper procedure for selecting a new chief of police. The matter was finally resolved in 1990, and a pension plan was instituted for members of the police department.

❧ *Local Doctors*

Among the physicians who have served our community, listed here in chronological sequence, are Dr. Whipple; Dr. Frederick Sutphen (1827–1884), known to be practicing circa 1850; Dr. Thornton; Dr. Edward Perry (1820–1892); Dr. Edwin Farrow (1851–1913), known to be active circa 1898; Dr. Keating; Dr. Clarence Kay (1909–1950); Dr. Mahlon Smalley; Dr. H. W. Pierson, who also served as mayor from 1955 to 1960; and Dr. Jerome Vogel (ca. 1935–1992).

Dr. Sutphen's home and office were in the old stone house on Pottersville Road in Gladstone, across the brook from Chatfield's Restaurant. Built in the late 1700s, the house is one of the oldest in the borough and is said to occupy the site of an old Indian trading post. Dr. Thornton lived there after Dr. Sutphen.

Dr. Sutphen's daughter married Dr. Mahlon Smalley, who also had his practice in Gladstone for fifty years in the house on the corner of Mendham Road and Jackson Avenue. Dr. Smalley was sure his son Clarence would follow in his footsteps, as he attended the University of Pennsylvania Medical School. Clarence, however, became a civil engineer instead.

Reference is made to Dr. Farrow in an 1898 issue of the Somerville *Unionist Gazette*. He bought property, "beginning at an iron pin driven in the ground in the eastern line of Main Street a corner to John H. Belton's lot,"[18] from Eveline and

Harriet Apgar in Peapack on April 26, 1892, for three hundred dollars.

Lydia Ann Sutton and Phillip Sutton conveyed property to George Perry October 7, 1865, one acre for $500.00 "bounded by G. F. Crater's wood lot."[19] On March 22, 1867, James M. Todd conveyed to George Perry for $630 "a property bounded by property formerly owned by George Lawshe's line."[20]

Dr. Clarence Robert Kay opened his medical practice here in 1909. In 1913, he and his wife, (née) Sara Ellen Gulick, purchased a house at 89 Main Street from George S. Van Arsdale, as a residence and office for Dr. Kay. The doctor was also an active contributor to the community at large, serving on many committees in a voluntary capacity. In 1950 he was honored with a testimonial gift of $6,322 from his friends to commemorate forty years of medical service. The money was used to fund a medical library at Somerville Hospital. A plaque in the library bears the following inscription: "This library is donated by patients and friends in the Somerset Hills as a tribute to Clarence R. Kay, M.D." In 1988 the former Kay home was renovated and converted for use as a restaurant; the restaurant closed in 1991.

Dr. Jerome Vogel started his Peapack practice in 1965 while continuing a private practice in Livingston, New Jersey, where he was also chief surgeon at Livingston City Hospital's emergency unit. As his practice in Peapack grew, he gave up the Livingston practice. Dr. Vogel, the son of a Newark fireman, eventually became medical director of the New York Institute for Child Development, a member of the New Jersey Council on Disability Benefits, a teacher at Somerset Hospital, a consulting physician at Wellking Neurological Hospital for Multiple Sclerosis, president of the Peapack Board of Health, and consulting physician for many private schools and the United States Equestrian Team. He administered fertility shots to Peggy Jo Keinast of Liberty Corner, the mother of the first set of quintuplets to be born in New Jersey. Dr. Vogel continued his practice in Peapack until his death in 1992, although he and his wife, Dolores, and their eight children moved to an early nineteenth-century house in Tewksbury Township after they outgrew their Peapack house. Dr. Vogel had many other occupations, including antiques dealer, art restorer, gun dealer, radio and TV personality, carpenter, and author. He also enjoyed yachting, fishing, and collecting rare wines and nineteenth-century paintings.[21]

🌢 The Peapack-Gladstone Library

Although the Peapack and Gladstone Library opened officially in 1936, sentiment favoring the establishment of a public library dates back as far as the turn of the century. On April 29, 1903, a play was given at Van Arsdales Hall, Peapack, for the benefit of a public library and gymnasium, the purpose of these being to afford a place of healthy recreation and amusement for all the citizens of Peapack and Gladstone. According to the records of the Woman's Club, the play presented was *Uncle*, written by Henry J. Byron. Reserved seats for the performance were thirty-five and fifty cents, and during intermission vocal duets, character songs, and an exhibition of "rapid crayon drawing" were presented.[22]

In 1925 Rev. John M. Harper, rector of St. Luke's Episcopal Church, proposed to turn over the collection of books housed in the church basement as the foundation of a public library on the condition that a proper building be procured and a permanent association formed for the purpose of financing the library project. He asked that the Peapack and Gladstone Woman's Club, which had been organized in 1921 and federated in 1922 under the motto "Not for Ourselves but for Others," assume responsibility for operating the existing library system until the project was a reality. Under the administration of Mrs. Sara Gulick Kay, first president of the Woman's Club, and Board of Education member, the library became a reality. The Woman's Club launched a fund drive and collected nearly all of the three thousand dollars needed to purchase a building. The remainder of the funds was donated by Mrs. Kay's husband, Dr. Clarence Kay, and by her brother, Ronald Gulick.

The Borough Council offered to turn over the first floor of the Riker house, a two-family dwelling located in Liberty Park, to be operated by the Woman's Club as a public library; the borough would furnish light, heat, and water. The offer was gratefully accepted, and the project was finally underway. The building was remodeled with a large front room with bookshelves lining the walls and a librarian's desk near the entrance. A middle room was designated as a reading room, and the small room at the rear was fully equipped as a kitchen.

The library officially opened on January 15, 1936, with a tea and public reception. Miss Sara Akew, state librarian, and Miss Dorothy VanGorder, county librarian, were the principal speakers. The Junior Woman's Club presented three dozen folding chairs, to be placed in the reading room so that it could be used as the meeting place of the Woman's Clubs.

In January 1939, the decision was made to incorporate the library for financial reasons: the Borough Council could legally contribute five hundred dollars yearly toward the maintenance of the library if it were incorporated. Incorporation of the Peapack and Gladstone Public Library provided for maintenance, purchasing of books and supplies, the hiring of a librarian and assistants, and holding title to property located in the borough. A board of trustees was formed consisting of three members of each of the Woman's Clubs: Seniors, Progressives, and Juniors.

The library opened with an inventory of 2,724 books; one

year later the number of volumes had increased to 3,345. Numerous donations from the private libraries of surrounding estates increased the number of reference, historical, and other books. The library also received many donations of money and books, as well as magazines from the Legion Auxiliary, the Valley Club, the A.B.C. Club, and the Y.M.C.A. A wreath for the front door at Christmas was donated by the Girl Scouts.

On the death of Mrs. Sara Kay in 1945, Mrs. Oscar Smith assumed leadership of the Woman's Club and Library Board. During World War II books and magazines were sent to New Jersey army camps, the Veterans' Hospital, the Merchant Marine Rest Center at Hamilton Farm, and the Victory Book Campaign.

The library continued to grow, and as a result more space was needed. A remodeling and expansion project was approved by the borough. The kitchen was converted into a children's room; arrangements were made to store surplus books upstairs; a meeting room for the board and a thrift shop in the rear were added. The council financed the decoration of the hall and board room; Boy Scouts and former scouts assisted in moving books; and a phonograph for the children's room was donated by one of the trustees. A large oil painting of George Washington was presented by Mrs. Cutting of Hamilton Farm. The thrift shop opened in November 1953.

When the Peapack-Gladstone public school building was converted into Borough Hall, a new library facility was incorporated into the plans. After nearly fifty years at its original site, the Peapack-Gladstone Public Library moved across Main Street to its modern facility in the municipal building in March 1983. In 1982 the library became a part of the Somerset County Library System, an affiliation that provided access to the card catalogues of all libraries included in that system. The library offers borough residents the use of a computer, a copy machine, and a facsimile machine, and it is part of the IBM Inter-Library Loan System. In 1990 the Peapack-Gladstone Library inventory included some sixteen thousand books, video and audio cassettes, compact discs, and books on tape.

♣ *Liberty Park*

In the heart of Peapack-Gladstone is Liberty Park where graceful swans, ducks, and geese swim on a tranquil pond. The park is widely used by residents and visitors seeking a pleasant place for a walk, a picnic, or quiet contemplation.

In May 1919, a group of public-spirited town fathers met at the local firehouse to discuss creating a park in honor of area men who had served their country in the Great War. They proposed to raise the funds necessary to acquire the property then known as Riker's meadow, to develop it, and

The swans at Liberty Park. Photograph by Jan Gordon, October 1990.

to maintain it as a memorial to these World War I veterans.

At that first meeting the group agreed to form the Liberty Park Association and elected the following officers: Mayor John Bodine, president; Dr. M. C. Smalley, first vice president; Fred P. Crater, second vice president; Garner F. Hill, treasurer; and Rev. John Mitchell Harper, secretary. Other trustees were Elmer P. Courter, William Trimmer, W. C. Horton, Nicholas T. Ballentine, and Thomas Howard.

The proposed project met with general enthusiasm, and donations from the community at large began to accumulate. The Women's Committee canvassed the entire community and solicited contributions. John Sloane donated one thousand dollars, and six hundred dollars was raised "from the sale of the House Guard Carbines." By June of the same year the association had formalized agreements to purchase the Riker meadow and the Huber house that stood in the corner of the property, as well as "the mill property (including the mill, millpond, mill race, tailrace, all water rights and lands, and the house in which Mr. H. N. Miller now lives.)"[23] (For further details about the millrace see the sections on the early mills in "Early History.")

Mrs. Sheldon Martin oversaw the plans for landscaping the park along lines suggested to her by C. Ledyard Blair. Blair proposed that William Symmes Richardson be the landscape architect for the project. "By unanimous vote Mrs. Martin was extended the thanks of Liberty Park Assoc. for

her untiring efforts in furthering the advancement of its purposes; not the least of which was her communication with Mr. Blair."[24]

The focal point of the park was to be a swimming and skating pond, to be formed by the construction of a concrete dam on the brook. This major project was completed in time for winter skating in December 1920.

Treas. Statement
Dec. 15, 1920

Receipts	
Subscriptions, dances etc. in Borough	$ *763.48*
Donation from P.V. Fire Department	*550.00*
G. R. Hill—loan	*100.00*
Subscriptions from summer people	*5050.00*
House Guard Rifle Fund	*602.49*

Expenditures	
Riker property (in full)	$*2,500.00*
" " recording deed	*2.00*
Interest on note	*6.25*
Sec. book	*.95¢*
Printing	*2.25*
"	*3.20*
G. F. Hill—loan	*100.00*
L. Huber—on property purchase	*275.00*

M. C. Smalley—on Mill Race	400.00
" " bal. " "	1,100.00
Eddy Valve Co. Valve for dam	54.70
Construction of Dam—Labor	72.00
" " Teams	240.85
" " Overseer	110.00
" " Mason work	1,307.50
Total Expenditures to date	$6,171.50
Bal. on hand	$894.47

❧ *Fire House, June 16, 1921*

A meeting of the Trustees was called to order by Pres. Crater at 9 P.M. The Trustees present were Messrs. Bodine, Courter, Crater, Harper, Hill and Smalley.

After careful consideration the following rules were formally adopted:

1. All boys and men are required to wear two-piece bathing suits.

2. All girls over twelve years of age and all women are required to wear bathing suits with skirts.

3. No bathing is allowed later than one hour after sunset.

4. No profane or indecent language nor boisterous conduct is allowed.

5. No so called "ducking" or any other interference with bathers is allowed.

6. No bathing on Sunday is allowed.

7. Anyone committing a nuisance, defacing any part of the property of Liberty Park Asso., or violating any of the rules, now or hereafter in force, will be prosecuted according to law and deprived of the use of the Park.

8. A reward of $5.00 will be paid for information leading to the conviction of anyone violating the rules laid down by Liberty Park Asso.

Mr. Bodine moved that 25 copies of the foregoing rules be printed on cloth and posted. Sec'd by Dr. Smalley. Carried.

❧ *Fire House, Jan. 10, 1922*

A meeting of the Trustees was called to order . . .

Mr. Trimmer moved that the Waw Waw Camp Fire Girls be given permission to plant an evergreen tree in the Park to be used as a permanent Community Christmas Tree, the location of the tree to be decided by the Comm. on planting. The motion was seconded and carried.

❧ *Fire House, May 31, 1922*

A meeting of the Trustees . . .

Mrs. Martin moved that the Township Committee be invited to place a tablet in Liberty Park in memory of those who served the World War: and that, if possible, this tablet be placed on July 4, 1922: and that the Township Committee be informed that they feel free to remove the tablet at any time in case they find a more desirable location. Seconded By Mr. Bodine, Carried.

❧ *Fire House, Aug. 3, 1923*

A meeting of the Trustees . . .

Mrs. Martin sent a report of the Planting Comm. as follows:

Trees and shrubs planted last autumn	*$180.40*
Sidewalks, d[r]ains, grading, this spring	*284.96*

    Concrete steps into the Park will be built next week. Mr. Barnes will give ten or twelve benches for Park.

Electric-light pole will be moved very soon.

    At this meeting there were present several representatives of the various women's clubs who have kindly consented to take charge of the stands at the Smith picnic, and give the net proceeds for the new sidewalk fund.

       Ice cream and cake—Ladies Social Circle.

       Candy and Fruit—Women's Club.

       Hot dog and sandwiches—Ladies Aid Society.

       Fancy table—Aux. to the Fire Co.

       Novelties—Ala. Blackberries.

       Soda & water melon—Fire Co.

       General discussion. Adjournment.

The Annual Meeting was then called to order. . . . On motion it was decided to prohibit fishing in the lake during the present season. The reason for this action is that strangers came from various towns & cities last summer and abused this privilege. Mr. Courter agreed to print some signs and post our property. A motion to adjourn carried.[25]

In April 1927 Liberty Park was deeded to the borough by the association. The care and upkeep of the property had gone beyond the means of the association, and it was financially advantageous that the borough maintain the park through taxation.

The early summers in the park saw activities centered primarily around the swimming pond. An August 1935 edition of the *Peapack-Gladstone Exponent* announced a "water meet" to be held at the "Peapack-Gladstone Park Lake." Long-time residents recall the old swimming hole. Marcus Canfield tells of being an anchorman on the swim relay team, and Mayor Mary Hamilton remembers her father swimming there with Marcus. A lifeguard was employed for the swimming season each summer. On the darker side, a local woman chose to drown herself in the pond in 1936, and for some years thereafter the lake was referred to by some as Suicide Lake. In the late 1930s, swimming was discontinued because the pond had become polluted by waste from the development of home sites. That was long before there was a municipal sewage system.

    The swans made their appearance around 1955, the gift of Mrs. Edgar Rosenblatt, who pictured them as the finishing touch to an idyllic setting. The birds' arrival at the pond brought new responsibilities to the then superintendent of roads, Clyde Manning, who often had to round them up from the sidewalks and return them to the water. When babies didn't appear after several years, Manning journeyed to Spring Lake to consult with experts on how to encourage breeding.[26]

On warm summer days the park is always busy with

families, picnickers, fishermen, people basking in the sun, or strollers enjoying the shady paths.

The flashing blades of ice skaters swirling on the frozen pond add sparkle to the long winter season in the park. The frosty scene invariably includes children gliding on their first pair of skates; gleeful youngsters and teenagers wielding hockey sticks; and the more sedate, but graceful, figure skaters of all ages.

Visitors to the park in spring enjoy the flowering trees and shrubs; in the fall, the brilliant autumn foliage. Of course, one can always feed the ducks.

Park House, the former Huber property acquired by the association when the park was being planned, became the headquarters of the Peapack-Gladstone Woman's Club in 1938, and subsequently, the community library. When the library moved to new facilities in Borough Hall, the house was sold to Dr. Bittner, a local dentist, for his office. The house was originally a bakery, and the location of the large brick baking ovens is still visible at the back.

Ceremony is the element that unites a community. Liberty Park has been the focal point of the events that bring us together year after year.

Most significant of these have been the annual Memorial Day services, which are in keeping with the intent of the founders of the Liberty Park Association. These solemn ceremonies have been conducted each May from the grand-

stand in the park at the conclusion of the parade. In 1948 a new memorial honoring the veterans of World War II was placed in the park. The newest monument, honoring Vietnam War soldiers, was erected in the mid-1980s. Through the efforts of Borough Council member Ann Winston, and her fund-raising committee, aerating fountains were added to the pond in 1990.

Perhaps the sentimental favorite among the special occasions in the park is the annual lighting of the Christmas tree and the carol sing. Each year, in conjunction with a live nativity tableau, sponsored by the Methodist Church, community carolers of all ages gather around the nativity scene at the church and travel in procession to Liberty Park to await the arrival of Santa Claus and the subsequent tree lighting.

On any given Saturday, weather permitting, bridal parties choose to pose for their wedding portraits against the serene background of the Peapack pond.

Residents of this community look with gratitude to the town fathers of 1919 who had the foresight to plan Liberty Park, and to the volunteers who carried out their plan. To many minds the image of this serene oasis in our midst has come to typify what is best in Peapack-Gladstone.

❧ The Community Center

Sara Gulick Kay was the first president of the Peapack and

Gladstone Woman's Club, a member of the Board of Education, and the representative from the Woman's Club who oversaw the development of the public library. She was a vital and active woman, and when she died in 1945, the loss to the community was keenly felt. The members of the Woman's Club sought an appropriate memorial to honor her contributions to the community. A committee proposed to acquire the old two-room schoolhouse on Willow Avenue which had once stood on Main Street (the site is now a parking lot for the Peapack Post Office and other commercial buildings across the street). At that time the building was the headquarters for the Junior O.U.A.M. (Junior Order of United American Mechanics). It was proposed that the acquired structure would serve as a meeting place for the three Woman's Clubs of the borough: the Seniors, Progressives, and Juniors; and to operate as a community center for meetings, dances, plays, dinners, wedding receptions, and private parties at a nominal fee. All services and funds required for the acquisition of the property were donated, title was acquired, and major structural improvements were begun. Once rehabilitated, the building was rented to organizations and private parties to raise funds, at first to pay for the cost of the improvements, and thereafter, to defray operating costs. In later years new wiring and a new kitchen and bathrooms were installed as a result of a one-thousand-dollar donation by the Kiwanis Club, and manual labor provided by Kiwanis members. The

kitchen equipment was a gift of Kate Macy Ladd. These major improvements were followed in later years by a new roof and heating system and periodic refurbishing.[27]

❧ The Cemeteries

There were several early cemeteries in and near Peapack. According to Snell, there was a burial place on the west side of the road before entering Peapack, "near Watson Allen's property" about 1810, but nothing remained of it by 1881. He also noted that around 1812 there was a burial place on the west side of the road in Upper Peapack "a short distance north of the Reformed Church," that too having disappeared by 1881.

The early village interments were first held on property belonging to the Methodist Church, and later at the Reformed Church. "In 1875 four acres were purchased of Elias Philhower and William Hilliard on an elevated spot in the upper part of the village for a 'union cemetery.' The grounds were handsomely laid out, and many remains were removed from the other burial-places and deposited in the new ground."[28] The charter for Union Cemetery was filed in 1872, and since it is indicated on the 1873 map in the *Atlas of Somerset County*, it seems likely it was the proposed site for the cemetery before 1875.

The cemetery charter reads as follows: "The Peapack Union Cemetery Association is a corporation of the State of

Early cemetery still to be seen on the grounds of the Reformed Church. Photograph by Jan Gordon, October 1990.

Union Cemetery, circa 1910. From the Reverend Paul Walther collection.

The old Jeroleman family cemetery located on the northeast corner of Main Street and Highland Avenue. Victorian home built by James Irving Ludlow circa 1900 in background. Photograph by Jan Gordon, October 1990.

New Jersey, having filed a certificate with the Secretary of State and with the Clerk of Somerset County as of June 18, 1872 under the New Jersey Rural Cemetery Act of March 7, 1851 and amendments thereof."[29]

The Jeroleman Family Cemetery, which stands on the northeast corner of Main Street and Highland Avenue, was a private burial ground for the Jeroleman family who came to Peapack in 1808 and operated the mill across the street.

❦ Notes

1. "January 11, 1838 a meeting was held at the home of Moses Craig, in Peapack and the following trustees were elected: Abraham Wortman, Philip Lawrance, Stephen Rush, David Apgar, Moses Craig, John Jeroleman and Hugh Runyan, Jr. These persons certified that they had taken upon themselves the name of 'Free Christian Society.' A stone church was erected on the west side of Main Street and services were conducted by the Rev. Moses Cummings and Austin Craig and others for a year or two, then discontinued. The building was afterwards used for services by the Baptists for a time, and these also were discontinued." From Rachel Potter, "Historical Facts and Places of Interest in Peapack-Gladstone."
2. *Weekly Exponent*, November 19, 1897.
3. *Peapack and Gladstone Fire Department: Our First Seventy-five Years*, 1905–1980.
4. Ibid.
5. Ibid.
6. Ibid.
7. Ibid.
8. Tiger's Lumberyard was located along the Delaware Lackawanna & Western Railroad tracks, between what is now the Gladstone House parking lot and the Gladstone station.
9. The Tiger Hardware Store occupied what is now known as Conover Corners, opposite Gladstone House.
10. *Peapack and Gladstone Fire Department: Our First Seventy-five Years.*
11. The property was located across from Rudolfo's Ristorante on Lackawanna Avenue.
12. *Peapack and Gladstone Fire Department: Our First Seventy-five Years.*
13. Minutes of First Aid and Rescue Squad of Peapack and Gladstone, 1936.
14. Ibid.
15. Ibid.
16. Copy of the original ordinance, Archives of the Borough of Peapack-Gladstone.
17. *Morristown Daily Record*, November 23, 1968.
18. Deed book 1, vol. 7, p. 391.
19. Deed book R3, p. 357.
20. Deed book, vol. 3, p. 247.
21. Vic Kalman, *Sunday Star-Ledger*, November 14, 1982.
22. The Peapack and Gladstone Woman's Club, *The History of the Peapack and Gladstone Public Library and the Sara Gulick Kay Memorial Building.*
23. Minutes of the Liberty Park Association, June 18, 1919.
24. Ibid., December 9, 1919.
25. Ibid., April 7, 1926.
26. *Bernardsville News*, April 29, 1976.
27. The Peapack and Gladstone Woman's Club, *The History of The Peapack and Gladstone Public Library and The Sara Gulick Kay Memorial Building.*
28. James P. Snell, *History of Hunterdon and Somerset Counties, New Jersey*, p. 724.
29. Peapack Union Cemetery Association, *The Minute Book.*

The Class of 1923, Peapack
Elementary School. From the
Borough Archives.

🕯 *The Schools*

The Peapack-Gladstone Elementary School

*I*n 1980, after nearly 150 years of continuous public school operations, Peapack-Gladstone's only public school closed its doors, and the borough became a non-operating school district. For several years the local school board had researched plans for modernization of the elementary school. Several referendums for remodeling and enlarging the school had been rejected by the voters. Declining enrollment and the high cost of renovating an outdated facility were factors cited by opponents of the referendums. As a result, the Peapack-Gladstone Board of Education entered into an agree-

The Peapack
Elementary School,
circa 1904. From the
T. Leonard Hill
collection.

ment with the Bernardsville Board of Education effective July 1, 1980, under which Bernardsville was to provide education in its facilities for all Peapack-Gladstone public school students.

To honor the old school, the Peapack-Gladstone Board of Education prepared a commemorative sheet for all the students, which featured a drawing by Peter Smith and the following poem by Herta Rosenblatt:

The linden trees are in bloom
again scenting summer;
the windows in the school let in the sun
and the light—always the light—
you celebrate the end of another year
a year of—
learning;
and now you must learn leaving.
Leaving, yet remembering
this place of gathering,
where the two boroughs come together
and the street knows
the bicycle bells and the hellos of friends;
where the stars glitter in the water of the pond
and the swans glide;
where the shouts of skaters ring on winter days
into evening.
High are the ceilings in the classrooms
and the walls gay with book or picture.

The wide hallways know running and whispers;
the gym—oh, the gym—
and the field, the games (who has not played here?)
and celebrations—
bicentennial, first aid, fire company, community gathering;
parades ending here—remember? remember!
And your father and your mother before you
making friends through year after year
of learning and growing together—
Now it is June, again,
time for commencement, the beginning;
of all of you.
Don't forget the rooms of light
where you discovered and mastered
the secrets and delights
of reading, of using your mind—
Keep throwing your ball, high and sure;
keep catching and returning—
aim high—.
Between the park with its pond and your school
is the street,
tree-arched and the sidewalk with its—watch-it-bumps—
your street,
your home street
where again
the linden trees are in bloom.

Public high school students from the twin borough have attended Bernard's High School since 1912. The older students in grades seven through twelve travel between Bernardsville, Peapack, and Gladstone via the Erie Lackawanna Railroad. Their railroad tickets are mailed to them monthly by the borough Board of Education office.

> *"The cry is still they come!" At a meeting of the Board of Education of Peapack-Gladstone it was decided that all high school pupils be sent to Bernardsville this term. The State authorities do not encourage small high schools and therefore this term the new borough will be devoted very much to the pupils for the eighth grade to try and produce high school scholars for the coming years.*[1]

The early school records of Bedminster Township are not available, probably having burned in a fire in the 1800s. Research at the Somerset County and Peapack-Gladstone Borough archives yielded few documented records of early schools. A historical overview of the borough by Rachel Potter (undated and largely based on Snell's *History of Hunterdon and Somerset Counties*, published in 1881) speaks of the first schoolhouse in Peapack as being on Holland Road: "Ellis Tiger attended this school. His father had to pay for his tuition and books."

In 1866 this school was located near the entrance to the stables of Mr. Thomas Kissel.[2] According to Rachel Potter, the children of Upper Peapack attended a one-room school on the site of the C. P. Conover home on Mendham Road, which was closed in 1900. The students were then compelled to attend the Peapack school "much to their displeasure." Snell's *History of Hunterdon and Somerset Counties* includes mention of a schoolhouse that once stood on the site of Union Cemetery, the teachers there being John Herod and Stoffel Logan. Frederick Walter, in *The Township of Bedminster*, states that these two teachers taught at a school in Peapack in the 1820s. Snell further notes that the first blacksmith shop of William Logan, father of Captain John Logan, stood "opposite the schoolhouse, where Robert Layton now lives." The public school in Peapack was originally located on the corner of Broad Street (now Main Street) and Branch Road (now Willow Avenue). That corner is now the site of the public parking lot opposite the post office and commercial buildings. The land was purchased from Nicholas Jeroleman and conveyed to the trustees of the Fourth School District in Bedminster in 1834. In 1855 that land was sold to Abram [sic] Smith. In 1890 the one-room school was moved north about 325 feet across Branch Road to land purchased from the David Apgar farm, where it stands today as the Sarah Kay Memorial Building. At the time of the move, the old school bell was bought by Abram Smith, and was part of a collection of school bells gathered by Mrs. Oscar Smith. A larger room was added for seventh- and eighth-grade students, and an addition was built in 1906 for kindergarten and first-grade children.

The girls' basketball team, Peapack Elementary School, 1904. The names penciled on the back of the photograph do not identify each lady as she appears but read as follows: Elizabeth Gulick (Compton), Ella Mapes (Philhower), Rodenbough, Sarah Gulick (Kay), May Belton (Hill), Ann Tiger (Smith), May Cooper (Kitchen). From the Ruth Thomson collection.

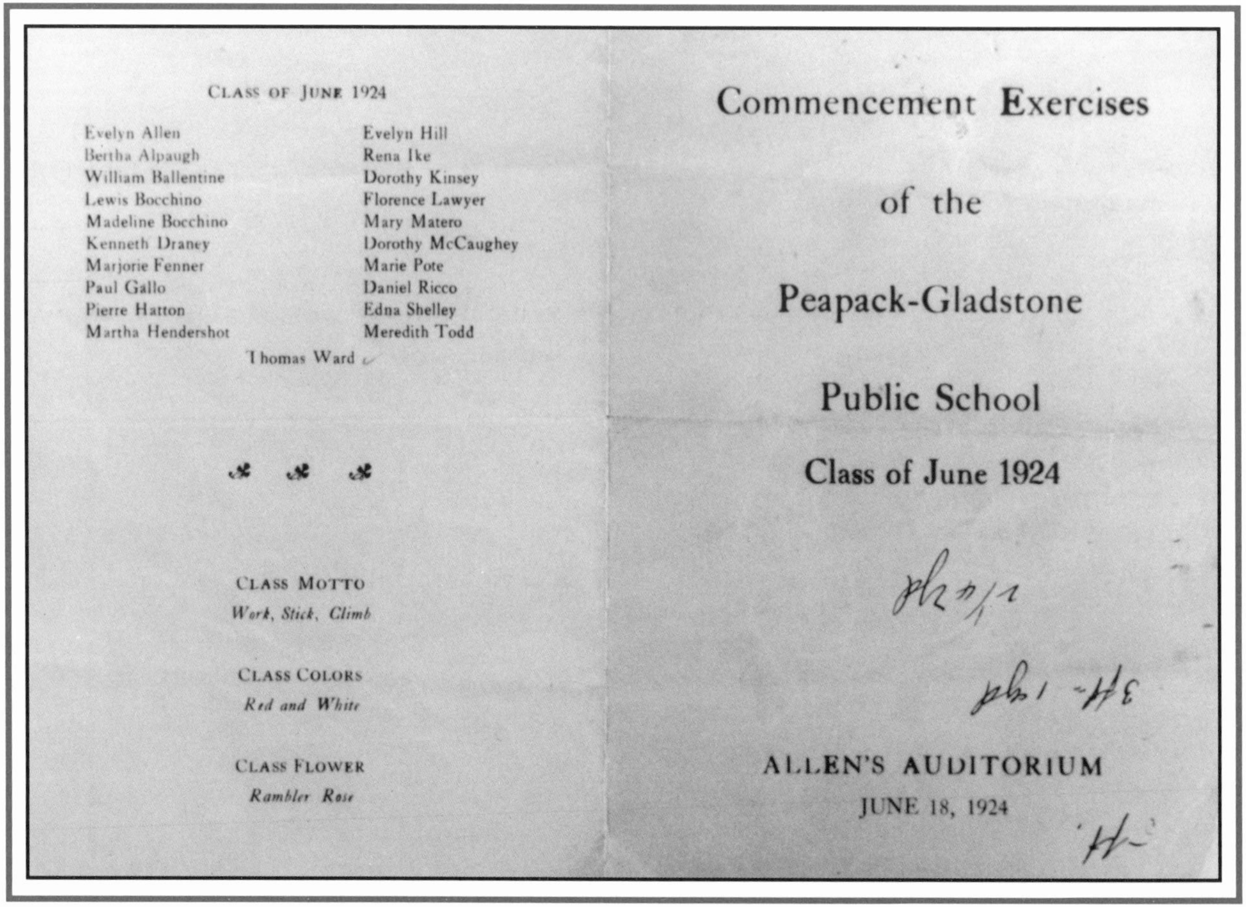

Program for
commencement
exercises of the
Peapack-Gladstone
Public School, Class
of June 1924. From
the Thomas Ward
collection.

CLASS OF JUNE 1924

Evelyn Allen   Evelyn Hill
Bertha Alpaugh   Rena Ike
William Ballentine   Dorothy Kinsey
Lewis Bocchino   Florence Lawyer
Madeline Bocchino   Mary Matero
Kenneth Draney   Dorothy McCaughey
Marjorie Fenner   Marie Pote
Paul Gallo   Daniel Ricco
Pierre Hatton   Edna Shelley
Martha Hendershot   Meredith Todd

Thomas Ward

❀   ❀   ❀

CLASS MOTTO
Work, Stick, Climb

CLASS COLORS
Red and White

CLASS FLOWER
Rambler Rose

Commencement Exercises

of the

Peapack-Gladstone

Public School

Class of June 1924

ALLEN'S AUDITORIUM
JUNE 18, 1924

Ellis Apgar (his father was probably David Apgar, owner of the Apgar farm) was born in Peapack on March 20, 1836. A graduate of Rutgers University, he became the first state superintendent of schools when the State Board of Education was established in 1866. "In this position he was able to influence many changes for the better, in school buildings, furniture, etc. For efficient operation he established the office of Superintendent in each county."[3]

According to Snell, Bedminster Township contained the following school districts in 1867: Pluckemin, Lesser Cross Roads, Union, Peapack, Lamington, Central, Foot of Lane, Larger Cross Roads, Dutchess, Pottersville, and Union Grove. The total number of students attending that year was 633; the county surplus revenue interest $294.73; state appropriation $292.23; township appropriation $1,266; the total $1,852.96.

Snell listed the districts for 1879 as follows:

Peapack	No. 1
Union Grove	No. 2
Bedminster	No. 3
Larger Cross Roads	No. 4
Foot of Lane	No. 5
Pottersville	No. 6
Lamington	No. 7
Pluckemin	No. 8
Burnt Mills	No. 9

The archives of the Somerset County Board of Education include records of teacher certification. Entries that relate to the Peapack Public School include May 31, 1879, Silas N. Gorsuch, Peapack, educated at Michigan University; February 25, 1888, Augustus Ballentine, eighteen years old, educated at Peapack; May 26, 1888, May Woodruff, sixteen years old, educated at Pottersville; and Emma Wingett, eighteen years old, educated at St. Normal.

Financial records for the Peapack School from 1888 to 1890 bear the signature of Oscar Smith, and in 1891 that of A. B. Van Derbeek. The September 15, 1895, issue of the Somerville *Unionist Gazette* reports the Peapack school opened and a Miss Van Zandt and Miss Mamie Moore as the teachers.

The need for a larger schoolhouse in Peapack became evident at the end of the nineteenth century. On March 3, 1898, the *Unionist Gazette* reported that the Board of Education at its yearly meeting would submit a proposition to the voters to build a new schoolhouse in Peapack, the existing one being too small. The measure was defeated by the voters. Somerset County archives include certificates dated 1898, issued to the county superintendent of schools, stipulating the necessary taxes to be raised in the Bedminster school district in the amount of twelve hundred dollars to enlarge the schoolhouse of Peapack. In April 1900 the county superintendent was petitioned for five thousand dollars for a new schoolhouse or nine hundred dollars to build an addition to

The Class of 1969, Peapack
Elementary School. From the
Borough Archives.

the old school. In 1901 the Bedminster school district was authorized to raise two thousand dollars and to use the proceeds of the sale of the old school property to complete the proposed new school building at Peapack, one thousand to be raised by district tax and one thousand to be borrowed and repaid the following year. The new school was completed in 1907. It was substantially remodeled and enlarged in 1950.

In 1902 H. S. Miller was school principal; he was assisted by three teachers: Beatrice Chadwick, Anna Sarson, and Lillian Brown. The 1904 minutes of the Somerset County Teachers' Association found in the county archives recorded the following: "The Annual Meeting of the Somerset County Teachers' Association was held at Peapack, May 21, 1904. The members of the Association journeyed to Peapack in stages, and as the weather was fine, everybody enjoyed the trip very much." Miss Cecilia Hurley, Peapack teacher, presented an exercise dealing with first year numbers. From 1911 to 1912 John White was principal at Peapack, assisted by Beatrice Chadwick, Frances Benjamin, Lillian Brown, Eva Moke, Susan Lehr, and Anna Tiger. The Directory of Somerset County Teachers for the year 1931–1932 listed William S. Twichell, Jr., principal, assisted by eight full-time teachers of grades one through eight and two part-time teachers of music and manual training.

❧ Gill St. Bernard's

St. Bernard's School, founded in 1900, was a product of the imaginative educational concepts of the Reverend Thomas A. Conover. In 1894 Dr. Conover interviewed for the position of pastor of St. Bernard's Episcopal Church in Bernardsville. While there he mentioned to the parish board of trustees his dream of founding a "farm school" similar to St. Paul's School in Concord, New Hampshire, where he had been educated. According to school history, after the board meeting, R. V. Lindabury, one of the parish trustees, promised, "Mr. Conover, if you will take the parish with our ideals of missionary work, I will see that you will get the farm and the buildings for the school."[4]

Reverend Conover did become pastor of the Bernardsville parish in 1899, and, as promised, with the help of Mr. Lindabury, the Henry Hillard farm in Gladstone was rented from the executors of the Hillard estate as a campus for the new "farm school." Mr. Conover and his new wife, Charlotte Green Conover, moved into the old homestead (now called Hillard House) on their wedding day, June 2, 1900.

The school opened in September of that year with nine students enrolled—five boarders and four day students; tuition was one hundred dollars per year. At first Reverend Conover, the only teacher, held classes in the old homestead.

The school's work-study format included a full academic

Children at St. Bernard's Farm School, circa 1915. From the Reverend Paul Walther collection.

program; religious instruction and attendance at church services during the week; and a work skills program which taught farming, housework, and, in winter, carpentry and book printing.

School enrollment increased and expansion followed: Founder's Hall was built in 1909 and included a chapel, classrooms, a study hall, a reception and reading room, and dormitories housing thirty-six boys and one master. In 1925, the Richard V. Lindabury Building was constructed as a memorial to the man who had had such a large part in creating the school. It housed the carpentry and print shops. A Scout Cabin and tennis courts were built by the boys, and a swimming pool, said to have been the first in Somerset County, was constructed on an old building foundation.

The farm flourished under the hands of hired help and the students. By 1935 the farm produced 20,000 gallons of milk, 150 pounds of butter, 500 bushels of oats, 1,000 bushels of corn, 75 tons of hay, 13 tons of straw, 170 dozen eggs, 250 pounds of chicken, and 1,280 pounds of beef and veal; the garden produced 265 bushels of potatoes and 75 bushels of turnips, beets, and other vegetables stored for the winter. In later years, farm inventory expanded to include a herd of registered Guernsey cows (6 cows, 2 calves), three sows, pigs, and one team of horses.

Arthur Page, a graduate of the St. Bernard's class of 1933, recalled life as a student in the Depression years: Students were "required to work two hours a day, for which [they] earned fourteen dollars a month for [their] accounts from which [they] were allowed to draw, and each received a monthly allowance of five to twenty cents depending upon age level."[5]

Mr. Page remembered grooming the horses, milking cows and making butter, doing laundry, and cleaning Founder's Hall or the bungalow. The sports program at the school included basketball, baseball, and football. The social program was limited, but there were two dances a year, the junior and senior proms.

A new chapel, built in 1942, was a gift from Mrs. Charles M. Chapin, in memory of her husband, who was a founder of St. Bernard's School and a trustee for twenty-four years.

Colonial in style, with Greek details, it was designed by F. Burrall Hoffman from New York City. The contractor was John Bodine Co. of Gladstone, and the mason was H. Pantley of Bedminster. The approach to the chapel is replete with special gifts donated in memory of Charles M. Chapin by many Somerset Hills people. Flanking the stone court are apple trees donated by R. Stuyvesant Pierrepont. Inlaid in the bricks between the cornerstone and the door are a stone brought from Nazareth and one from the Island of Jersey. Also inlaid on the west exterior wall is a cross of stones from twelve English schools donated by a Harrow graduate, Denys Cadman, and his sisters. In the tympanum above the door there is a statue of St. Bernard sculpted by Mme. Maryla Lednicka and given in memory of Percy Rivington Pyne, Jr. The chapel interior was filled with treasures, including a stone from the Jordan River and a font from the home of Thomas Arnold, headmaster of the Rugby School. A crucifix, originally in the first chapel in the old homestead, was brought from Oberammergau, and a white altar cloth made by Miss Jane Hall was said to have won the prize for best ecclesiastical embroidery in the centennial of 1876. Many gifts in memory of former students, including a processional cross in memory of Gilbert Dymock, an alumnus who died in World War 1, were donated to the school. The altar and reredos were moved from the old chapel in Founder's Hall. The altar, originally in Trinity Church, Princeton, was given to the school by the rector when the chancel in Princeton was enlarged. The reredos triptych above the altar was designed by R. Clipston Sturgis and carved in Italy by Angelo Lualdi, the reredo painting done by Rachel Richardson, who was also the artist of the murals in Trinity Church, New York City. Today, although no longer a consecrated sanctuary, the beautiful little chapel is favored by many couples for weddings. The altar and reredos are now in St. Luke's Episcopal Church in Peapack, which was also founded by Reverend Conover.[6]

The school continued to grow, and facilities and programs expanded. The gym was built with contributions from the alumni of St. Paul's School in Concord, in memory of "the boys who died in the great war." An addition was completed in 1981, and the building now houses the art gallery and the theater.

The St. Bernard's School Horse Show, a tradition that continues today, was started by Reverend Clayton, headmaster from 1946 to 1953. A dormitory, called Conover Hall, was built in 1950 and today is used for classroom space. The new gym, called the "Hall of Events," dates from 1963. The Chapin Math-Science Buildings were built in 1968, adding a two-story library, four laboratories, and new classrooms, connected by an underground walkway.

In 1971, under Headmasters John Wright, Jr. of the Gill School for girls in Bernardsville and Rev. Henry A. Tilghman of St. Bernard's School, the trustees of the two schools decided to merge the two schools for practical and economic reasons. The schools officially merged July 1, 1972, as Gill St. Bernard's, with John Wright remaining as headmaster and Henry Tilghman as his assistant. The religious affiliation was discontinued, as was the boarding school format. In the seventies a new curriculum and a revised format featuring the Unit Plan, whereby students studied the same subject all day for five weeks, were instituted. In 1979, the Unit Plan was modified, and a format adopted that was traditional for independent high schools.

In May 1986, Christine Gorham was named head of the school. Under her guidance the school has made an effort to revive some of the early traditions: work days have been reinstituted; the gym is known again as the Hall of Events; a peer leadership program has been developed whereby upperclassmen are chosen to act as role models and mentors for younger students; and for the first time in more than twenty years, the chapel bell is rung for weekly all-school assemblies and on Christmas and New Year's eves.

For a list of the heads of school for St. Bernard's and Gill St. Bernard's, see the appendix.

✦ *The Matheny School*

The Matheny School was founded in 1946 by Walter and Marguerite Matheny as a center where their son Chuck, who was born with cerebral palsy, and other children with similar physical disabilities could acquire an education along with needed therapy. Their goal was to help the children develop the self-help skills needed to live as members of their families and communities. The program was therefore planned to be short so that the children could return to their homes following a comprehensive evaluation and intensive therapeutic work.

By virtue of their educational and occupational backgrounds the Mathenys were eminently suited for the circumstances thrust upon them, and they met these challenges in a courageous manner. Walter Matheny had served as a physical training consultant to the air force during World War II. He had been in charge of both British and American cadets in the Advanced Flying Training School in Valdosta, Georgia, and was later transferred to Massachusetts to Army Special Forces to rehabilitate injured service men. Marguerite had been trained as a teacher.

Their primary concern was for their son Chuck, and they searched for a school that would help him reach his full potential. The Mathenys finally heard of a school for cerebral-palsied children in Florida. Since the tuition for the school was $175 a month, an unmanageable sum for them on Walter's first lieutenant's salary, they were forced to borrow the money so that they could enroll Chuck in the school. In later years the Mathenys were proud to state that no child had ever been turned away from their school because of lack of ability to pay. When Chuck was three years old, the school moved from Florida to Long Island, and Marguerite agreed to work at the school. She taught school during the day and acted as a nurse's aide during the evening. It was a strenuous regimen during which she learned first hand the many problems involved in caring for the cerebral-palsied child.

Before long it became clear to the Mathenys that a school of their own would be the ideal way to handle their concerns. Walter's work in rehabilitation was featured in a newspaper, and he was approached by a mother for help in caring for her cerebral-palsied daughter. The daughter, along with a paraplegic woman, moved into the Matheny home to receive daily therapy. After an unsatisfactory term in a California institution for the cerebral palsied, the Mathenys determined that the time had come to start their school. They had moved to New Jersey when the California school opened an eastern branch in Far Hills and Walter was asked to head it. When he determined that the school's goals were inconsistent with their own rehabilitative theories, he severed all ties with the institution and proceeded to found the Matheny School.

Having secured a three-thousand-dollar GI loan, they rented a shabby boardinghouse in Burnt Mills. They placed an ad in *Good Housekeeping Magazine* and, as a result, enrolled their first two students at a fee of fifty dollars each.

All of this happened in December. In January, another student arrived, making, with Chuck, four in all. At this time Walter discussed their situation with Dr. George Deaver, of the Institute for Crippled and Disabled, in New York, who, together with Dr. Rusk, was associated, later, with the Department of Rehabilitation Medicine at the New York University Medical Center. Walter had met Dr. Deaver through his work in the army. Dr. Deaver said, "If you are damned fool enough to start a school for these kids, I'll be damned fool enough to help you." Dr. Deaver was an acknowledged authority in the field of rehabilitation, so this was encouragement of the highest order. Dr. Winthrop Phelps of Baltimore also consented to help. Dr. Phelps had his own clinic in Baltimore and one in Jersey City, New Jersey. Later on, Walter studied with Dr. Phelps in Baltimore. The fact that these two eminent physicians were willing to become involved with such complete newcomers in the field is evidence of two things—the dearth of aid for these unfortunate children and the instinctive trust inspired by the Mathenys.[7]

In those early years the Mathenys managed to persevere in spite of constant financial difficulties. They moved to a larger building in Far Hills and eventually began a search for a large property for their own plant. In 1950, just when the Blair estate in Peapack was being divided for sale, the school received a grant of twenty-five thousand dollars. The palatial house was beyond their means, but they were able to buy a thirty-eight-acre parcel with outbuildings. This property included Blair's stables, the carriage barn, and three brick houses, which had served as living quarters for the employees of the estate. It was the Mathenys' intent to rehabilitate the beautiful old buildings, but John Terry, a local contractor, convinced them that the cost of doing so would be prohibitive, and that they would be better advised to build. In 1954,

acting on Terry's advice, the Mathenys elected to erect a single-story brick structure adjacent to the older building. They moved into one of the brick houses. Another wing of similar construction was added in 1964.

Mr. Terry's involvement was another circumstance in the long list of fortuitous things that happened to the school. Always helpful in situations like this, he had great imagination. He could look at a drawing and visualize the finished product, as most builders can. But, to him, nothing was impossible. And he was infinitely kind. Not only did he tailor his bill to their circumstances—he didn't even present it until much later when he knew they had the money to pay it.[8]

In the early 1950s the school incorporated as a non-profit organization governed by a voluntary board of trustees. Walter Matheny set out to acquire funding from the private sector, a formidable task. He applied to all the foundations that seemed promising, sending them documents and often making presentations.

Walter remembers an appointment with the Trustees of the Kresge Foundation. He told his story. The directors seemed to be listening but gave no indication of sympathy or understanding. At the end of his talk, Walter showed some pictures of the children. One of the directors quickly picked it up and asked Walter to explain it. When told that the children were saying "grace," he said, "Do they do it every day?" When assured that grace was said every day before every meal, the director said, "Let's talk some more." He was a Methodist minister, and three days later a pledge of $25,000.00 came in the mail. The Mathenys *called that their million dollar picture because the boost it gave their morale was worth much more than the actual grant. The picture still hangs in the school.*

The Mathenys' next big boost came from the Marguerite Doane Foundation. And here, again, one senses that manipulation in the wings. They had been given a grant of $10,000.00 from the Foundation. Walter was in Newark on business and, on his way home, decided to stop at Mrs. Doane's house and thank her, in person, for the grant. A secretary answered his ring, told him Mrs. Doane was too ill to see him, but invited him to come in. He told her he wanted to thank Mrs. Doane and tell her how things were progressing. The secretary listened to him with much interest. Finally, she said, "This Foundation has given many grants and this is the first time, ever, that anyone has done anything more than to send a 'thank you' note. You will be hearing from us." At the year's end, a check for $10,000.00 came in the mail and, in January, an additional $25,000.00 was received. Walter again wrote, thanking the Foundation for its help. He told them that their goal still had not been reached but, thanks to the Foundation, they could now start building. By return mail, he had a letter advising him of an additional grant of $50,000.00 to "get the building started." . . .

Later, excitement was added to their days by the Olin Foundation. This group, rather than granting funds, preferred to give complete buildings. One of their grants had been to a small college in Iowa, where keys were handed over to a building equipped to the last desk and chair. Walter had described the school and its needs to three Trustees. Three months later, a member of the Board inspected the school. Walter

had requested a grant of $54,000.00 to build a wing. This wing was already under construction, and the grant was made. Two trustees, Mr. Wynn and Mr. Horn, came out to see the building and said, "Now that you have the building, how are you going to move your children about?" Walter said, "In my car." "If you are foolish enough to start a building with no money to equip it, you must have a lot of faith. We think we'd better help you." And they provided another $35,000.00 for equipment. This would also cover a station wagon for the children.[9]

Approximately eighty children, ranging in age from five to sixteen and exhibiting a variety of physical disabilities, were students at the Matheny School during its first decade. Many of the students were ambulatory with the aid of braces; others were capable of feeding themselves and assisting with their daily personal care needs. Most were able to articulate their needs through some degree of intelligible speech.

The 1970s saw the growth and development of regional centers and mainstream programs where children who had traditionally been served by Matheny could acquire their education and other necessary support services closer to home. Matheny's population shifted to include children with the most severe physical and neurological disabilities. In the latter half of the 1970s a follow-up study was conducted to determine the circumstances of former students. The study concluded that although many of the alumni had done well, many others had returned home to lead passive, nonproductive lives as adults. It was determined that a need existed for a program to aid in the transition between teen and young adult years, for these young people to lead more self-directed lives. The Life/Work program was started as a result.

Between 1979 and 1981, the original carriage house and outbuildings were renovated to accommodate the new program, to house and train up to twenty students at a time. The purpose of the program was to determine and develop the potential for the young adult with severe disabilities to make critical decisions concerning life style and vocational alternatives.

Today, Matheny offers a comprehensive treatment program for children and young adults, providing the following services: occupational therapy; physical therapy; speech and language therapy; music therapy; recreation therapy; rehabilitation engineering; dietary, nursing, and personal care; and a full complement of medical specialties, as well as social and psychological services. While at Matheny, each child receives an accredited educational program according to the sending school district's Individual Education Plan.

Walter Matheny served as executive director from the school's founding in 1946 until 1975, when he retired. Marguerite Matheny, who had been assistant director during that time, assumed the position of acting executive director until a new one could be named. David Sutton was named executive director in 1975, and remained in that position until 1982. Elaine Baumeister followed him as executive director

in 1982. In 1990 Robert Schonhorn was named president of the school.

In 1988 the Matheny School embarked on a major renovation and expansion of its facilities and programs. Plans provide for an upgrade of student housing, including more spacious accommodations and private modern bathroom facilities; renovated therapy, hospital, administrative, clinical, and educational facilities; the replanning of dining, rehabilitation engineering, administration, family center, and day-care center facilities; and the construction of a respite housing facility. Few of these changes are evident on the exterior of the existing facility; the majority involve a reworking of existing interior space.

The directors of the Matheny School have taken a keen interest in preserving the beauty of the magnificent site the school occupies. A concerted effort has been made to keep the character of the original brick structures intact, "recycling" them for new uses as unobtrusively as possible. Important architectural details of the beautiful brick and limestone structures built at the turn of the century have been carefully retained. Arches, masonry walls, herringbone brick floors, glazed tiles are there to remind us of a once-grand era. Future plans include a Founders' Garden and a Trustees' Garden; an atrium; and the relocation of parking facilities to the rear of existing buildings. The Matheny School, sitting on its beautiful hilltop site, is a source of great pride to the community of Peapack-Gladstone. It is appropriate that it looks out on a landscape of magnificent vistas. Such were the visions of Walter and Marguerite Matheny.

❧ *Notes*

1. *Bernardsville News*, September 5, 1912.
2. Peter Ellis Van Doren, *Combined History of the People of Peapack-Gladstone Born before* 1900.
3. Frederick Walter, *The Township of Bedminster*.
4. "The History of Gill/St. Bernard's," a slide presentation, with text; on file in the Gill St. Bernard's School archives.
5. Ibid.
6. Robert C. Conant, '43, "The New Chapel of St. Bernard's School."
7. Madeline Borman, *How Far!*, pp. 13–14.
8. Ibid., pp. 21–22.
9. Ibid., pp. 23–24.

ABRAHAM LINCOLN

"The town did not support Lincoln at first, but after he was elected the residents held a meeting and decided to back the new President. On property that is now [Chatfield's Grill], they raised the American Flag on the tallest pole they could make to show their support."

—J. H. Van Horn, comp., *Historic Somerset*, p. 173

GLADSTONE M. E. CHURCH, PEAPACK-GLADSTONE,

Postcard of Methodist Church, circa 1916. Note automobiles on Jackson Avenue. McKinstry's grocery store, located on the northwest corner of Roxiticus Road and Jackson Avenue, can be seen in the background. From the Harold Chesson collection.

🕯 *The Churches*

Gladstone United Methodist Church

*T*he Gladstone Methodist Church, which celebrated its 150th anniversary in 1988, is our borough's oldest religious institution. In 1837 "Pioneer Preachers" rode a circuit on what was then known as the New Germantown and Somerset Mission. The congregation in this area was a regular stopping point on that circuit. Riders would come to preach every four weeks, often preaching in the home of John Philhower, a farmer who owned most of the land that is now Gladstone.

On March 27, 1838, a meeting was held to found and erect the Methodist Episcopal Church of Peapack. Present at the meeting were James Melick, Robert A. Craig, John Philhower,

Tunis Cole, Philemon D. Lawrence, Peter Rowe, and William Groendyke. The Reverend Abraham Gearhart was named as the first minister.

John Philhower donated the land on which the church stands. His gift was matched by the trustees of the congregation who provided funding for half the cost of a frame building and one hundred dollars. Philhower boarded the mason and the carpenters working on the church in his home free of charge. The building was completed and dedicated on November 11, 1839. A balcony and steeple were added in the late 1850s, and a parsonage was built toward the end of the nineteenth century. The structure was solidly built, and so proven in 1860, when it was raised up to accommodate the digging of a basement, and turned from facing south to face, instead, due west.

As late as 1848, only six families lived in what is now Gladstone. But by the late 1800s church membership rose to 154 when 40 new members joined "on probation." Alas, according to church records, many failed to live up to the strict moral code imposed by the church. "Scandal-mongering, no attendance of divine worship, and no-support of the church" were grounds for expulsion.[1]

In 1899 the Reverend W. S. Coeyman organized the Women's Christian Temperance Union and the Young Men's Christian Temperance Union at the church.

At the beginning of the twentieth century further changes in the church building were made: steam heat and acetylene gas lamps were installed, a new porch was built, and stained-glass windows, many of which were paid for by individual parishioners, were added. One window was donated by the Bodine family.

William Trent Mellick (b. April 1821, d. January 1898), who was married to Rachel Philhower, donated the bell in the church steeple. His obituary in the Somerville *Unionist Gazette* included the following testament: "Each Sabbath morning his voice will still call to the people of this village, 'come, come' by the ringing of the bell."

In 1939, the name of the church was changed from the Methodist Episcopal Church of Peapack to the Gladstone Methodist Church, and in later years changed again to its present name, the United Methodist Church of Gladstone.

In 1955, the church pastor, Rev. William Lufburrow, was featured in *Life Magazine* because in order to

> *"understand the bum as well as the businessman" [Reverend Lufburrow] posed as a homeless person on New York's bowery for three days. The magazine devoted a four-page spread to the pastor, who was shown in photographs resting on the floor of a homeless mission, standing on a bread line and attending a mission revival service with other homeless people on the bowery.[2]*

A later addition to the church was a new building on the grounds for church social activities and for Sunday School classes, built by James B. Thomson, of Peapack.

The church is an ecumenical presence within the community, at no time more so than at the Christmas season, when it presents a beautiful "Live Nativity" each year. Parishioners and their children and farm animals pose in the straw-covered stable, constructed faithfully each year for the occasion. Swarms of people converge on the scene and stand in silence before the tableau. At a given time the crowd departs, and the people sing carols as they make their way to Liberty Park, where they await the lighting of the town Christmas tree, and the arrival of Santa Claus.

As church historians Rebecca Bertz and Barbara Tomlin have phrased it:

> *Many ministers have served the Gladstone church, many projects have been planned and executed, many persons have become members of the church, many weddings, baptisms and funerals have been held. Yet, amid all the changes brought by the passing years, the United Methodist Church of Gladstone remains.*[3]

For a list of the ministers who have served through the years, see the appendix.

❧ The Peapack Reformed Church

The white steeple of the Peapack Reformed Church towers majestically in the landscape as one approaches our borough from a distance. Within the boundaries of Peapack-Gladstone it is an ever-visible presence, an appropriate symbol of the enduring spirit of community embodied by its congregation through the years.

The church had the germ of its beginning in 1738, when a petition to hold religious services in Peapack was presented to the Presbytery of New Brunswick. The petition was apparently disregarded as it went unanswered. Twenty years later, in 1758, a Reformed Church was organized, not at Peapack, but at Bedminster. Peapack belonged to that congregation, a situation that continued until 1844. In that year, owing to the influence of the Reverend George Schenck, pastor at Bedminster, "The Lecture Room" was built on land leased from Shobel Luse for seventy-five years at a cost of ten dollars. It was from that building that the Reformed Church of Peapack was organized on October 31, 1848. It was incorporated November 6, 1848, as the Peapack Protestant Reformed Dutch Church.

> *There were received 31 from the church of Bedminster; four from the Presbyterian Church of Lamington, and one from the Congregational Church at Chester. Jacob Tiger, Peter De Mott, Abraham Cortelyou, and Nicholas Tiger, elders, and Henry H. Wyckoff, James S. Todd, John S. Felmley, and Jacob A. Clawson, deacons, formed the Consistory.*[4]

Within two years the church had acquired a pastor, a building, and a rectory. Land for a graveyard and church was donated by Shobel Luse, and an additional half-acre was bought from Jacob J. Tiger for seventy-five dollars. The cornerstone of the church was laid July 10, 1849, and Rev.

Reformed Church parsonage, circa 1915. From the Reverend Paul Walther collection.

William Anderson was installed as the first pastor on September 9. The church, which was modeled after the First Reformed Church in Irvington, New Jersey, was dedicated on January 15, 1850; the ceremony was attended by many New Jersey church officials. The church cost forty-one hundred dollars to build, the parsonage four hundred.

The first choir organized by the church was led by John B. Demond, who taught singing classes at the Lecture Room. Until the church acquired its first organ, the choir used pitch pipes borrowed from Mr. Demond's singing school. The first organ, willed to the church by "Aunt" Lillian Wikoff, remains in the church today and is used in worship services from time to time.

In February 1872 a plan for enlarging the church was approved by the consistory. Major A. Hudson of Mendham contracted the work at a cost of $4,221.36. The church was reopened on December 5, 1872, but just over a month later, on Sunday morning, January 12, 1873, a disastrous fire struck. The blaze, caused by an overheated smoke pipe too near a piece of timber, was discovered at 3:30 A.M., when it was too far advanced to bring under control. Imagine the dismay of the parishioners, who, upon arriving for Sunday services, found themselves without a church. Their pastor, Rev. Henry P. Thompson, comforted them with words from Deuteronomy 31.6: "Be strong and of good courage," a verse he had selected while the church was in flames.

Plans for a new building were submitted on January 30, 1873. The second church was to be modeled after one at Schooley's Mountain. The church was rebuilt at a cost of fourteen thousand dollars by John Cole, a Mechanicsville contractor, and furnished for four thousand dollars. It was dedicated on January 8, 1874, just under a year after the fire.

Jacob J. Tiger left one thousand dollars in his will to the Reformed Church, the interest on which was to be used each year to help pay the ministers' salaries. (For a list of the congregation's pastors, see the appendix.)

Through the years, as the size of the congregation has increased, the church has undergone a series of organizational and structural changes. A synopsis of some of the important additions and improvements accomplished during the terms served by the church pastors includes (for the precise dates the pastors served, see the appendix):

& Ladies Aid Society organized: Reverend Scarlet

& Organ purchased: Reverend Davis. Missionary Society formed by Mrs. Davis

& Steam heat installed, envelope system of giving instituted: Reverend Hasbrouck

& Individual communion cups purchased, slate roof installed, major interior redecoration, new pews and cushions purchased, chapel planned: Reverend Simonton

& Chapel erected at $7,000, equipped at 1,000, funds donated by Mrs. William H. Horton: Reverend Baeder, who did volunteer war work at Quantico, Va., for six months. During that time the congregation was served by the Methodist Church; Reverend Baeder returned and died of ill health, being the first pastor to die while in service.

⚜ Steeple struck by lightning, damage repaired at $1,200: Reverend Prochnau

⚜ First rectory sold in 1955: Reverend Renskers

⚜ Sanctuary substantially renovated from Victorian Gothic style to Colonial: Reverend Bayer

⚜ Fire in kitchen, area remodeled: Reverend Johnson

⚜ New wing added for an enlarged kitchen, offices, meeting rooms for Sunday School and Youth Group; alterations included to provide barrier-free access; total cost $300,000; dedicated, debt free, in 1985: Rev. Paul Walther

The Reverend Walther was pastor of the Peapack Reformed Church during a time of great change within the community. The congregation from its very beginning has been civic minded and involved. That characteristic endures, although the make-up of the congregation has broadened as the borough has undergone a significant increase in population. The church is a focal point for various community activities, many of which are of an ecumenical nature. The Youth Group has attracted participants from nearly all of the denominations in the area, and the church is a meeting place for Brownies and Scouts. The Willard Arntz scholarship fund was established in memory of a member of the congregation

killed in Vietnam. Recipients are chosen from throughout Somerset County, and need not be members of the Reformed Church at Gladstone to qualify as candidates.

In 1989 the congregation of the Reformed Church at Peapack consisted of 275 adults and children. Active within the church is a variety of organizations and programs, including the senior choir, a youth choir, adult bible and book study, junior and senior high youth groups, evening Discovery Group dealing with timely issues, Sunday School for children, a local mission and outreach, a world mission and outreach, ecumenical services, ecumenical Vacation Bible School, and fellowship opportunities.

From its humble beginnings in the little Lecture Room (which most unfortunately was demolished in the early 1970s) to the imposing edifice that stands at the center of our community today, the history of the Reformed Church of Gladstone is coincidentally a history of the Borough of Peapack and Gladstone. Is it conceivable that the original eight members of the consistory and the thirty-one who made up the congregation in 1844 could have had such great expectations and vision?

⚜ *St. Brigid Roman Catholic Church*

St. Brigid Roman Catholic Church began as a mission to St. Elizabeth Parish, which had been established in Far Hills in

The facade of St. Brigid Catholic Church on Main Street. Photograph by Jan Gordon, October 1990.

1906 through the generosity of Grant B. Schley. In 1923, because of the increasing number of Catholic families in the neighboring towns of Peapack-Gladstone, Bedminster, and Pluckemin, a Sunday mass was initiated and said at Amerman's Hall in Peapack. Rev. Thomas Maher, the pastor of St. Elizabeth at the time, traveled to and from Peapack in his convertible, carrying all the articles necessary to say mass, which included vestments, linens, chalice, and Communion hosts. He was often accompanied by the altar boys who are said to have enjoyed the bumpy ride.

In 1936, when Rev. William Lannary was pastor of St. Elizabeth, it was announced that Mrs. Charles Suydam Cutting, formerly Mrs. Helen McMahon Brady, wished to build a church to honor the memory of her late first husband, James Cox Brady. Brady had been a generous contributor to the Catholic Church, having donated many buildings, including St. Elizabeth School in Bernardsville. F. Burrall Hoffman, from New York City, was selected as the architect for the project, and Joseph Dobbs, Inc., of Bernardsville was named general contractor.

Hoffman's design for St. Brigid took its inspiration from the sixteenth-century stone churches of Ireland. The windows were handcrafted and copied from a detail of one of the famous stained-glass windows in the cathedral of Chartres. Their simplicity of design was intended to ensure that they not detract from the unique mosaics that were to be the focal point of the interior church design.

The architect's plan called for an edifice 103 feet long and 56 feet wide on the exterior, with interior measurements of 68 feet by 35. The exterior was to be built of whitewashed, native fieldstone capped by a dark slate roof, this to be supported by hammer and beam trusses. Stone buttresses were to serve as the overall support system. The plans included a sacristy and vestry with separate approaches on either side of the sanctuary and an assembly hall under the main body of the church. The sanctuary was to have a wooden vaulted ceiling and be separated from the nave by a massive arch. An organ gallery would hang over the interior entrance. The site on Main Street was excavated in 1936, and construction was soon underway.

On a joyful Sunday in December 1936, ceremonies were held in conjunction with the blessing and laying of the cornerstone of the new church. Msgr. William I. McKean, rector of Our Lady of Perpetual Help Parish, Bernardsville, officiated at the ceremonies, which were attended by nearly six hundred people. Mrs. Charles Suydam Cutting and Evander B. Schley were sponsors of the blessing. The cornerstone was placed in position by Fred W. Kampmier, Jr., of Joseph Dobbs, Inc. A wooden cross was blessed and erected on the planned altar site. There was a special blessing of the new church bell donated in memory of Mrs. Helen Parker Jones. Following the ceremonies, Msgr. Edward C. Griffin of St. Mary Church, South Amboy, preached the sermon. Monsignor McKean was assisted during the dual ceremonies by a number of priests.[5]

In the spring of 1937 the mosaic Stations of the Cross were installed and blessed. A year later, on May 22, 1938, a mass was said by Father Lannary to celebrate the blessing and installation of the altar frontal. These wonderful mosaic pieces were created by Elsa Schmid, an artist from Rye, New York, who was born in Germany and had studied in Italy. The colored tesserae used in the designs were procured by her from Vatican City and various other places in Europe. The altar front, which depicts events in the life of St. Brigid, was on display at the Museum of Modern Art in New York from January 1938 until its installation in the church. The pieces were considered unique at the time for the linking of a modern approach to the subject matter of the stations, using the ancient craft of mosaic out of Byzantium. The works have been widely admired for the broad, though subtle, spectrum of colors used, and for the vibrant effect created by the play of light on the varied surface planes used in the delineation of the figures.

The numerous works of art that adorn the church were gifts of the Brady, Griffin, and Clucas families and other members of the parish. It is noteworthy that some of the generous donors were not members of the Roman Catholic faith.

Mrs. Howard Fowler presented the thirteenth-century Byzantine crucifix over the altar. The tabernacle and candlesticks were specially designed to reflect the design of the cross. A fourteenth-century Italian copper gilt and enameled plaque of God the Father was applied to the tabernacle. The sixteenth-century bronze candlesticks were presented by Evander B. Schley.

The frescoes on either side of the altar depict events in the life of St. Brigid. They were executed by artist and critic Jean Charlot. Also donated was a pair of Jacobean chairs which sit at each side of the altar. All of the old beams in the church were presented by Arthur Fowler and Kenneth Schley.

The remarkable pieces of statuary adorning St. Brigid were donated by the friends of Helen McMahon. The sculpture of Our Lady, at the left of the altar, was presented by Mrs. Barney Schley. It is a rare masterpiece of the sixteenth century, believed to have been stolen by Napoleon from Ventimiglia, Italy. On the other side of the altar is the Spanish St. Anthony the Abbot, a seventeenth-century work of polychromed wood presented to Mrs. Cutting by the duke of Alba, the leading duke of Spain. Two works that grace the church vestibule are noteworthy: an exquisitely carved seventeenth-century wooden madonna, presented by Marjorie Dalmien; and an antique polychrome figure, the gift of the late Dowager Countess of Limerick, grandmother of Mrs. Cowperthwaite and Mrs. Anderson Fowler. The late Polish sculptor Maryla Lednicka executed the figure of St. Anthony that stands outside the church. (Rusponi, a Florentine nobleman, was supposed to have posed for the statue.)

Mrs. Rivington Pyne designed and crafted the missal cover displayed on the altar of the Blessed Sacrament. It was a remarkable labor of love, for Mrs. Pyne went to England to learn a special stitch used in the border of the work. She used an emerald and the pearls from one of her own bracelets to form the cross on the cover.

In her reminiscences of St. Brigid, Helen Cutting included the following:

> We received 600 Iris bulbs from Mr. Herman Kinnicutt, a neighbor, Protestant friend now deceased. They alas were washed away in a heavy freshet one year. I have endeavored to plant roses and forsythia and a little dam. It is to be hoped that the Parish will try to keep this superb little church free of commercial ugliness and mediocrity. That is my fervent prayer.

The congregation of St. Brigid has been a vital spiritual body from the early days, when it was a mission church, until the present time in which it functions as a parish associated with St. Elizabeth's of Far Hills.

Through the years parishioners have benefited from the services of a number of pastors and assistants. Rev. George Everitt came to the parish in 1956 and undertook the task of raising funds to build a new school. Ground was broken for the school on March 27, 1960, and St. Brigid Parochial School officially opened on September 7, 1960. Father James Q. Bittner was pastor from 1967 until 1984. During this time declining enrollment, transportation problems, and financial difficulties forced the decision that the school be closed.

A program of total parish religious education was instituted when Father Brembos (now Monsignor Brembos) was assigned to the parish. Together with Sister Christyn Fodor, c.s.s.f., pastoral assistant, he reorganized the elementary and high-school religious program and brought it to the parish center (formerly the Catholic elementary school that had closed in the late 1960s). A large enrollment in the program continues. Adults of the parish participate in special information sessions that include Gospel and Bible studies and those relating to Catholic life. Organizations that are active within the parish include the Art and Restoration Committee, a youth group, a choir, altar boys, prayer groups, the Council for Financial Affairs, the Parish Council of Consultors, the Christian Action Committee, the Education Committee, the Liturgy Committee, the Public Relations Committee, the Social Committee, and the Spiritual Life Committee.

For a list of the pastors of St. Brigid, see the appendix.

❦ St. Luke's Episcopal Church

St. Luke's Episcopal Church has fostered a unique stability within the community of Peapack-Gladstone. The winged ox is the symbol of St. Luke, and it is also an appropriate symbol for the slow and steady growth that typifies the parish and congregation. The landmark, ivy-covered church is remarkable in that it has had just four rectors in its ninety-year history. St. Luke's was founded in 1900 as a mission of St. Bernard's Church, Bernardsville, by that church's rector, the

Reverend Dr. Thomas A. Conover, who appointed the Reverend John Mitchell Harper as first vicar of the Gladstone congregation. The first services were held in a grove of woods owned by the Apgar family. In inclement weather the homes of parishioners or the old schoolhouse served as meeting places. A lot was purchased from the Misses Apgar, and the church cornerstone was laid in July 1904. The first service was held in the new church in October 1904; the building was officially dedicated in January 1905.

Bernardsville, N.J.
March 4th, 1905
Rev. John M. Harper,
Columbus, Indiana

My Dear Mr. Harper:

I write to ask you formally to take up the work as senior curate in our parish, to be in charge of work at Gladstone, Far Hills and the neighborhood. Your salary, as I wrote you, will be $1000.00 a year, $100 more towards keeping of a horse. You would also be provided with a horse, harness, and carriage.

The work is largely missionary in character, and is small to begin with, but I am confident of its rapid and good growth. We are about an hour's ride from New York, situated most beautifully in the hills of northern New Jersey. The climate is excellent and I am sure the life here would be agreable [sic] to you, or to any one loving the country.

May I ask you to let me know, as soon as possible, whether you will accept this work, and try to take it up as soon as possible. I have been without a curate now for a number of months and the work sadly needs your attention.

I think you would be interested with the services at Gladstone and Peapack, which is practically the same village, they being held in a church we have just built, which is called St. Lukes Hall. It is practically a Parish House, with a chapel in it. It is very churchly in appearance and it is so arranged that the Hall can become the nave of the Chapel, by simply opening doors.

There is a debt upon this of $3500., but of course you will be in no way responsible for the debt, except that you, I know will be eager to help me in meeting the running expenses, and doing what we can to reduce the debt.

The Hall is used for basket ball, a gymnasium, library, entertainments, &c. My idea is to make it a center of healthful and educational amusement, for the people of the community in general, and a number of them may be led, I hope, through the Hall, into the Chapel.

I can only say, that if you consider this proposition favorably, that I shall do my best to make you and your wife comfortable and happy in this work. You will find in me, I trust, more of a brother, than a rector.

Your faithful friend,
J. A. Conover [6]

Fortunately, Reverend Harper accepted the offer. When he arrived he found a plain rectangular building with no tower

St. Luke's Rectory and Church, circa 1906. Note carriage houses between the church and rectory for parishioners' vehicles. From the Canon R. J. Morrow collection.

The facade of St. Luke's Episcopal Church. Photograph by Jan Gordon, October 1990.

or chapel. Huge doors screened the nave from the choir and sanctuary. When Reverend Harper became vicar of the church he found "four walls, the roof, and the mortgage!" There was no grass, no finished floors, no church decorations. Local boys could, and did, fish for frogs through knotholes in the floor above a wet basement. After improvements, the nave, which held a stage, served as a multipurpose space for meetings, plays, and bazaars attended by the congregation and the community at large. It was there that the Peapack-Gladstone Library was founded and the Peapack Valley Fire Company first met (see "Community Services" above). There was a basketball court where lively games were played, and in 1908 the *Whitehouse Weekly Review* noted the opening of a bowling alley in St. Luke's basement. An item in a 1913 issue of the *Weekly Exponent* announced that in the evening following St. Luke's Christmas Bazaar there would be dancing to Berrell's Orchestra, gentlemen dancing for fifty cents, ladies for twenty-five.

> *In 1908 the first improvements were made with the installation of hardwood floors and the raising of the Chancel and Choir. Three years later a lot was given in the back of the Church for a Rectory and in 1912 Father Harper gratefully moved his family into their new home. In 1916 the mortgage on the Church was finally paid off and four years later, December 21st, 1920, St. Luke's became a Parish, elected its first Vestry and confirmed Father Harper as its first Rector.*
>
> *It was about this time that the interior began to take on the appearance of a Church. For the next twelve years one permanent improvement was made each year, and as the stained glass windows, the pews, the Altar, the lighting, the pulpit, the paneling and various other articles of Church furniture were put into their permanent place, St. Luke's began to look as we know it today. With the purchase of a new organ—to replace the one some kind soul had LOANED some twenty-five years before—the building of the Tower in 1932, the addition of the Parish House in 1958, which necessitated the removal of the Rectory which had stood behind the Church, and the building of Anne's Chapel in 1965, St. Luke's Church was complete.[7]*

Anne's Chapel and Anne's Garden were erected as a memorial to Mrs. Clarence Dillon. Anne's Garden, designed by James Hazelton, is for children and is entered through the Sunday School rooms and adjoins the chapel. Bilevel in design, it is completely enclosed, with fieldstone walls broken by wrought iron gates. It is paved with bluestone, bordered with flowering shrubs and small trees, and underplanted with pachysandra and spring bulbs. Religious symbolism has been used throughout, and it is a peaceful haven which has been used for several weddings.

The Reverend Harper was a remarkable man, a "town father" in every sense. He was one of the organizers and a charter member of the Peapack Valley Fire Department; a contributor to the founding of the Peapack-Gladstone Public Library; a founding member of the Liberty Park Association; the first president of the Peapack-Gladstone Board of Education; and the organizer, in 1910, of Peapack's first Boy Scout troop. He wrote to the Gladstone family in England to obtain formal permission for use of the name as a town name (see "The Naming of Gladstone" in "The Grand Estates and the Resultant Changes" above). He often entertained friends at musical evenings, where his wife, an accomplished operatic soloist, sang for the guests.

St. Luke's has maintained the community awareness that has characterized its programs throughout the years. In addition to a strong community outreach program, the parish is very involved in ecumenical mission work.

The most recent community effort undertaken by St. Luke's is the innovative senior citizens residence, the Ethel Stantial House, which was conceived and constructed through the dedicated efforts of Cannon Morrow and the congregation. The nine-unit facility, located on Main Street near the church, provides elders of the parish community with convenient low-income housing and has been recognized by the State Council on Affordable Housing as a "unique" development. The plaque on the front of the Ethel Stantial House, named for the long-time church bookkeeper who directed in her will that her house be sold and the proceeds given to St. Luke's, contains the biblical text, Isaiah 32:18, "My people will abide in a peaceful habitation, in secure dwelling, and in quiet resting places."

For the names of the four vicars who have served the congregations of St. Luke's through its ninety years, see the appendix.

❧ Notes

1. *Bernardsville News*, April 14, 1988.
2. Ibid.
3. Ibid.
4. James P. Snell, *History of Hunterdon and Somerset Counties, New Jersey*.
5. *Bernardsville News*, December 17, 1936.
6. Letter from the archives of St. Luke's Church, Gladstone, N.J.
7. *St. Luke's Church (Episcopal) Gladstone, Jersey*, 1900–1975, p. 4.

WARS

"A parishioner, listed in the church records: 'Teets, James (single) killed at Petersburg, Va., July 28, 1864 in his 24th Year.' He was one of several young men who served the Union Army from the parish."—*Bernardsville, News*, April 14, 1988

During World War I local women and girls made quilts and army blankets and knit woolen caps and leg warmers for our soldiers.

"The United States Defense Savings Bonds and Postal Savings Stamps will be placed on sale in the main Post Office at the opening of business today (Thursday) as part of the national effort to make America impregnable."—*Weekly Exponent*, May 1, 1941

Anonymous poem published in the *Somerset Messenger*, November 21, 1872; handwritten in the ledgerbook of Dr. Fred C. Sutphen 189-.

In the town of P——, there lived an old hen
Whose feathers are fine, Still she's despised by all men
This old hen is spotted all over her face,
Though not natural to one of her race,
Yet she's as proud as the original one,
Had she laid a dozen eggs from sun [illegible]
And the people know from near and from far
That she cackles and blows as bad as a steam car

This hen like wolf in sheeps' clothing dressed
Scoffs at all others and disturbs their sweet rest
She intimates that she is all kindness & love,
And one would believe her as meek as a dove.
Yet she's so scornful and full of deceptions
That she deceived a great many by professing redemption
But the people all know, who inhabit the place
That the cackling and blowing is inherited from her race

This old hen, one day, got a new notion
Her nest was well worn and all out of fashion
She resolved to build a new one close by the old,
And being very jealous large stories she told
The new nest was built after a very common style,
Just because she was ignorant, yet she became very rile
But the people all knew, who knew her of old
That she cackles and blows and rejoices to scold

Old speckle is a professor of good works and of fame
But she's a very wicked sinner and bears a hard name
Her appearance is bold, she delights much to boss
She'd frighten you badly, but her talk is all dross
Her position is high, [as] if perched upon a cloud,
That says she has the best nest of any in the crowd
But all the folks know from the eldest one down
That she cackles and blows about everyone in town

Now long years have passed o'er the subject of this story
Yet she thinks herself quite young, in her prime and glory
Some say she's almost sixty, perhaps not quite so old
But her locks are turning grey. The story is true when told
We know it hurts her much, she looks as cheerful as she can
For she possesses much gold and she'd like to get a man
But the people know that like opinions are rare
That she'll cackle, and she'll blow and she'll curse and she'll snarl

Now one thing more is certain, she can simmer down a little
And then have brass enough to mar a kettle,
She can drop her wings too, for her character is plain
She a professor of religion, but she draws [in] backwood rein
An enemy to the poor she would take their last penny
And lay it [in] with hers though they [illegible] number many
We know she's enough in store and she loves a good dinner
But she's a liar and a thief and the truth is not in her

🌿 *Appendix*

Three Prize Essays

In 1932, the Bicentennial Committee of the Borough of Peapack and Gladstone sponsored an essay contest, choosing as its topic "The History of the Peapack Valley from the Original Grant to 1900." There were three awards: a prize of ten dollars for the college group was awarded to Miss Evelyn Hill; the first prize of six dollars for the grammar school grades went to Gladys Smith, and the second grammar school prize of four dollars to Gladys Trebilcock. The essays were judged by the Historical Society of Basking Ridge. They were published in the *Peapack-Gladstone Exponent* in December 1932.

The History of the Peapack Valley from 1700 to 1800

EVELYN HILL

Foreword

The following imaginary diary, which makes up this essay, is used solely as a device. The fictional writer of the diary is a person built up after reading the thrilling and romantically intimate tales of the founding of the Peapack Valley. All allusions to abstract characters and experiences have no factual authenticity.

However, any mention of specific names of places, and all historical facts have been secured from source references, and are true.

My main reference was "The Story of an Old Farm" by Andrew D. Mellick, which book was kindly loaned me by Mr. David Mellick of Peapack.

After reading the tales of this little valley which I have always known as "home," and after picturing the struggle against environment coupled with the "glamorous," eighteenth-century American society, I gasp to think of my proximity to such gripping history which apparently seems to have been left unsung up to this year.

In an attempt to show my keen personal interest in the material I have been able to acquire, I have made use of the diary form which allows unlimited excuse for the personal reaction which cannot be restrained in writing of something so dearly familiar to me.

No attempt has been made to use the contemporary English language of the time due to lack of any worthy source and a lack of the ability to write in that medium if any source were available.

Entries from the Diary of an
Eighteenth-Century American Girl

November 1761

It does seem strange that the family took to reminiscing tonight, for it was just ten years ago today (and I was only ten) that father, along with Johannes Moelick and others, received their portion of land in this beautiful valley. How impossible it all appeared then to turn the wild woodland and old trails that were here in 1751 into the farms and clusters of homes which now make up our little hamlets of Pluckemin, Bedminster, and Peapack.

In England, we were often wont to wonder at the evidences of the old Roman and Norman founders of the island, but how much queerer it is to know that up until 1701, this section was one of the great natural thoroughfares running East and West, and called by those quiet, bronzed men who traversed it—"Peapack Path."

It was amusing, tonight, to notice the tremor of pride in father's voice as he retold the deeding over of this property to our good old Scottish ancestors, John Johnstone and George Willock. Like all land in the New World, it was acquired from royal proprietors this piece being deeded "on the seventeenth day of June, in the thirteenth year of the reign of William, the Third, over England, Scotland, France, and Ireland, King etc., Annoque Dom. 1701."

As shrewdly economic and morally brave as these good Scotsmen were, they never ventured farther than Perth Amboy to settle, and so it was when the Peapack Grant was broken up into small grants by the families of these two men, that we few, who desired small, permanent settlements, ventured into this beautiful, but wild section.

As proud as the two Scotch squires must have been of their "Peapack Patent," which I read in the records, "embraced nearly the entire township of Bedminster, and extended from below Pluckemin to somewhere near the Morris county line, and from the north branch of the Raritan on the east to the Lamington river on the west," and that it included, "surveys number 59, 62, 88, 120, 122, and those marked Daniel Axtell, and Doctor Johnstone Lewis and Mary Johnstone, as laid down on the map accompanying schedule III.," they could not have been one mite prouder than we were when we started our first home in America which we could call our own.

It makes me shiver now to think of the cold nights spent in our log cabin with its thatched roof, and cock-loft above— a primitive cabin, which like many others scattered along the trails and tracks of this newly opened country sufficed as homes until our more permanent stone homes could be built.

As hard and cold as that first winter was, it gives me a feeling of pride now to look at stones in the walls or beams in the ceilings and know that I helped dress them so that they were ready that next spring to start the new home.

What fun we children had—thrilled with curiosity and shivery with expectation—when the "redemptioner" came to help father build in the spring. This feeling, I remember, soon turned to one of respect—for although he was, like the rest of the "redemptioners," working off the price of his passage to America and his debts which were the cause of his being brought to America as more or less of a slave—he was of that sturdy, hard working type which is bound to prosper when given a chance. Only yesterday I recall hearing father say that this very man had bought a tract of land, and was a prosperous farmer of our own middle class. This experience, so typical of so many other redemptioners, seems to me to be a proof of the strength of the New World with its virile ruggedness to show up the true worth of a man.

I truly believe, however, that although the redemptioner was only a helper, he was every bit as proud of our growing home as we were. Even to our childish eyes, I can remember how inviting the double Dutch door in the front of the house seemed to us with its complicated lock which came from our old home across the Atlantic.

Parts of the house have lost their interest for me with my growing familiarity with them—but not so two spots. They are the hill in the back and the deep chimney fireplace. Perhaps it is because of the friendly jealousy existent over these two features which are part of every settler's home. I can recall father pondering long and seriously over the location of our home—it must be on the south side of a hill, . . . [illegible] the cold . . . [illegible] winds could be shut off, and it was a keen experience to choose the loveliest souther [*sic*] exposure in this country of rolling hills.

Of no less importance to my young mind, nor has it lost any of its flavor now, was the fireplace. There is such strength and simplicity in this spot which is the heart of our home, with its great crane swinging out over the flames from the hickory boughs.

As I sit by the fireplace now with the fire no more than glowing embers, and look out of the tiny window which is one of the few in the whole house (mother feared a window tax like that in the old country and demonstrated against larger ones or more of them). I can feel only happiness and contentment in this countryside which hints so much of Devon country in England and which is to be my home forever. It has meant hardships on all our parts to create a home from a wilderness, but our joy in this simple, fine life is a hundred fold reimbursement.

April 1762

So tired tonight but so thrilled! Two days ago father and I left for Amboy for the mail. It is a joy to know that now that spring is here our mails will be received at least once a week instead of every two or three as in those long winters months. It was a lovely ride through the broad pathway hemmed in by trees, and our horses seemed to sense our excitement as they carried us on their backs through the dew drenched country side past our neighbor's farms to our first stop—Pluckemin. I love the excitement of pulling up to the "Barracks," Christian Eoff's tavern. Father told me that it was a rare party from New York or Philadelphia en route to the famous water place—Schooley's Mountain—which does not stop over night at the "Barracks."[1] It was for this reason that I looked with such awe at those handsome, aristocratic coaches with the family arms emblazoned on their panels drawn up to the tavern in such glory by four or six horses. It was with not a little resentment that I acquiesced to father's insistence that we must "start on" and leave behind the excitement and bustle of the tavern.

Our trip from Pluckemin to New Brunswick was far from boring, however, for all along the shadow speckled way, we caught glimpses of bears, deer, and saw evidences of foxes and wolves. It is little wonder that the province offers from ten to sixty shilling for the capture of those sly beasts. It is well worth it!

I know that father grew impatient with my unrestrained eagerness to get to the "Great Raritan Road." But after the quiet of a winter on the farm, a day's travel on this great colonial thoroughfare, which has been in use since 1700, is a treat to be coveted. We followed this immensely interesting route into New Brunswick at which place I was more than ready for the dinner that awaited us at [the] tavern on Water Street.

The last lap of our journey was even more enticing to me than the first, for it lay along the most famous of all routes—"The King's Highway." My mind, which is so full of the revolutions of youth (so father says), does revolt most emphatically at the name of this thoroughfare. Its existence cannot be accredited to any white man. Instead, its first faint imprints were made by the impress of the moccasined feet of the Lenni-Lenape on their way to the Delaware River. I kept my silence to father as to my views on the naming of the highway which took us so quickly out to the shore panorama of Amboy with its sea-shore, bays, and rivers.

It was good to spend the night in Amboy and talk with acquaintances of trading, commerce, and discuss the news brought in by the mails from the Old Country—subjects which grew remote today we rode homeward where time and conversation were taken up with the problems of farming and stock preservation.

May 1762

All troubles seem to fall on one day, and today has been one of those days. To start the day with the feeling of dogged determination to the end—it was wash day! Brother and I built a roaring fire along side the wash house—on the bank of the brook—and suspended the heavy iron pot over it for boiling the clothes. With the late work in the fields and the plowing, most of the clothes had to be put in the pounding barrel and thumped and pounded, until all the dirt was eliminated.

A morning taken up with such labor was not a happy setting for father's news that the crops were not doing so well this year, and that Doctor John Reeves of this county (Somerset) believed it was due to the continual planting of one crop in one field, and he has already sent all the way to a quarry on the Delaware for some lime to enrich the soil. Not only was father discouraged by this news, but his bad luck turned on him in the form of a broken plow, and he and brother had to make a new one before any of the later plowing could be started.

There . . . [illegible] the day, and that was the fresh . . . [illegible] we had tonight. Our neighboring farmer slaughtered a "critter," and the fresh meat was a real treat after a winter of the hams, bacon, and smoked meats. Although my lips still pursed at the thought of those hams cured over the fragrant smoke of burning hickory and oak which gave them that rich, nutty flavor so delicious with beer, cider, or Jamaican rum—father's favorite drinks.

After we ruminated from one subject to another over our repast and beer, none of us was loathe to climb upstairs to those red cedar four posters that brother and father have just finished, and which mother has stuffed thick and high with feather-beds. I feel especially proud of mine, and with its valances of dimity to the floor, it looks particularly inviting to my sleepy eyes as I say "Good night."

October 1763

Tonight was one of the gayest nights the valley has seen. We held a husking bee and killing frolic—all in one too! The men were here at the house early in the morning, and spent the entire day hog-killing. Although this is a usual custom among the neighboring farmers in Bedminster and Pluckemin, it is the first time father has ever held one here. Tonight, all the women came for the husking bee and frolic.

After all the ears were husked, the dancing began, and I can assert with no shyness that my head and feet are still awhirl. Beside having the excitement of the "frolic," everyone was astir over the two new projects in the vicinity this year.

There were some very knowing accusations and "I told you sos" over the "Hogback Folly." Although William Allen was the first one to establish a mill in Bedminster township, his family could not retain the honor. Many persons now travel the road over the spine of the Hogback to see the aqueduct and reservoir which Mr. Allen's family built in order to put more power into their mill, and which, according to "neighborly gossip" of the well-meaning [illegible] is

most certainly only a folly, and will put the Allen family to ruin.

There was too much excitement about the new church, however, to keep speculating the success or failure of the Hogback proposition. Everyone felt a glowing pride and satisfaction in the new edifice which had only recently been completed. There had been considerable discussion over its location, both Mr. Sutphen and Mr. Vander Veer had personal opinions on the subject. Mr. Vander Veer's choice was final, however, and the church was erected in Bedminster just below the Lesser Cross Roads.

I heard whispering that Mr. Vander Veer donated the two acres of land, fifty pounds sterling and one-third of all the oak timber. But others say he was not alone in this privilege, for Mr. Sutphen gave the same amount of money and one-half of all the timber for the frames.

Despite all the gaiety of the evening, I could not help but notice a catch in many voices as they thought of the solemn, inspiring services in the lovely Old World cathedrals compared to the simple, yet no less sincere meetings we now hold in the prosaic, bleak little church. But I know that every man who was here tonight learned to love this whole vicinity which has become our home.

October 1776

I can't realize whether it is a dream or a bad reality that we must all prepare for war. All the dissension and uneasiness about the Revenues and Stamp Act seem so remote, and loyalty toward England remained as much a natural feeling as ever in our neighborhood until recently.

Even then I could believe that it was only the unrest of a few agitators.

But the stark reality came upon hearing this morning when Mr. Hunt, the owner of the mills near Schomp's and the Hogback, announced that he had been promoted Lieutenant Colonel Stephen Hunt to command the first Somerset Battalion.

Before we had time to recover from this shock, brother came running in with the news that all citizens between the ages of sixteen and fifty must enroll themselves into militia companies that the several committees of safety were directed to form. There was a tremor in the excitement with which brother went about furnishing himself with the required weapons which are to be a "good musket or firelock, and bayonet, sword, and tomahawk, a steel ramrod, worm, priming wire and brush fitted thereto, a cartridge-box to contain twenty-three rounds of cartridge, twelve flints, and a knapsack."

It is all so nerve wracking, so cruel to think of the quiet, happy life which has only just begun in this country to be broken up by the harsh commands and iron sounds of war. We can only hope and pray that Jersey might be spared any of the real fighting.

December 1776

We are now a captured province! Howe and Cornwallis did manage to force Washington to retreat across the Delaware and leave New Jersey at the mercy of the British—and what little mercy they have shown. Although Somerset lays far north of the actual British cantonments in Trenton and New Brunswick, we have not escaped the miseries inflicted by the enemy.

Father just returned from Pluckemin with the sickening tales of the actions of a squadron of British cavalry, who in their attempt to secure Captain Van Arsdale, grossly insulted some of the women, robbed homes, and even went so far as to batter down the doors, break up the pews, and hack the pulpit of the Lutheran church.

We have not finished discussing the atrociousness of these acts when we receive word from a passing neighbor that Elias Vander Veer, the spirited patriot in Bedminster, had been carried off as a prisoner to Trenton.

We know now that this is the time to stand by the principles of the colonies and not allow these discouragements to make us swerve to the easier task of turning Tory in our sympathies. Let us hope it will all end soon.

I could not wait to enter this exciting bit of news in my diary right away tonight while I remember every detail. The bitter cold could not stop us all from walking over to Peter

Mellick's land in Bedminster to view by moonlight the cannon and baggage wagons, horses, campfires, and the tired, sorry looking soldiers of Gen. Charles Lee's army which is encamped there for tonight. As strange a sight as this seems tonight, if the war continues, it will become a beaten path for soldiers going from Morristown to Trenton.

January 5, 1777

The thrill, the honor, and the glory of war reached me today as never before. At news of Washington's being encamped on the Pluckemin hillside last night on his march from Princeton to Morristown, we all arose at break of day this morning, and with friends from Peapack, Bedminster and Lamington made our way to Eoff's Tavern in Pluckemin where there was much confusion and excitement. Many of us lost no time in peeking in at the gloomy British soldiers who were held prisoners in the Lutheran church which they not so long ago insulted.

But as interesting as all these sights were none caught us so much in its grip as did the face of the great commander-in-chief as he walked with his knightly attitude of lofty, yet kindly courtesy and the calm reflective tranquility of conscious power. His spirit seemed to prevail at the affair of ceremony which was held this afternoon.

"At the beat of muffled drum, and the wail of fife, the men presented arms as the corpse of the British soldier Captain Leslie was given military burial." The escort reversed arms and breaking into columns of four marched in slow time and solemn steps to the graveyard in the Lutheran churchyard where they laid the body of the twenty-six-year-old soldier to its last honored rest. Few will forget his bravery at Princeton. And I am thinking now, how typical of our Washington to pay "due respect to bravery, tho' in an enemy."

Although this great leader will leave Somerset county tomorrow to take up winter quarters in Morristown, many soldiers assured us that there would be much use made of the hospitality of all our homes during these next few months by soldiers traveling between Morristown and Trenton.

February 1779

Not since long before the war began has Pluckemin seen such a sight as it saw last night (the twenty-eighth) when General Knox, who has had his company quartered here all winter in training, held the grand fete and Ball on the first anniversary of the French alliance.

We all went in to see the commander-in-chief who, with his escort and staff, rode on the parade at three o'clock, followed by Mrs. Washington.

It was a gay scene for staid Pluckemin—all the scarlet coats, satin short-clothes, and striped waistcoats, gleamed as their wearers stepped to the graceful and stately steps of the minuet.

General Knox said of it himself this, "We had a most genteel entertainment—everybody allows it to be the first of its kind ever exhibited in this state at least, we had about seventy—all of the first 'Ton' in the state—we danced all night—between 300 and 400 gentlemen—an elegant room—the illuminating fireworks, etc. were more than pretty."

As devastating as the ministers of the Bedminster and Pluckemin churches feel the war has been to the churches, all these spectacles make life enticing in these small villages, and only a few less families are going to be seen each Sunday noon on the church grounds eating their lunches before going in for the afternoon sermon.

The war has changed few of our regular habits, but it is a thrilling adventure.

April 1789

Eight years have passed since Cornwallis' surrender in Yorktown, but it is only this spring that our little farms and villages have begun to take on a habitual, peaceful, prosperous time.

There was the dissension and indignities suffered by both Tory and Whig, there was loss of loved ones who would never return to help heal the ravages of the war both in the fields and homes. There has been little sign of any financial prosperity in this section until John Malick set up the first Inn in Bedminster township—at the corner of the Lamington and Peapack roads.

It was in this tavern today—so popular because of the tales of the farmers who were buying slaves, and that they were especially used at the tannery in Bedminster. This set father

to thinking that he must have some for it is becoming a worthy custom.

As rapidly as this custom is coming into favor, so is another going out. There had been much talk, and father said many strong opinions were expressed today on the advisability of some Temperance reforms. I cannot understand, however, how the government could ever regulate a man's personal production of beer and rum.

There seemed to be much of the old semblance of neighborly happiness and contentment tonight as we sat around the fireplace discussing these questions, and we all felt that this spring had ushered in a new regime of a "joy in just living." And how can we help ourselves after taking one look at the glorious beauty which surrounds us in these hills that have always been, and always will be full of a natural loveliness that is typical of the Somerset Hills.

The History of the Peapack Valley from the Original Grant to 1900

GLADYS SMITH

The native Indians sold a very large tract of land in 1708 to a company of people for Peter Sommons, who was one of the proprietors and agents to the rest of the proprietors of this division of New Jersey. This tract conveyed by the Indians was bounded by lines from Popatcong to an Indian town called Pepock, thence to Elizabethtowne, thence to a point on the

Whippany River and thence again to Hopatcong. Morristown was situated in the center of this large tract. The original deed which is still carefully preserved by J. S. McMasters of Jersey City states that the Indians received for this tract thirty pounds in cash, ten strand water blankets, fifteen kettles, twenty axes, twenty hoes, ten duffel blankets, half a barrel of wine, one barrel of rum, two barrels of cider, three . . . [four lines are illegible here] colarette of powder, ten white blankets, twenty shirts, and one hundred knives. This rare and valuable deed contains all the Indians' names and their marks which are very queer looking.

My great-great-aunt Rachel Melick told that a tribe of Indians used to live along the stream which we know as Van Derbeek's meadow and now owned by St. Bernard's School. The Chief's name was Paul. When he died they buried him on top of the high hill near Rocksiticus. A pine tree was planted to mark his grave. This spot can be seen for miles around and is now owned by Mr. Owen Winston who named his estate "Mt. Paul Farms."

Among the early colonists was a man named George Willock. He was much respected and bought up large tracts of land from the proprietors in Middlesex, Monmouth, Hunterdon, Bergen and Somerset Counties. Among the bodies of land he acquired was one lying in Somerset County known as the Peapack Patent. It is evident this Peapack Patent embraced within its boundaries nearly the entire township of Bedminster and extended below Pluckemin and from the North branch of the Raritan River to the east to the Lamington River to the west.

Peapack is supposed to be an Indian name. It was spelled Pepock in the deed of 1708. There was an Indian thoroughfare which ran from east to west through northern New Jersey, crossing the Lamington River at its falls called the "Peapack Path" and was frequently mentioned as the boundary of early grants.

The New Jersey Historical Society's map of George Leslie's grant made in 1751 by Samuel Willmot shows that a grist mill and a saw mill were standing on the west side of Peapack Brook. There is little doubt that these mills were erected by William Allen. He died in 1761 and the new owner soon found that Peapack Brook did not have enough water for the mill wheels so they decided to divert the water from the North Branch of the Raritan. Peapack or Lawrence Brook, about one quarter of a mile above its mouth, runs parallel with and some three hundred feet distant from this branch. These streams are separated by a long narrow hill known as "Hogback." The highway used to climb this ridge and run along its spine, instead of following the bank of the larger stream as it now does. At this point a dam was built which created a reservoir. The hill was then tunnelled and a considerable quantity of water was led into the smaller stream to serve the mills below. This piece of work has always been known as "Hunt's Folly" as it was built by Stephen Hunt, a

Colonel in the Revolutionary Army. Mr. Walter G. Ladd now owns this land.

Across the brook from the mill stood the eighteen tan vats and great piles of drying hides and sacks of ground oak bark, for this was the site of the earliest tanneries in America. It was owned by the Moelick (Melick) family who had been tanners in Germany. Johannes Melick had selected this spot for his new home. He purchased the land from George Leslie. In 1751 he built a stone house which is still standing and is now owned and occupied by a Mr. Willets. In the "Story of an Old Farm" it says the tannery developed into one of the most important industries of that character in the province. A large frame structure was erected adjoining the house, in which the leather was curried, both negroes and whites aided in the work and in grinding the bark.

The little stone house at the Walter Ladd Estate entrance at "Hogback" was once a stopping place for the stage coaches.

During the first years of life on the farm there was much beside clearing the land and tillage. Gun and worm fences were built, great barns and mows erected. Orchards were set out and water power improved. Mills were built. Gardens were planted. The vegetables were potatoes, cabbage, beans and Indian corn. The tables were well supplied with ham, bacon, and smoked meats. Wild animals were killed when needed.

The best of Bedminster lands were considered worth $1.56 per acre in 1726.

There was a great deal of limestone in Peapack. This was used for burning into quicklime and has been an active industry.

The Presbyterian Church at Lamington was organized in 1740. People from Peapack, Lebanon, Readington and the surrounding country worshipped there. In 1756 St. Paul's Church at Pluckemin was built. It was used as a prison for British soldiers captured at Princeton. A young officer by the name of Hon. Captain William Leslie is buried in the cemetery adjoining the Church. The inscription on his monument states that he fell at the battle of Princeton on January 3, 1777.

Squire McEown, a Pluckemin merchant, was a commissary for the army. He bought and delivered flour on a large wagon drawn by four yoke of oxen. This was conveyed to Morristown and other places where Washington was . . . [several lines are illegible here].

My great-grandfather John Opdyke had a list of the names for this vicinity of the reserved militia for the Civil War. He said many of the farmers could not leave their families but paid men to go to war as their substitutes.

Jacobus Van Derveer gave the land for a Dutch Reformed Church at Bedminster in 1758. The people of Bedminster and Peapack were pleased to have a church so much nearer than Lamington and Pluckemin.

The Methodist Episcopal Church of Peapack was built in

1839. The land was donated by John Philhower. Later more land was purchased and a parsonage erected.

On July 10, 1849, the cornerstone of the Peapack Dutch Reformed Church was laid. My great-grandfather Jacob Tiger was one of the first elders. This church burned in 1873 but was promptly rebuilt. Rev. William Anderson was the first pastor and served until 1856. Rev. Charles Anderson, a later pastor, edited a quarterly newspaper called "The Pastorial" in 1875. This paper gave news, births and deaths of the people.

Among the early settlers of Peapack we find the names of Aaron and John Van Doren. They established an industry known as "Van Dorn's Mills." In 1832 William Van Dorn introduced and operated the first threshing machine in Bedminster. The Van Dorens also operated a distillery and general store. Across the road was a blacksmith shop. The Masonic Lodge held secret meetings in the upper room.

My great-great-grandfather Zachariah Smith built a log cabin about the year 1800 on the Raritan River, a mile east of Peapack. Shortly thereafter he built the house where my father was born and the famous "Smith Family Reunion" was held. This farm is now owned by Mr. A. Turnbull.

Daniel Jeroleman conducted a feed mill in 1808. This mill was situated where the Hagan farm now is. A mill race carried water along the main street of the village to run this mill.

The early school records were destroyed but according to some old inhabitants Pluckemin had a school in 1810. The teachers wore gowns and wielded the birch with vigor. In 1818 a school was conducted opposite the Bedminster Church. My grandfather Ellis Tiger attended a school in 1866 on Holland Road at the entrance to Mr. Thorne Kissel's stables. Later he attended school on the main street opposite where the drug store now stands. This school was moved to where the Junior Order Hall now is.

A wheelwright shop stood where Amerman's Auditorium now stands and a blacksmith shop adjoined. A short distance below Mr. Theodore Allen conducted a general store for many years.

The Rockaway Valley Railroad ran from Whitehouse to Upper Peapack. Later this road was continued to within a short distance of Morristown. It was called "The Rock-a-bye-baby," as the tracks were not level and the train rocked to and fro.

In 1890 after much discussion and through the influence of Mr. G. B. Schley, the Delaware Lackawanna Railroad continued its line from Bernardsville to Peapack. It was then found necessary to have two post offices. Mr. William Hillard selected the name of Gladstone for the upper end of the village. Evidently this did not meet with the approval of everyone. Mr. L. Van Dorn wanted to send the first telegram but when he found he had to address it "Gladstone" he tore up the telegram and would not send any.

Mr. John Stevens drove a stage and carried the mail between Peapack and Somerville for many years.

About the year 1898 construction was begun on the building of Ravine Lake. Foreign labor was brought in to help with this work. Mr. C. L. Blair bought the choice farms of Dr. Perry, Morris Crater, Bartine Melick and I. Philhower and began the erection of his beautiful summer home.

At about this time some of the village people had steam heat and telephones installed in their homes.

The History of the Peapack Valley from the Original Grant to 1900

GLADYS TREBILCOCK

In 1701, just thirty-seven years after the state of New Jersey was settled, a grant was given to John Johnston and George Willocks, which was known as the "Peapack Patent."

There were also some Indians who claimed title to the land, and they conveyed whatever title they possessed by a conveyance dated October 29, 1701 to Johnston and Willocks; so it may be said that a very complete and honest title was obtained.

The "Patent," as printed and copied from original grant, was published by the *Somerset County Historical Quarterly* in October, 1915, and an exact copy of same follows: . . .[see "The Peapack Patent" in "Early History" above].

It might be better understood if I should tell what this grant took in by using the names we have today. The lines ran along the Morris County line on the North, Bernardsville on the East, Pluckemin on the South and Lamington on the west.

I am sure that our own towns of Peapack and Gladstone are of more interest to us than the history of the entire grant.

While I was gathering material for this essay, I visited Mr. John D. Conroy of Union Grove, who is seventy-five years old and has a wonderful memory. He told me a great many things of interest as they were told to him by his grandfather who died sixty years ago at the age of ninety-two. Among his stories were the names of the former owners of properties around our own town.

The first school ever built in Peapack was built on the corner directly opposite our A and P market. The next one at the head of Long Lane, next on the Holland Road just beyond Mr. Johnson's drive. The farmers around what is now Union Grove School, cut lumber and hauled it together and built the Union Grove school in 1861.

The name of Jerolaman seems to be about the oldest familiar name that I could learn much about. Nearly two hundred years ago, a man named Nicholas Jerolaman bought a piece of land running from Mr. Gambrill's residence down what is now Main Street over to Mr. Johnson's new home, this included our mayor's home and the Essex Hunt Club.

The old house opposite Blairsden entrance is the oldest house Mr. Conroy has any record of and it was the Jerolamen homestead.

About this same time, a Mr. Arrowsmith bought the section running from the former Mosle estate, just east of the Jerolamen property, down to Maple Cottage. The house is now occupied by Mr. Korzdorfer.

A short time before the Revolutionary War, a man named Jacob Tiger bought the property that is now Vernon Tiger's farm. Mr. Tiger had eight sons, one being Captain John Tiger of the Revolutionary forces, who later served in the war of 1812, with his father, a civil soldier being under his command.

There are a great many direct descendants of Jacob Tiger still living in the Peapack Borough.

The road leading from Gladstone to Pottersville was an old Indian trail which they used as a direct route from Pennsylvania to Long Island. The present road follows the old road, so I think that is why it is so winding and crooked.

The stone cupola that stands along the new highway on the Hamilton Farm, was built about 1785 by an Englishman named Thomas Barker.

It seems that what is now Hamilton Farms has always been quite a show place. Ninety years ago this property was owned by Madame Tenairs, a French lady who was the owner of a circus and kept this farm for its winter home and training quarters.

The house now owned by George Bowers was built by Shuble Lewis about 1780. Mr. Lewis was a trader and hauled lime from the Peapack lime kil[n] to New Brunswick and traded it for groceries and brought them back and sold them to the people around here.

In 1755, a Mr. William Van Doorn from Van Doornville, Holland, settled on the property now known as the William Vanderbeek corner. Mr. Van Doorn built the house of which the original foundation is still used, and had a store there, and just across the street was a saw mill and grist mill. The long brown house now owned by Mr. Boschi was a school house about one hundred years ago.

In the year 1828 the old stone building known as "Lewis Little's blacksmith shop" was built and used as a tailor shop until 1848 when the "Free Masons" bought it and held their meetings there until 1855, and since that time it has been owned by the Voorhees family and used as a blacksmith shop.

The stone bridge over the brook by the old blacksmith shop was built in 1829 by John Philhower who a few years later gave the property for the Methodist Church to be built on.

The church was built in 1839 and remodeled in 1859. The cemetery was just back of the church, but in 1872 when the

Peapack Union Cemetery was started, the bodies were moved and taken to the new cemetery.

Peapack being a very long narrow town was divided into two towns, the northern half being called Gladstone after the English Statesman William Ewart Gladstone.

The first postoffice in upper Peapack (or Gladstone) was in an upstairs room in the house now occupied by the Trebilcock family.

In 1890 the first railroad came in here. It was the D.L. &W., and the next year the Rockaway Valley came through.

In a small book I have, being loaned to me by Mrs. Susan Blazure, a very funny chapter is written about the "Rock-a-bye" as it was called. It follows:

> *We are also favored with another railroad concerning which travelers say, "there is nothing like it." The original owners of the road believed in doing things quickly and accordingly laid the rails without grading. We therefore have the pleasure of rising to Alpine Heights and viewing the surrounding country, and then taking a toboggan slide to the valley below. A more accommodating road is not to be found for people can signal the engineer from yonder orchard, and the wide awake engineer who scans the fields and meadows and mountain summits is certain to pass no one by.*

Mr. Conroy has at his home a number of ledgers owned by Henry Kennedy who ran a country store in the stone house on the Parish Estate. Some of the entries and orders are very funny. One order was, 1 lb. tea, 3 lbs. candles, 1 Gallon molasses, 1 qt. whiskey. A Dutch Reformed Church was built in Peapack in 1849—burned down in 1873 and rebuilt in 1873.

A great many of the old names are still heard today, such as Smith, Honeyman, Van Dyke, Wortman, Jerolamen, Melick, Tiger, Van Arsdale, Van Doren, Voorhees, and Ludlow.

I am sure that anyone interested enough in the history of our valley to read "The Journals of Andrew Jackson" [Johnston] will find a great many things of interest.[2]

❧ Ravine Lake Clubs

In 1894 a group of men joined in an effort to form a country club. J. Herbert Ballantine, George B. Post, Robert L. Stevens, and Edward T. H. Talmage each pledged eight thousand dollars toward a fund to purchase real estate in the Peapack area that would be a viable site for the proposed private club. A significant part of the plan involved the construction of Ravine Lake by building a dam across the North Branch of the Raritan River at the location then known as Hub Hollow, because of the hub factory that had operated there.

Allison Wright Post, a lawyer and founder of Post and Reese, a real estate and insurance firm, was employed to

The Ravine Lake Club, 1903. Courtesy of Charles Ashmun, treasurer of the Ravine Lake and Game Club, via Mrs. John Ryan, Bernardsville, N.J.

carry out the purchases of farms for the proposed club. With the help of Abraham Smith, Post acquired 364 $^{781}/_{1000}$ acres of land at an average cost of about $80 per acre. In 1896 a real estate corporation, The Ravine Association, was formed to hold title to the land.

In 1897 work was begun on a clubhouse on the hill overlooking the future Ravine Lake. A nine-hole golf course was laid out, as well as three grass tennis courts. In 1899, the last stone in the Ravine Lake dam was placed, and the Somerset Hills Country Club was organized and obtained a yearly lease of all properties from The Ravine Association. The lease included the clubhouse and grounds, golf links, tennis courts, the lake, and the boathouse. C. Ledyard Blair was the first president of the country club.

The Somerset Hills Country Club continued at the same location until 1917—the search for a larger property having been initiated about 1915. The desire to expand the nine-hole golf course at the original club site could not be accommodated, as there was no adjoining property available. In 1916, 210 acres of land near Bernardsville were purchased from the heirs of Frederic P. Olcott. A new clubhouse was erected there, and an eighteen-hole golf course and six grass tennis courts were laid out. In January 1918 the new Somerset Hills Country Club was complete.

The Somerset Hills Country Club gave up its connection with Ravine Lake and the boathouse. In December 1917 the Somerset Lake and Game Club was organized for boating, bathing, fishing, skating, and conservation of game on Ravine Lake.[3]

❧ *Boy Scout Cabin*

Built with WPA funds, the Boy Scout Cabin was completed in 1934. Thomas Howard was the carpenter, and Somerset County's engineer, Oscar Smith, drew the plans in cooperation with the scoutmaster, Harold Horton. The latter two traveled to Washington to have the plans approved to secure the WPA funds.

The following undated ordinance pertaining to the property on which the Scout Cabin is located was discovered in the borough records.

An Ordinance Relating to the Purchase of Certain Lands for Municipal Purposes.

WHEREAS, *Mahlon C. Smalley has offered to sell to the Borough of Peapack and Gladstone, for a consideration of Twenty Five Hundred Dollars ($2500.00), for municipal purposes, all that tract of land and premises in the Borough of Peapack and Gladstone more particularly bounded and described as follows:*

Beginning at a stake in the southeast corner of the lot deeded to Louis Rosenthal and following the Southern boundary of said lot on a line running South fifty-six degrees and thirty minutes West, three hundred and twenty feet to a stake, said stake being one hundred feet south of the southwest stake in David Philhowers lot; thence (2) South thirty-three degrees and thirty minutes east, ninety-six feet (be there more or less) to a stake in the northern line of Theodore Allen's line; thence (3) following the northern boundary of said lane or a line running north fifty-nine degrees east, three hundred and twenty feet to a stake; thence (4) North thirty-three degrees and thirty minutes west, one hundred feet to the place of beginning.

Containing seventy-two hundredths of an acre of land more or less. Four feet is to be taken from the width of the lots to widen the lane. Said party of the second part agrees to erect no buildings on these lots nearer the street than those already built there. He also covenants that no saloon, hotel or blacksmith shop shall be maintained on this property. It is understood that the said party of the second part shall build and maintain the fences on the property.

Being the same premises conveyed to Theodore Hill by Charles M. Quimby and wife, by deed dated the 27th day of April, 1905 recorded

The Boy Scout Cabin built in 1934 with WPA funds. Photograph by Jan Gordon, October 1990.

in the Somerset County Clerk's Office in Book M-10 of Deed for said county, page 381 etc.

Being the same premises conveyed to Mahlon C. Smalley by Theodore Hill and wife, by deed dated the twenty-third day of July 1913 which deed is unrecorded; and

WHEREAS, it is deemed desirable and necessary that the Borough of Peapack and Gladstone acquire for municipal purposes the aforesaid lands and premises.

Be it ordained by the Mayor and Council of the Borough of Peapack Gladstone:

1. That the Borough of Peapack and Gladstone purchase from Mahlon C. Smalley all that tract or parcel of land and premises hereinabove more particularly described, and the rights and appurtenances connected therewith; subject, however, to the terms conditions and covenants therein contained; the same to be maintained and used for such municipal purposes as may be deemed necessary, useful and desirable.

2. That the sum of Twenty-five Hundred dollars ($2500.00) or so much thereof as may be acquired, be and is hereby appropriated for the purchase and acquisition of the aforesaid lands and premises, said purchase price to be paid for by funds raised by general taxation.

3. That the Mayor and Council are authorized to accept delivery from Mahlon C. Smalley of deeds or other instruments to give effect to and to carry out the purpose of this ordinance.

4. That this ordinance is to take place immediately.

❧ *Andrew Johnston's Journal, 1743-1754*

P.A., Aprill 20th, 1743.—Sett out for Pepack in order to look over Axtells lands and to settle the amts. of rents with the tennants, etc, and to run the lines of the several lotts in the Pepack pattent; . . .

Lott No. 2, began at Pepack 10 ch. above the forks . . . 2 ch. more Wm. Hogland's house, . . . We ran throu clear'd fields all the way and the land very good. Above the corner the land grows poorer and seems to be very hilly, some of it indifferently well timber'd. From this corner we ran N. 76° East 28 ch. to a branch of Lawrance's brook, the land but indifferent; two settlements on ye other sid[e], and Drake's mill about 30 chains below the line. . . .

Return'd to ye corner of lott No. 6 and No. 5; ran S. 76° W., throu John Wortman and Peter Wortman's fields . . .

Apr. 22d.— . . . A considerable quantity of timber upward towards Peter Demond's. At 36 ch. a small brook in a deep gully by ye side of James Allen's wheat field; at 50 chain throu the field, his house to the southward of the line. I did not see it, but suppose about 20 chain; at 130 ch. in a field John Adams and Ephr. McDowell house; bears N. 10° West; about 20 ch. distant, Abra. Johnson's house . . .

April 23d.—Came to ye wallnut saplin markt yesterday on ye brow of ye hill near to Dan. McCoy's house; . . .

John Craig's house about 6 ch. up the river. . . .

25th April.— . . . I was greatest part of these days more in settling with the tenants on Axtell's lands. Some paid me and some have given their notes of hand as paym'ts in an acco't of rents. . . .

P. Amboy, Aprill 16th, 1744.—Sett out for Peapack in order to settle and call Axtells tenants to acco't, and to finish the bargains with some who are about purchasing part of ye Peapack lands, etc. I got to Mr. Dunsters at night and lodg there. . . .

I crost at ye N. Branch bridge and went to Thos. V. Buskirks to settle ye acc't between him and my fathers estate; . . .

Apr. 20th.—To lay out the land which the Wortmans are about buying we began at the white oaks near James Allens house markt for Mathias Lanes most northerly corner . . .

April 21.—Went from John Lawraueds [Lawrance's?] down the brook to look over the lands. Agreed with Josia Scudder to sell him a small lott where Drake had by my consent built a mill, to begin at a black or red oak tree standing on ye upper [lesser?] end of a small island in Lawrances brook, and to run N. 71° E. about 5 ch. to Peapack river; thence down the river about 24 ch. to where the river unites with Lawrances brook; thence up ye brook to where it began, containing about 18 acres (mines excepted) . . .

They have hired from Abr. Drake, being what he calls his improvements there. . . .

I am told the land is generally good from the house up to the Iron works for about 40 or 50 ch. wide. . . .

22d.—I went up to Rockistocus meeting and return'd to Lockharts that night. The land from ye 44 ch. last mentioned on Laurenses brook continues good both sides of ye brook, near to ye Iron works & some of it well timberd, I suppose about two miles & a half—some places 40 or 50 ch. wide. I am told that between the beforementioned black oak tree I markt "D.C." and the head of the brook where Duncan McCoy lives ther's a good deal of middling land and several settlements, some of which I could see from the top of the hill.

❧ *Mayors*

The following have served as mayors of the Borough of Peapack and Gladstone since its incorporation in 1912.

John Bodine	1912–1930
Reginald Rives	1930–1944
A. Alpaugh	1945–1948
A. Speight	1949–1954
Joseph Salvia	1954–1955
H. W. Pierson	1955–1960

W. J. Benjamin	1960–1964
Edward J. Van Wyck	1965–1968
Albert M. Sracic	1969–1979
Mary Hamilton	1979–

❦ *Local Ministers*

Gladstone United Methodist Church

Abram Gearhart	1837
George Hitchens	1837
Joseph Chattels	1839
Edward Hance	1840
William E. Perry	1841
Peter D. Day	1842–1843
Richard Vanhorne	1844
J. P. Dally	1845
Abram Owen	1845–1846
Isaac Cross	1846
J. P. Dally	1847
Charles E. Hill	1848–1849
Charles Larew	1850–1851
David McCurdy	1852
John S. Coit	1853
Robert B. Sutcliff	1854
David Walters	1855–1856
Thomas T. Campfield	1857–1858
Matthias F. Swaine	1859
John Davis	1859
J. B. Howard	1860–1861
B. D. Palmer	1862–1863
Jacob P. Fort	1864–1866
Edward M. Griffiths	1867
Thomas Rawlings	1868–1869
Samuel J. Morris	1870
William H. Haggerty	1871–1872
Joshua Mead	1873–1874
J. H. Runyon	1875–1876
J. N. Keys	1877
J. Thomas	1878–1880
Frederich Bloom	1881–1883
C. S. Vanelen	1884
A. L. Smith	1885–1886
W. H. Dye	1887–1888
E. T. Fowler	1889
W. S. Nelson	1890–1893
D. W. Ryder	1894–1895
George F. Illman	1896–1898
William S. Coeyman	1899
Richardson Gray	1900
Albert A. Andersen	1901–1904

Oscar L. Joseph	1905–1906
H. W. Ewig	1907
Ed. M. Compton	1908–1909
George M. W. Fulcomer	1910–1913
A. L. Fretz	1914–1916
E. G. VanLilburg	1917
P. C. Bascom	1918–1920
Ralph R. Roby	1921–1922
William Alten	1923–1924
P. C. Greenly	1925–1926
George Anderson Hill	1927–1928
James Jamieson	1929–1930
D.W.C. Ramsey	1931
Francis Kirch	1932–1936
Richard G. Jones	1935–1937
Herbert C. Lytle, Jr.	1937–1938
Alden L. Smith	1938–1940
Claude H. Thompson	1941–1942
Frank L. Reed	1943–1945
Wilbur H. Wilson	1946–1948
Edward S. McLaughlin	1949–1952
William A. Lufburrow	1953–1957
R. Douglas Merriam	1958–1959
M. Stanley Bain	1960–1961
Herman Soderberg	1962–1964
Bruce M. Stephens	1965–1967

David S. Warren	1968–1971
Ronald S. Sell	1972–1973
Judith Bennett	1974–1976
Duane D. Buddle	1977–1978
Lorna Lee Curtis	1979–1981
Susan G. Hill	1982–1984
Leo Collins	1985–1986
Kevan Hitch	1986–1987
Vicki M. Brendlar	1988–1989
Cindy K. Storrs	1990–

Peapack Reformed Church

Rev. William Anderson	1849–1856
Rev. Henry P. Thompson	1857–1873
Rev. Chas. T. Anderson	1874–1882
Rev. Geo. W. Scarlet	1883–1886
Rev. Geo. Davis	1887–1893
Rev. Howard C. Hasbrouck	1894–1900
Rev. William Johnston	1900–1903
Rev. Thos. M. Simonto	1903–1914
Rev. Fred. N. Baeder	1915–1920
Rev. Julius Prochnau	1920–1951
Rev. Armand Renskers	1953–1955
Rev. Russell Block	1956–1959
Rev. Arlen Salthouse	1960–1961
Rev. Lee Bayer	1962–1966

Rev. Charles Johnson	1966–1973
Rev. Paul Walther	1974–1991

St. Brigid Roman Catholic Church

Rev. William J. Lannary	1936–1946
Rev. Alfred F. Sico	1946–1952
Rev. Thomas A. Kane	1952–1953
Rev. John F. Walsh	1953–1956
Rev. George E. Everitt	1956–1964
Rev. Msgr. Charles E. McGee	1964–1965
Rev. Francis J. Coan	1965–1967
Rev. James Q. Bittner	1967–1984
Msgr. George M. Brembos	1984–

St. Luke's Episcopal Church

Rev. John Mitchell Harper	1900–1945
Rev. Emmet Paige	1945–1951
Rev. Canon L. Irving Greene	1951–1965
Rev. Canon John T. Morrow	1965–

❧ *Headmasters*

St. Bernard's School

Rev. Thomas A. Conover	1900–1906
Rev. James Conover	1906–1916 (presumed, undocumented)
Harold "Spike" Nicholls	1917–1945 (approximate)
Rev. Robert Clayton	1946–1953
Rev. William Penfield	1953–1954
Donald R. Williams	1954–1958
John Durwood	1958–1965 (approximate)
Rev. Henry A. Tilghman	1966–1972

Gill St. Bernard's

John Wright	1972–1978
William Cooper	1979–1985
Christine D. Gorham	1986–

❧ *Notes*

1. Here the spelling differs from the typewritten copy on file in the Peapack-Gladstone Library.
2. *Peapack-Gladstone Exponent*, December 22, 1932.
3. Historical information from Allison Wright Post, *Recollections of Bernardsville*.

AN ORDINANCE TO PREVENT AND SUPPRESS GAMING HOUSES OF ILL FAME AND TO PROHIBIT GAMING FOR MONEY OR OTHER VALUABLE THINGS, TO PRESERVE PUBLIC PEACE AND GOOD ORDER, TO RESTRAIN AND PUNISH INDECENT OR DISORDERLY CONDUCT OR DRUNKENNESS, AND TO SUPRESS [SIC] VICE AND IMMORALITY.

Be it Ordained by the Council of the Borough of Peapack and Gladstone:

1. No person shall keep or maintain a disorderly house, or a house of ill fame, or allow or permit any house, shop, store or other building owned or occupied by him or her to be used as a disorderly house, or house of ill fame, or to be frequented or resorted to by riotous or disorderly persons, prostitutes, gamblers, or vagrants.

2. No person shall set up, keep, or maintain, or permit to be set up, kept, or maintained in any house or premises any faro table, faro bank, roulette wheel, or other device or game of chance for the purpose of gaming, or any boxing ring, cock-pit, or other place for men or animals to fight, nor shall any person hold, or permit to be held, in any house or premises, any dog fight, cock fight, prize fight, or any sparring contest for a purse or money prize.

3. No person shall deal, play or engage in faro, roulette, or other game of chance, either as banker, player, dealer or otherwise for the purpose of gaming.

4. No person shall loiter on the streets in any public place, in any quasi-public place, or in or upon any private property not his or her own, being under the influence of intoxicating liquor, or, not being under such influence, shall there indulge in and utter loud and offensive or indecent language, or address or make audible and offensive remarks or comments upon any person passing along such streets, public places, quasi-public places, or private properties not his or her own, or abstruct [sic] or interfere with any person or persons lawfully being in and upon such streets, public places, quasi-public places or private properties not his or her own.

5. No person shall go about from door to door, or place himself or herself in the streets to beg or gather alms.

6. No person shall appear in any street or public place in a state of nudity, or in a dress not belonging to his or her sex, or in any indecent or lewd dress, or shall make any indecent exposure of his or her person, or be guilty of any lewd or indecent act or behavior, or shall exhibit, sell or offer to sell, any indecent or lewd book, picture or thing, or shall exhibit or perform any indecent, immoral, or lewd play, or other representation.

7. No person shall engage in any practice, sport or exercise having a tendency to annoy persons passing in the streets or on the sidewalks.

8. Each and every person violating any of the provisions of this ordinance shall, upon conviction, thereof, forfeit and pay a fine of not more than —— hundred dollars, or be imprisoned in the county jail for not more than ninety days; and the magistrate before whom any such person may be brought may impose such punishment by fine or imprisonment in the county jail as he may see fit, not exceeding the maximum herein fixed.

Presented May 12th 1931.

———————————————

Passed June 9th 1931.

———————————————

Borough Clerk

Approved June 9th 1931.

———————————————

Mayor

Bibliography

Barber, John W., and Howe, Henry. *Historical Collections of the State of New Jersey; containing a general collection of the most interesting facts, traditions, biographical sketches, anecdotes, etc. relating to its history and antiquities, with geographical descriptions of every township in the state.* New Haven: Benjamin Olds for Justus H. Bradley, 1844.

Barnes, Valerie. *The Strange and Mysterious Past in the Somerset Hills Area.* Bernardsville, N.J.: Bernardsville Book Company, 1975.

Becker, Donald William. *Indian Place Names in New Jersey.* Cedar Grove, N.J.: Phillips-Campbell Publishing Co., 1964.

Bedminster Town Committee Records, 1797–1806 (partial). Manuscript Collection of the New Jersey Historical Society, Newark, N.J.

Bernardsville News.

Borman, Madeline. *How Far!* Princeton, N.J.: Princeton University Press, 1979.

Conant, Robert C. '43. "The New Chapel of St. Bernard's School." *Spirit of Clairvaux*, February 1942.

Cross, Dorothy. *The Indians of New Jersey.* Trenton, N.J.: Archeological Society of New Jersey, 1953.

Cunningham, John T. *New Jersey: America's Main Road.* Garden City, N.Y.: Doubleday & Company, 1966.

Dalton, Richard F. *Caves of New Jersey.* Department of Environmental Protection, New Jersey Geological Survey Bulletin 70, n.d.

Deed books. Somerset County Hall of Records. Somerville.

De Forest, L. E., and De Forest, A. L. *James Cox Brady.* New York: De Forest Publishing Company, 1933.

Derson, Art. *Historical Sketch of the Gladstone Methodist Episcopal Church and a Short Biography of William Evart Gladstone.* Gladstone, N.J.: Methodist Church, 1902.

Ely, John Lawrence. "Supplement to *The Old Farm* by Andrew D. Mellick, Jr.: Regarding the Ancestors of Alice Louise Lawrence Ely & Interesting to Her Descendants." Peter Hogeboom Collection, Peapack, N.J.

Estate of Aaron Mellick Record Book, 1809–1818. Manuscript Collection of the New Jersey Historical Society, Newark, N.J.

Essex Hunt log, 1928–1937. Manuscript Collection of the New Jersey Historical Society, Newark, N.J.

Fascinating Blairsden. Pamphlet printed by the Sisters of St. John the Baptist, St. Joseph's Villa, n.d.

French and English Furniture: Property of the Estate of the Late C. Ledyard Blair. New York: Parke-Bernet Galleries, New York, 1950.

Genealogical Magazine of New Jersey.

Jason M. Cortell & Associates. *Bedminster Township: A Historical Analysis.* Compiled as part of the impact statement for AT&T Long Lines, Bedminster, N.J. Wellesley Hills, Mass.

Johnston, Howard E. *The Rockaway Valley Railroad Story.* Plainfield, N.J.: Printed by the Ocean Grove Times, 1958.

Jones, Frederick W. *Recollections of the Essex Hunt.* Gladstone, N.J.: James S. Jones, 1967. Spinning Collection, Bernardsville Library, Bernardsville, N.J.

Jones, James S. *Early Times.* Gladstone, N.J.: James S. Jones, 1971.

"Journals of Andrew Johnston." *Somerset County Historical Quarterly*, vol. 1, 1912.

Kay, John L., and Smith, Chester M., Jr. *New Jersey Postal History: The Postoffices and First Postmasters, 1776–1976.* Lawrence, Mass.: Quarterman Publications, 1977.

Lane, Wheaton J. *From Indian Trail to Iron Horse: Travel and Transportation in New Jersey 1620–1800.* Princeton, N.J.: Princeton University Press, 1939.

Lesser Crossroads. Edited by Hubert G. Schmidt from *The Story of an Old Farm* by Andrew D. Mellick, Jr. New Brunswick, N.J.: Rutgers University Press, 1948.

Lytle, Reverend Herbert Clyde, Jr. *Gladstone's First Century of Methodism.* Gladstone, N.J.: Methodist Church, 1938. In the archives of the Morristown Library.

Mellick, Andrew D., Jr. *The Story of An Old Farm: or Life in New Jersey in the Eighteenth Century.* Somerville, N.J.: Unionist Gazette, 1889.

Minutes of First Aid and Rescue Squad of Peapack and Gladstone, 1936. First Aid and Rescue Squad Archives.

Minutes of the Liberty Park Association. Archives of the Borough of Peapack-Gladstone, Peapack, N.J.

Morison, Samuel Eliot. *The Oxford History of the American People.* New York: Oxford University Press, 1965.

Mount Saint John Academy Commemorates the Sixtieth Anniversary of Its Foundation. October 1986. Pamphlet from Mount Saint John Academy archives, Gladstone, N.J.

Myers, William S. Lewis. *The Story of New Jersey.* New York: Historical Publishing Co., 1945.

Nemeth, Tom. *The Gladstone Branch: Affectionately Known As the P & D (Passaic & Delaware).* Reprinted from *The Block Line*, Official Newsmagazine of Tri-State Chapter, National Railroad Historical Society. Bernardsville, N.J.: Hill Press, 1978.

New Jersey Transit Authority. *A Brief History of the Lackawanna Electrics: 1931–1984.* 1984.

O'Brien, Anne. "From Primitive Man to Planning Master: A Tale of the Township of Bedminster." 1982.

—————. "Pleasant Valley." July 1985.

Our Home: A Monthly Magazine of Original Articles. Edited by A.V.D. Honeyman. Vol. 1. Somerville, N.J.: Cornell & Honeyman, 1873.

Peapack and Gladstone Fire Department: 1905–1955. Fiftieth anniversary celebration souvenir booklet. 1955.

Peapack and Gladstone Fire Department: Our First Seventy-five Years, 1905–1980. Seventy-fifth anniversary celebration souvenir booklet. 1980.

The Peapack and Gladstone Woman's Club. *The History of the Peapack and Gladstone Public Library and the Sara Gulick Kay Memorial Building.* Archives of the Peapack-Gladstone Library, Peapack, N.J., n.d.

Pomfret, John E. *The New Jersey Proprietors and Their Lands, 1664–1776.* New Jersey Historical Series, vol. 9. Princeton, N.J.: Van Nostrand Company, 1964.

Peapack Union Cemetery Association. *The Minute Book.* Archive of John Keith, Gladstone, N.J.

Post, Allison Wright. *Recollections of Bernardsville, New Jersey, 1871–1941.* New York: J.P. Little & Ives, 1941.

Potter, Rachel. "Historical Facts and Places of Interest in Peapack-Gladstone." An undocumented history of Peapack in the Peapack and Gladstone Library archives.

Rawson, Marion Nicholl. *The Old House Picture Book.* New York: E.P. Dutton and Company, 1941.

Scannells, J. J., ed. *New Jersey's First Citizens and State Guide.* Paterson, N.J.: J.J. Scannells, 1917–1918.

Schumacher, Ludwig. *The Somerset Hills; being a brief record of significant facts in the early history of the hill country of Somerset County, New Jersey.* New York: New Amsterdam Book Company, 1900.

Smith, William Francis Smith, and Smith, Beverly B. *John Smith 1718–1791: Descendants.* Bethesda, Md.: William Francis Smith, 1987.

Snell, James P., comp. *History of Hunterdon and Somerset Counties, New Jersey; with illustrations and biographical sketches of its prominent men and pioneers.* Philadelphia: Everts and Peck, 1881.

Somerset County Historical Quarterly.

Somerset Messenger Gazette, July 1949. Clipping on file at New Jersey Historical Society, Newark, N.J.

St. Luke's Church (Episcopal) Gladstone, New Jersey 1900–1975. Printed by the church in 1975 for its seventy-fifth anniversary.

Stevens, Stephanie. *The Forgotten Mills of Readington.* 1987.

The Story of Hamilton Farm. Bedminster, N.J.: Beneficial Finance, n.d. Clarence Dillon Library archives, Bedminster.

Sypher, J. R., and Apgar, E. A. *History of New Jersey from the Earliest Settlers to the Present Times.* Philadelphia: Lippincott and Co., 1870.

Tabor, Thomas T. III. *The Rock-A-Bye Baby: A History of the Rockaway Valley Railroad*. Muncy, Pa., 1972. Ruth Thomson Collection, Gladstone, N.J.

Thompson, Henry P. *History of the Reformed Church at Peapack, New Jersey.* New York: Board of Publication of the Reformed Church in America, 1881.

Throop, Octavia. "The Essex Fox Hounds." Photocopy of article. In the Peapack-Gladstone archives of the Morristown Library.

Unionist Gazette. Somerville, N.J.

Van Doren, Peter Ellis. *Combined Recorded History of the People of Peapack-Gladstone Born before 1900 with Children.* Peapack Gladstone Bank, ca. 1987. Clarence Dillon Library archives, Bedminster, N.J.

van Horn, J. H., comp. *Historic Somerset.* Published by the compiler for the Historical Societies of Somerset County, New Jersey. New Brunswick, N.J.: Uniman Printers, 1965.

Voting Register, Bedminster, New Jersey, 1797–1803. Manuscript Collection of the New Jersey Historical Society, Newark, N.J.

Walter, Frederick. *The Township of Bedminster: Published for the New Jersey Tercentenary (1664–1964).* Bedminster, N.J.: F. Walter, 1964.

Weekly Exponent. [Later called the *Peapack-Gladstone Exponent* and the *Somerset Hills Exponent.*] Special Collections and Archives, Rutgers University Libraries.

White, E. B. *The Fox of Peapack and Other Poems.* New York: Harper & Brothers, 1938.

Typeset in Aldus digitized Baskerville and Centaur by
Martin-Waterman Associates, Ltd., Highland Park, New Jersey

Printed by Princeton Academic Press, Inc., Lawrenceville, New Jersey, on Mohawk Superfine, an acid-free paper,
and bound in Brillianta cloth